Exclusions in
Feminist Thought

Exclusions in Feminist Thought

CHALLENGING THE BOUNDARIES OF WOMANHOOD

Edited by
MARY BREWER

sussex
ACADEMIC
PRESS

BRIGHTON • PORTLAND

2 4 6 8 10 9 7 5 3 1

First published in 2002 in Great Britain by
SUSSEX ACADEMIC PRESS
PO Box 2950
Brighton BN2 5SP

and in the United States of America by
SUSSEX ACADEMIC PRESS
5824 N.E. Hassalo St.
Portland, Oregon 97213-3644

British Library Cataloguing in Publication Data
A CIP catalogue record for this book is available from the British Library.

Library of Congress Cataloging-in-Publication Data

Exclusion in feminist thought : challenging the boundaries of womanhood / edited by Mary Brewer.
p. cm.
Includes bibliographical references and index.
ISBN 1–902210–63–8 (alk. paper)
1. Feminism. I. Brewer, Mary F.

HQ1206 .E98 2002
305.42—dc21   2002021717

Typeset and designed by G&G Editorial, Brighton
Printed by TJ International, Padstow, Cornwall
This book is printed on acid-free paper.

Contents

Contents

Introduction

What does feminism mean at the millennium? Can we say that such a thing as a women's movement exists anymore, and, if so, in what form? Why are so few women willing to identify as feminist; are we really *post-*feminism, or do we still need a woman-centered political discourse? And what might a feminist theory and practice capable of addressing the aspirations of *all* women look like? These are the fundamental questions about women's needs, experiences, and ideas explored in this volume.

Since the nineteenth century, women in the West have fought for women's interests under a variety of feminist banners. There have been and indeed are as many different kinds of feminism as there are different communities of women. Experience has shown that placing too big an umbrella over feminists' social and political activism is not necessarily something to be desired, for coalitions among different social groups of women have often as not led to a "one-woman's-move-ment", a movement that caters to the needs and interests of only some women, those whose class, race, ethnic, and sexual identities are most closely allied to that of the dominant culture.

Since the advent of second-wave feminism in the 1960s, a corpus of ideas, concerns and strategies, consistently repeated in a variety of media and institutions, has amalgamated into capital-*F* Feminism. Historically throughout the 1970s and into the 1980s, one version among the many feminist perspectives on offer enjoyed a privileged hold on what the women's movement was and should be about, and, despite the proliferation since the 1980s of competing explanations concerning what women need and want to live meaningful, productive lives, in some cultural quarters this remains the case. In Western democracies, liberal feminism, dedicated primarily to enabling some women to succeed economically as well as some men in a consumer capitalist system, continues to form the basis of legislation deemed of particular benefit to women. Among the majority of organized women's groups, especially in the United States and Britain, for the time being at least, bourgeois feminism has won out over more equitable alternative visions of feminist movement. Moreover, most of the albeit modest attention paid to so called "women's issues" by the popular press and media focuses on what one might call "white-bread" feminism: a commercially palatable brand of feminism that is non-controversial in its demands and which generalizes straight, able-bodied, white middle-class values as representative of all women's views.

The promotion of mainstream feminist ideology is not limited to the legislative arena, the odd journalistic article or brief hearing from a celebrity feminist pundit on a high- or low-brow chat show. Mainstream feminist discourse reproduces itself on a number of fronts, including many women's and gender studies programs and feminist organizations, those spaces where radical, liberatory practice ostensibly takes place. Of course, its appearance and the manner of its reinforcement in feminist locations differs from the way in which it gets reproduced in heteropatriarchal law or the popular media.

Whereas the general absence of recognition of differences among women within most media genres makes the narrow vision of corporate equality fostered therein difficult to challenge, most educational institutions in the United States for instance now offer a range of programs and individual courses dedicated to the histories and cultural production of diverse peoples. Although Ethnic Studies is in a much earlier phase of development in the UK and, in recent years, Women's Studies programs have struggled to maintain a foothold in some British academic institutions, different cultural perspectives are beginning to appear more frequently as part of individual courses, particularly in the burgeoning field of Media and Cultural Studies, as well as Gender Studies, and a range of fields in the Humanities. I would not deny that the inclusion of work by different groups of women as part of academic women's programs, though regrettably still piece-meal in places, represents a significant step forward in feminist institutional practice – the particular way in which feminists inhabit and produce work within extant institutional spaces. Nevertheless, even where the experiences of diverse groups of women are taken into account, the centrality of "Universal Woman" can prove difficult to contest. In fact, depending on the manner in which different perspectives are included in any feminist endeavor, the status quo can end up being reinforced.

First, let us consider how multiculturalism has impacted on institutionalized academic feminism. Although the work of Latina or lesbian women, for example, now regularly forms part of syllabi and appears on reading lists, these women's voices continue to be denied agency: because – as the essays in this collection clearly illustrate – the potential for transforming the structural methodologies of feminist theory and practice afforded by the knowledge produced within the full range of feminist communities, academic or otherwise, largely gets ignored. The inclusion of work by women marked as culturally different in feminist institutional practices tends at best to affect change only at a surface level, or, in a worst-case scenario, its inclusion works to further marginalize some women. Because so much feminist theory and practice today emerges out of women's work in the academy, the knowledges about women produced in this cultural space operate with great force in constructing the boundaries of womanhood. Women cannot afford to underestimate the vital role this knowledge will play in determining whether third-wave feminism proves able to move beyond what Margaret Villanueva identifies as the "processes of *erasure, invisibility, tokenism,* and *denial*" that continue to inform contemporary feminist theory and practice (see p. 47).

The same case can be made for many grass-roots feminist activities, as evidenced by Angela Slaughter's documentation of Aboriginal women's experiences in the Canadian Women's Movement included in this volume. Slaughter illustrates how attempts to "integrate" Native women into the mainstream movement have generally served to replicate racial and class hierarchies, with Aboriginal women "having to explain and defend" why they are different and require different things from a feminist movement than white, middle-class Canadian women (see p. 175). Such observations unfortunately are hardly new. Since the 1970s, women who have felt marginalized or wholly neglected by the women's movement have protested that what some groups of women say is either not being counted, or heard and misconstrued, within feminist debates as well as male-stream culture. Gerda Lerner's *Black Women in White America* (1972), Angela Davis' *Women, Race and Class* (1981), and bell hooks, *Ain't I A Woman* (1982) were among the first critiques of the women's movement to point out that when feminism fails to challenge racism or classism, some women may be marginalized thrice over. Charlotte Bunch and Nancy Myron's *Class and Feminism* (1974) and Christine Delphy's *Close to Home* (1984) also helped open explorations into feminism's middle-class bias. And Adrienne Rich's seminal article, "Compulsory Heterosexuality and lesbian existence" (1980), illustrated the erroneous and harmful assumption of women's heterosexuality in feminist discourse.

There are many more such resistant texts available that address the problem of exclusion in feminist thought, including work by Gloria Anzaldúa, Wini Breines, Barbara Christian, Ruth R. Frankenberg, Gloria Hull, Aída Hurtado, June Jordan, Audre Lorde, Biddy Martin, Trinh T. Minh-Ha, Chandra Talpade Mohanty, Cheríe Moraga, Toni Morrison, Minnie Bruce Pratt, Barbara Smith, Valerie Smith, Elizabeth V. Spelman,

Gayatri Spivak, and Vron Ware – to name but a few. And these works have been incorporated, at least in an abstract sense, into the catalogue of mainstream feminist theoretical inventory. The problem lies in that a great deal of work by feminist-identified women still stops at what can only be a first step in a progressive women's movement. It is not enough simply to acknowledge, even respect differences among women, for even where feminist theory and practice has recognized difference, often difference has remained ex-centric to feminist thought.

Recently, however, a growing number of feminist writers and activists, including many of those named above, have begun to make theory and suggest practices that challenge the deep structural inter-relation of gender subordination with other kinds of social oppression. The emphasis in progressive feminist work – that work which engages with the concerns and experiences of the masses of women and the different communities of children and men to which they share a bond – has shifted away from a recovery of marginalized women's experiences and a corrective response to inaccurate representations of some women in feminist theory and practice; now the progressive focus is geared toward a deconstructive critique of the forms of privilege that accrue to some cultural models of femininity and the cultural foundations that construct and support these models. Progressive feminist work recognizes that feminine privilege is not universally and histori-cally the same for any group of women anymore than patriarchal privilege is always alike for any one group of men. At the same time, crucially it reveals how in a large number of cases women who prove able to forward the most "convincing" definitions of feminine identity remain those who possess the greatest cultural assets in terms of their race, economic status, etc. This means that women who challenge non-progressive strands of feminist thought – that body of feminist theory and practice focused primarily on the needs of women who occupy the cultural mainstream – frequently still get relegated to the limits of insti-tutional and organizational margins.

At present, many women are stuck in a Catch-22 situation, in which some of us at least seem likely to be damned whether or not we sign on to that remaining fraction of the women's movement. Outside of some form of an organized women's movement, progress toward social justice for women, as well as men and children, appears a daunting task. At the same time, to identify oneself with a movement that fails to truly value most of the significant differences that separate the needs of any one group of women from another seems both personally and politically unwise. It is axiomatic that subordinated peoples can go farther toward achieving some aims working together rather than alone in small and often under-resourced groups. As for any socio-political endeavor, broad-based alliances remain crucial for feminist movement. The task, then, to which progressive feminists must address themselves is the development of new non-exclusionary theoretical and organizational principles and more equitable consensus-based ways of enabling all women to act as Subjects of feminist discourse. This will not happen until, Julia Balén argues here, all women who advocate liberatory feminism interrogate their own individual and social groups' relation to power and privilege and reflect on the way each of us utilizes or fails to employ the variety of skills and power we do possess in order to foster a broad feminist campaign for social justice.

This collection is premised on the view that a feminism which is capable of forming the basis for a theory and a politics of social change can only develop from within a cultural framework that offers women space to engage in a dialogue of critical dissent as well as scope for affirmation and agreement. Further, it makes the case that the skeleton for this cultural framework must be made up from the plurality of feminine genders extant in society. The essays included here form part of the on-going struggle to reconceptualize a number of dominant paradigms and theoretical and practical methodologies informing feminist thought. The contributors to this collection seek to build upon the groundwork of progressive feminist theory by providing strategies for de-normalizing dominant cultural and exclusionary feminist constructions of womanhood. As a whole, *Exclusions in Feminist Thought* offers a close examination of a selection of cultural representations of femininity in critical theory and philosophy, literature, theatre, and film, cultural anthropology, sociology and psychology. The book critiques historical and contemporary representations of femininity in women's auto/biographical narratives, explores the relation between feminism as theorized in the academy and feminism as lived by women in their particular communities, and questions feminist pedagogical practices as well as a range of feminist critical theoretical methodologies.

The essays are divided into four sections, according to their primary focus: feminism in the Academy; "Woman" and representation; creating strategic alliances through narratives of localized resistance; re-writing the female self. However, feminist perspectives are rarely singular, and, certainly, the women's voices represented here speak about their chosen topics from a diversity of lived experience and a multiplicity of locations in culture. Each of the fourteen chapters explores from an interdisciplinary perspective various problems of exclusion in feminist discourse, interrogating the social, political, and economic factors that produce the power divisions between women of different cultural groups. Therefore, many of the essays have a number of things in common with more than one of the book's categorical divisions.

Introduction

Julia Balén's *Practicing Difference Differently*, **Susan Jackson's** *Ivory Towers and Guardians of the Word*, and **Margaret A. Villanueva's** *TransForm/ando Women's Studies*, which form *Part I*, put forward strategies for transforming power relations in the academy. Their projects seek to foster a liberatory feminist consciousness that can be translated into different forms of feminist practice both inside and outside of Academe, one able to afford all women access to the discourse of feminist subjecthood, without erasing, universalizing, or otherwise leveling the different racial/ethnic and sex-gendered categories across which women are defined.

The writers in *Part II* – **Melissa Chinchillo, Kathleen Iudicello, Doreen Piano**, and **Mary Brewer** – address systematic alternatives to prevailing ways of interpreting the materiality of gender(s). **Chinchillo's** *(Post)Colonial (Dis)Orders*, **Iudicello's** *"See, I've got my tit out!"*, **Piano's** *Leaving Las Vegas*, and **Brewer's**, *Violating the Seal of Race* tease out the complexities of gendered representations and their relation to hegemonic and mainstream feminist cultural theories and practices in a range of literary and performance contexts. The essays demonstrate both an awareness of how some feminist constructions of womanhood continue to reflect and sustain dominant cultural biases while pointing to the potential force of alternative feminist representations.

The essays grouped together in *Part III* – **Alyssa O'Brien's** *Theorizing Feminisms*, **Angela Slaughter's** *Aboriginal Women and the Canadian Feminist Movement*, and **Rebecca Walsh's** *Where Metaphor Meets Materiality* – aspire to develop a more progressive feminist theory that would foster a commitment to women's cultural particularities. At the same time, the authors explore the way in which feminist micro-narratives can work for and against the development of strategic alliances among women of diverse subcultural groups. Finally, the writers in *Part IV* examine women's relation to language and the performativity of gender. **Bella Adam's** *Feminism and the Aesthetic*, **Liz Barry's** *Bodily Transactions*, **Michele Hunter's** *"Doing" Judith*, and **Ashley Tauchert's** *Mary Wollstonecraft* engage with a variety of vocabularies and models for formulating gender as a site of difference. These critical definitions of gender and/or gendered practices are queried with the aim of destabilizing not only dominant categories of race, ethnicity, and sexuality, but also challenging the boundaries of professed feminist conceptualizations.

Acknowledgment

I am grateful to Ruth McElroy and Angela K. Smith for commenting on several drafts of this Introduction.

6

Selected References

Anzaldúa, Gloria. 1987: *Borderlands/La Frontera: The New Mestiza*. San Francisco: Spinsters/Aunt Lute.

——. 1990: *Making Face, Making Soul/Hacienda Caras: Creative and Critical Perspectives by Women of Color*. San Francisco: Aunt Lute.

Breines, Wini. 1992: *Young, White and Miserable: Growing Up Female in the Fifties*. Boston: Beacon Press.

Bunch, Charlotte. 1974: *Lesbianism and the Women's Movement*. Oakland, CA: Diana.

—— and Nancy Myron (eds). 1974: *Class and Feminism*. Baltimore: Diana.

Christian, Barbara. 1985: *Black Feminist Criticism: Perspectives on Black Women Writers*. Oxford: Pergamon.

Davis, Angela. 1981: *Women, Race and Class*. New York: Random House.

Delphy, Christine. 1984: *Close to Home: A Materialist Analysis of Women's Oppression*. Amherst: University of Massachusetts Press.

Frankenberg, Ruth R. 1993: *White Women, Race Matters: The Social Construction of Whiteness*. Minneapolis: University of Minnesota Press.

hooks, bell. 1982: *Ain't I A Woman: Black Women and Feminism*. Boston: South End Press.

——. 1984: *Feminist Theory: From Margin to Center*. Boston: South End Press.

Hull, Gloria, Scott, Patricia Bell and Smith, Barbara (eds). 1982: *All the Women Are White, All the Blacks Are Men, But Some of Us Are Brave: Black Women's Studies*. Old Westbury, New York: Feminist Press.

Hurtado, Aída. 1996: *The Color of Privilege: Three Blasphemies on Race and Feminism*. Ann Arbor: University of Michigan Press.

Jordan, June. 1985: *On Call: Political Essays*. Boston: South End Press.

Lerner, Gerda (ed.) 1972: *Black Women in White America*. New York: Pantheon.

Lorde, Audre. 1984: *Sister Outsider: Essays and Speeches*. New York: Crossing Press.

Martin, Biddy. 1996: *Femininity Played Straight: The Significance of Being Lesbian*. London: Routledge.

Minh-Ha, Trinh T. 1989: *Woman, Native, Other*. Indiana: Indiana University Press.

Mohanty, Chandra Talpade, Russo, Ann and Torres, Lourdes (eds). 1991: *Third World Women and the Politics of Feminism*. Bloomington, Indiana: Indiana University Press.

Moraga, Cheríe and Anzaldúa, Gloria (eds). 1981: *This Bridge Called My Back: Writings By Radical Women of Color*. Watertown, Massachusetts: Persephone.

Morrison, Toni. 1992: *Playing in the Dark: Whiteness and the Literary Imagination*. Cambridge, MA: Harvard University Press.

Pratt, Minne Bruce, Bulkin, Elly and Barbara Smith (eds). 1984: *Yours in Struggle: Three Feminist Perspectives on Anti-Semitism and Racism*. New York: Long Haul Press.

Rich, Adrienne. 1980: Compulsory Heterosexuality and lesbian existence. *Signs* 5 (4), 631–60.

Smith, Barbara. 1980: *Toward a Black Feminist Criticism*. New York: Out and Out Books.

Smith, Valerie. 1998: *Not Just Race, Not Just Gender*. London: Routledge.

Spelman, Elizabeth V. 1990 [1988]: *Inessential Woman: Problems of Exclusion in Feminist Thought*. London: The Women's Press.

Spivak, Gayatri. 1987: *In Other Worlds: Essays in Cultural Politics*. London: Methuen.

——. 1990: *The Postcolonial Critic: Interviews, Strategies, Dialogues*. London: Routledge.

Ware, Vron. 1991: *Beyond the Pale*. London: Verso.

Part I

Feminism in the Academy: Making Room for Different Subjects

I N *Practicing Difference Differently: Cyborg Consciousness and Political Practice*, Julia Balén suggests ways of facilitating group work and alliance building among women that avoid reproducing oppressive identities and discourses. Using her own pedagogical practice as case study, she explores the importance of self-reflection for enabling a feminist theory and practice that recognizes women's problematic relation to power – both inside and outside the academy. This essay argues that through "power shame and denial" women risk wasting or abusing the power they do possess. Drawing upon Donna Haraway's theory of cyborg consciousness, Balén makes the case that, if feminists are to successfully negotiate the relation between power, identity and difference in their theory and practice, they must risk creatively playing with their investment in the concept of identity; through provisionally suspending this investment, feminists may begin to develop group work strategies that resist reproducing hegemonic identity formation processes, those which depend on the "othering" of difference.

Susan Jackson 's *Ivory Towers and Guardians of the Word* addresses how the language of the academy is ideologically constructed to encode only masculinist reality; hence, if women are to succeed in a university environment, they must perform a kind of gendered "doublethink": that is, learn to produce knowledge using the approved language of the academy, a language that is antithetical to women's multiple subjective truths. This essay interrogates a range of feminist theory, including French and Black feminisms, to determine what solutions they offer to this dilemma. Jackson suggests ways whereby women can challenge and reconstruct academic discourses and, in the process, create new feminist ways of being "academic".

The final essay in this section, Margaret A. Villanueva's *TransForm/ando Women's Studies: Latina Theory Re-Imagines América*, provides an overview of the cutting-edge research, theory, creative production and pedagogical practice of Chicana/Latina women in the academy. Villanueva presents a compelling case for how the theory and practice being developed in this feminist community holds the potential to generate a paradigm shift in Women's Studies and academic feminism. With reference to the theory on canon-formation produced by Edward Said and Marcus Embry, she argues that Women's Studies must undertake a re-reading of its own canon – while thoroughly reading and integrating the insights of Latina theory and practice; only a deep-structural transformation of feminist theory and practice will result in a renewed and invigorated discipline that no longer has any "borders" to defend against those marked as different.

Chapter 1

Practicing Difference Differently: Cyborg Consciousness and Political Practice

JULIA BALÉN

The theoretical and practical struggle against unity-through-domination or unity-through-incorporation ironically not only undermines the justification for patriarchy, colonialism, humanism, positivism, essentialism, scientism, and other unlamented -isms, but all claims for an organic or natural standpoint. (Haraway 1991: 157)

"Networking" is both a feminist practice and a multinational corporate strategy – weaving is for oppositional cyborgs. (Haraway 1991: 170)

Progressive social movement is anything but easy. Hegemonic groups have the relative privilege and ease of organizing themselves in ways more "natural" to our social training, that work within and reproduce the discourses that produce "us". People in such groups are not constantly required to operate outside of their emotional or ideational comfort zones. They can enjoy the pleasure of a sense of cohesiveness between the way they perceive themselves and the ways in which most others perceive them, or the way they produce themselves and the ways in which most others produce them. This is why there is such privileged hue and cry, such swift and angry backlash whenever progressive movements manage to produce counter-hegemonic identities/ discourses. It forces those living the norm to live, if only minutely, where those working for social justice must live, without the ignor(e)ant comfort that the fiction of a stable identity produces. While few individuals actually live this fiction comfortably, we desire it powerfully. But progressives cannot afford to enjoy such comforts because it is precisely the production of hegemonic identities/subjectivities that we must resist for social change to work. Moreover, while the language of this paragraph produces a "them" and an "us" for the purpose of emphasizing some important differences, the danger of maintaining such a production of identities is that it supports the idea that "the problem" is with "them" rather than accepting the reality that normative identities and discourses are constantly re-articulated through everyone's daily actions, through every process of relating unless we are consciously resisting such reproductions. Many theorists have articulated the relationships between power, discourses, identities, and differences,[1] but few have offered concrete interpretations of how to apply such theories.[2] This piece begins a part of the project to articulate some of the ways that we might apply such thinking to our practices.[3]

Those working for social justice have only idealism and/or a personal desire to grow to motivate the self-reflection necessary to developing practices that resist reproducing oppressive identities/discourses – and both idealism and a personal desire to grow too often fail when up against the inevitable resistance to change. Moreover, given the fact that such idealism is often, at least in the US, tied to notions of freedom (and for many this means the freedom to be "who we are"), the focus becomes to change the world around us rather than ourselves when, in fact, both must change. For those of us whose identities are in any part defined by our knowledge of our own oppression, the notion that we may be part of the problem is not an easy pill to swallow. The world is wrong, after all, not us. However wrong the world may be, insofar as we produce it and are produced by it, this attitude works against developing the ongoing movement necessary to produce enduring social change. So while corporations are, ironically, learning to harness cooperative practices that selectively acknowledge the differences that CEOs know to be the increasing reality of the workforce and society that supports them, social change activists too often cling to no more than a common cause in hopes that it will see us through our differences. But, as many activists for social justice have found out the hard way, common causes do not negate the differences between us. In fact, the desire to erase or ignore the differences is part of the problem.

For those of us who perceive ourselves to be oppressed, our relations to power are problematic at best. The belief that others have it and we don't tends to leave power as a marker of the "evil" other and progressives in denial about what power we have, making that which we do wield all the more dangerous. It is this under-theorized level of group work and alliance building that I would like to address. In fact, our failure to address power at the interpersonal level as an important part of activism for social justice is related to our unwillingness to acknowledge our own power and our feelings about that power – especially as it changes. Through power shame and denial, we run the risk of failing to use and/or abusing the power we have. Acknowledging our own power while operating in a world in which we too often feel powerless requires developing a consciousness akin to what Donna Haraway refers to as cyborg: "a kind of disassembled and reassembled, post-modern collective and personal self" (1991: 163) that is "resolutely committed to partiality, irony, intimacy, and perversity. It is opposi-tional, utopian, and completely without innocence" (1991: 151). Developing such a consciousness is not easy because it goes beyond merely the ideological to the emotional and practical. Cyborg practices require suspending (or creatively playing with) our investment in iden-tity, at least provisionally, over and over again. It is not without risks, but then, nothing is.

This story is a microcosmic look at some of the lived dynamics that get in the way of building alliances for progressive movement. The chal-lenges that face anyone interested in making social change happen are great, though I believe not insurmountable. I believe this because I have witnessed effective action. I have also been repeatedly amazed and sometimes disheartened at how readily folks of good will and good intentions (myself included) sabotage our own and other's efforts through resistance to self-reflection, critical analysis, and a re-inventing of ourselves based upon this process. Too often we function on a simplistic belief that if our intentions are good, good results will follow, and as if everyone should put up with our quirks even though some of those "quirks" employ oppressive strategies of which we remain unaware. Such practices ignore not only the more theorized internal-ization of institutionalized identity-based oppressions such as sexism and racism (the ways in which those who experience oppression turn the oppression in on ourselves or on others of our own groups), but also the personal ways in which such internalizations structure our own uses of power in everyday personal relations – our practices of othering to define ourselves. Our relational practices are based on myriad complex, overlapping, interconnected interpersonal and group experiences, both normative and resistant, by which we define ourselves and our places in the world. By failing to address these relational practices, progres-sives reproduce the patterns of oppression we claim to want to change. Thinking alone will not make change happen. We all know too many intelligent people who can develop and describe anti-oppressive theo-ries with great complexity, but, failing the step of self-reflection, they/we consistently reproduce the dynamics they/we so intelligently critique in their/our own lives. Theory must be practiced.

My analysis of the case study below comes as much out of years of social change work in the "communities" that have been part of my life

13

Julia Balén

as it does from any theoretical frameworks. While I have worked at the level of state policy development – one avenue for social change, I have also facilitated community groups (as diverse as Take Back the Night organizers, nuclear protest action groups, work cooperatives, communes, and arts organizations) through difficulties that threatened to kill actions and alliances that many people had worked very hard to build – actions and alliances they all believed in, but for a variety of reasons members themselves were effectively sabotaging. It didn't take any outside agitator to come in and cause problems – the agitator and social power dynamics that we intend to change work from within in most devastating ways. It is easier to organize action/create movement when there is an immediate, obvious threat to focus activists' energies. But when the issues being addressed are diffuse, interconnected, ongoing, and pervasive – more like the polluted air we breathe – then activists must work all the harder and more creatively to resist the inevitable and ongoing reproduction of inequities that "the air we all breathe" creates. Naming the problem is not enough – it does not suddenly render us immune to participation in inequitable practices. The best we can do is develop practices consciously from self-reflective analyses and open discussion about our inevitable internalizations, practices that give us creative ways to move beyond our own denials and redefine what power with others might look like, what power that enacts social justice might be. Internalized power dynamics will continue to undermine effective social action until we choose to address them where we live. There are tools we can learn to use to develop such living practices.

A Case Study

> So my cyborg myth is about transgressed boundaries, potent fusions, and dangerous possibilities which progressive people might explore as one part of needed political work. . . .The political struggle is to see from [multiple] perspectives at once because each reveals dominations and possibilities unimaginable from the other vantage point. Single vision produces worse illusions than double vision or many-headed monsters. (Haraway 1991: 154)

The classroom experience that this piece grows out of was an experimental course developed with the help of the Institute for Public Media Arts (IPMA) grant for a curriculum and faculty development project called the "-ISM (N.) Project". Developed as a creative response to the dangerous hate speech and actions that take place on college campuses,

14

the -ISM (N.) Project grant asked that we develop a yearlong team-taught course that addressed "isms" (racism, sexism, classism, etc.) from any number of theoretical/disciplinary perspectives, and engaging in experiential learning and video production. Three of us – one Women's Studies and one Media Arts faculty member and one Media Arts graduate student, all white women activists from various class backgrounds – worked together with input from the first faculty institute, and materials developed by IPMA staff for the -ISM(N.) Project, to develop a year-long course syllabus. Given my own interests in cultural representations, power, and group dynamics and my team teachers' interests in social change through media literacy and video production, we developed a class called Crossing Boundaries: Diversity & Representation. The theoretical basis for the course was grounded in a media/cultural studies perspective informed by ethnic, social justice, and women's studies research. The first semester we focused on what it means to have a voice, who gets to represent whom and how, whose stories are told and whose are not, how one develops a resistant voice for change, and producing video diaries that addressed oppressive social forces in the students' own lives. The second semester broadened the scope to address group dynamics, "isms" on campus, institutional oppression, and strategies for alliance building through the experience of group video production. This was the general plan and we were very excited. I was personally excited about the possibility of teaching some of the group skills that I know work to a class of activist students. We knew that the practice/experience of the class would bring challenges, but like all risks, one never knows how the challenges will take shape until they happen.

Students had to apply to be part of the course. While this process alone created a lot of self-selection, we were looking for people who were able to articulate their own struggles with being socially silenced and/or who were interested in addressing such silencing. The course was designed as an upper-division honors[4] class that attracted three graduate students and twelve juniors and seniors with majors including media arts, women's studies, ethnic studies, anthropology, and fine arts. We lost three students, one graduate and two undergraduates, by the end of the first semester due to life changes, finishing the year with twelve. Over half of the class were ethnic minority students, about half were queer identified, one recently disabled, and about three-quarters female.

I want to say that I greatly admire the courage, tenacity, and dedication of both my team teachers and the students who dared to take part in this very challenging experimental course. We all came in with very high hopes, if differing, about what the course might accomplish. In fact, the class accomplished a great deal and is still accomplishing things far beyond the class boundaries as the videos the students produced are used for discussion and education on and off campus. Moreover, in spite of the very painful places some students wound up going with each other and with the teaching team, many remain in contact and some continue developing videos together. Even some for whom the class itself felt like a burnout experience have remained in various contact with both teachers and students. Clearly the experience was meaningful in all our lives in ways we could not have imagined. In evaluations at the end of the year, the majority of students reflected that this was "an experience unlike any other" and they knew that it would be "a rich mine for growth" for a long time to come.

We had a mostly glorious first semester during which students quickly developed an open rapport with teachers and classmates. We discussed readings with enthusiasm. We all shared experiences of being othered in a wide variety of contexts, and we found agreement and discussed differences over the readings, over cherished beliefs, over strategies for dealing with oppression. Students and teachers listened to each others' perspectives, added their own, and challenged each other to grow – to expand our own experiences to include a wider perspective on the operations of oppressions, their intersections, and ways to resist. We worked on listening skills as well as developing resistant voices. Moreover, several people in the group had experience with work shopping their artistic efforts and shared their considerable abilities generously – at one point effectively walking one student through the serious blocks she had to producing her video diary by offering astonishingly clear yet empathetic group critique of her ideas. While we were all tired at the end of such an intensely productive semester, students had produced amazing montages that critiqued cultural representations they found oppressive as well as powerful video diaries.

The second semester required us all to make a shift from the personal to the group on several levels: in the readings the topics shifted from the focus on voice to the ways institutions work to silence people and how people resist; and in practice the students would develop group videos rather than individual ones. This shift posed serious challenges. First of all, the shift from developing individual pieces to group projects is a big one in any medium. Secondly, given the glories of the first semester, the second had a great deal to live up to. Finally, the rapport that students had developed with each other and with the teaching team through all the sharing of the first semester had broken down boundaries – some of which we often depend on to protect us in difficult group situations. We tend to expect more of people with whom we have gotten close than those with whom we have not. The teaching team knew that the switch from the personal to the group would take some adjustment as group work requires a greater amount of trust and/or trusted practices for negotiating differences. Given that we had a preponderance of creative people pretty well accustomed to working on their own and generally disdainful of group work, several who claimed openly that they were usually the ones who wound up doing all the work, we knew that there would be some territory to cover before things might run smoothly. Nevertheless, we were very hopeful as the class had exhibited, developed, and practiced good workshop skills, high standards of participation, and respect for the teaching team and each other throughout the first semester.

We held a retreat at the beginning of the second semester to workshop some general ideas for group videos that we had outlined in the fall. The plan was to gain consensus on several key issues that the class felt needed addressing on campus and then organize several small groups of three or four that would each develop a video addressing one of the issues. By the end of the retreat we had two basic areas of interest which the teaching team expected would break out eventually into subgroups, but the class eventually divided into only two groups. We had planned for at least three and possibly four groups precisely because we were aware of the greater unwieldiness of large group decision-making, especially given the time-constraints.

While both groups struggled through difficulties, it was the larger group that consisted of the most openly affectionate members that ran into the most difficult problems in developing their project, or even working as a group. Both groups struggled with processes for how to make decisions, grew frustrated and sometimes angry with each other in spite of several in-depth sessions on group work that explored common problems to avoid and tools for heading problems off before they disrupt work. While during these preparatory sessions students readily articulated problem areas, brainstormed possible strategies for avoiding or negotiating a variety of group problems, and showed a high degree of comprehension of the possible pitfalls, when they began to work in groups, to different degrees, they failed to engage their own knowledge. Both groups had individuals who felt burned out at the end. Theorizing and practicing are definitely two different things. But the smaller group which, as a whole, practiced more ongoing self-reflection, maintained more freedom in their functioning, managed their group work with less rancor, and produced a video that integrated their points of view that clearly showed they had learned from and been changed by their interactions with each other.

The larger group wound up dividing into cliques, roughly along social class lines,[5] that allowed comparatively less room for free self-expression and much less productive self-reflection while creating inevitable out-members. In the end, they solved their problems by designing a project that required minimal group interaction and by scapegoating the faculty. While the end product videos are both wonderful in very different ways, my own desire for students to come away with positive experiences of group processing was in many ways thwarted and many of us suffered through tensions that are predictable products of the difficulties we face in attempting to ally across differences.

Looking back, there were several actions the teaching team could have taken to create an environment more conducive to effective practice of group process:

1   More consciously develop group work skills throughout the first semester rather than being seduced by what seemed like more organic group process development;
2   More fully develop and insist on the responsibilities that come with liberatory practices, especially within the inherently power driven context of a university classroom;
3   Insist on smaller groups;
4   Work out our own desires for the class and our own differences in approaches in even greater detail from the outset.

The first two actions would have been quite useful, but not something that we could do at the point at which problems arose. In fact, one could say that they were casualties of a domino effect of "oversights" that started with the national training, continued through our team efforts, and were replicated once again in our own students' actions. While I had expected our teaching team would be put through experiential learning paces at the faculty institute similar to those we would be expecting of our students, it turned out that the national trainers had been rebuffed by an earlier group of faculty for expecting the faculty to take part in experiential learning exercises. So the trainers chose to take a less experiential approach with us. Similarly, as I was the only teaching team member with extensive experience and particular interest in group dynamics and processes, I made the mistake of allowing group process skills development to be subordinated to, rather than consistently integrated into, the substantial theoretical content and video production imperatives that held much greater interest for my teaching partners and about which I was also excited. Though we were all interested in liberatory teaching practices[6] and, in fact, had exercised them in various ways in our past teaching, we made the mistake of not reflecting enough on what it might mean in this specific context. While I think our imaginations, even with the help of readings, might well have fallen short of what transpired, better reflection certainly would have helped.

Insisting on smaller groups would have been the easiest short-term solution, but this seemed to go against the grain of the liberatory structure we had developed that encouraged self-governance. If we are encouraging students to develop their voices against the backdrop of socially oppressive forces, it seems that the importance of encouraging them to develop their voices in relationship to each other becomes of greater importance. As Linda Holtzman, a member of another -ISM(N.) Project teaching team notes: "This is such a dilemma in teaching for social justice and working with people who are new activists – what's the appropriate balance between using what we know as instructive and allowing others to make the same mistakes we did"[7] (I would add, "and still do sometimes make" because it's always easier to see patterns of practice in others than it is in oneself.) In fact, the teaching team members encouraged the move to smaller groups several times, but the majority in the larger group insisted on working together expressing a sense that breaking into smaller groups would constitute some sort of failure. It did not help that the faculty too felt caught between time constraints and the desire for students to come to their own decisions even as their impasse was eating up precious time. But such time constraints are in no way peculiar to a classroom – they are the realities of any human endeavor. We attempted to facilitate them through their difficulties rather than merely (hegemonically) insist that the group break down into more manageable numbers. Nevertheless, their insistence on remaining a group offered a laboratory experiment in group process and all its glorious difficulties that shows how we tend to practice difference in ways that replicate the power paradigms we intend to change.

More concretely working out our (teaching team members') own desires for the class ahead of time would probably have produced all of the above and made the experience for everyone much richer without so much pain as, in part, some of the students acted out faculty differences over emphasizing production or process before the faculty identified that we had them. In any case, like children who know exactly how to play their parents against each other to establish their own identity and power as they moved into group projects, some students played on what they perceived to be our differences. The teaching team was not surprised by this tactic and, while it was not easy, we worked through our own differences to the best of our abilities, and refused to play the game. I certainly learned a great deal in the process about my own teaching style, articulating my own intentions, and the problem with wearing too many hats in a group situation (grant developer, faculty member, advisor, facilitator). The team-teaching experience will forever enrich all of my teaching and group endeavors.

In spite of our efforts, several students attached themselves to these differences – the focus on production as constructed against the focus on process difference – and refused the self-reflection necessary to disengage from this dichotomous production of identity and difference. They maintained these identities/discourses even as we actively mirrored the process of working through and with differences for them through classroom exercises (using ourselves and our real differences as models), as well as refusing to engage with their divisive strategies. For example, as we began to understand their production/process dichotomy, in one class session the teaching team members sat in the middle of the room with the students surrounding us as we discussed our own differences of opinion. Then we asked them what they noticed about our discussion, and we worked together to critique our own group process. This enacted for them – with the teaching team in the more vulnerable position and them in the more reflective position – the cycle of theorizing, action, reflection, re-theorizing that we wanted them to understand and incorporate in their own work with each other. Unfortunately, the resistance on the part of at least some of the class to the self-reflection that such a mirroring exercise is designed to stimu- late, was, it seems, too great.

Having empowered students to ask for what they wanted/needed, we failed in our insistence on reciprocation on that score for precisely the wrong reasons – in an attempt to lessen the power differential between students and faculty. No amount of "trading" – our voices for theirs – undoes the actual power differential when it comes to grades so it became an act of shame that denigrated the value of our own work with them. During their struggle to come to terms with their differences, rather than seriously considering suggestions from the teaching team, some of them began to interpret any faculty suggestions as institution- ally tied such that it became a righteous fight against hegemony to resist class requirements or teacher requests. In fact, there was a level upon which for some students the faculty members became the scapegoats for the pain of their own differences merely due to our roles. As we had left a great deal of room for them to be different with each other and stretched them to do more so as they faced greater difficulties in group project development, the scapegoat necessary to oppressive identity construction took form in the teachers. (It is that need of an Other to define oneself and thereby hang on to the type of power one knows in conjunction with the power difference between student and teacher.) The painful irony for the two faculty members on the team was that we should serve as the symbols of oppressive power despite all that we had done to encourage their empowerment. In fact, we had failed to adequately look out for our own. The graduate assistant team member's more liminal status in the students' perceptions allowed her somewhat more freedom of movement, keeping her from being perceived as authoritative. This made it possible for her to encourage students toward more productive practices.

While all of the group dynamics that developed could (problematically) be tied to oppressive "identity" categories, this would be a limited approach that ultimately reproduces the oppressive categories, does not create movement beyond them, and fails to address the complexity of our articulations of power in relation to each other. While such naming of institutionalized oppressions is absolutely necessary, too many of us use the naming as a way to distance ourselves as individuals from the hard self-scrutiny that effective social change work takes. Naming alone is as far as many of us go. Formulating power relations that enact and produce alliances for justice requires us rethinking not only our systemic identities, but how such identities – multiple and overlapping – become articulated as part of our personal practices – how we negotiate power on day-to-day interpersonal levels. Without such scrutiny (and the supportive environment that makes it possible) as well as theories & methods to address them, we will continue to either replicate the very power systems we critique and/or self-sabotage every time we come together to make social change happen. It was the articulation of this group's personal practices of power that severely limited their abilities to collaborate with minimal pain.

When they had struggled quite a bit as a group and gotten nowhere, I was asked to facilitate. Unfortunately, they had waited until substantial damage had been done. Several problems I have found to be very common made them wait too long: not actually hearing each other; denying that they had substantial differences until those not feeling heard were shouting; and one of the most common problems for people trained as individualists, believing that asking for help means weakness or failure. It is shameful and places one in a less powerful position, so we either ignore our need for help or do not ask for help until after damage to trust and relationships is already done. I think this might be a particular problem for those who have dared to resist normativity as doing so requires an ability to resist the constant suggestion that one should be something else. Strategies that are sometimes effective in personally resisting oppression – such as: hyper-individualism; hyper-resistance to any perceived form of disciplining; a sense of self as different, non-normative, and therefore not group oriented; trust resistance – are often counterproductive in creating cooperation. If one defines oneself as that which is "the different", then sharing difference

21

with others challenges that identity. This group's members shared individualized variations on all of these strategies that challenged their abilities to see each other as partners or even engage with what that might mean to them individually or as a group.

After assessing the group's difficulties through both group and individual interviewing, I felt mediation was necessary between two members whose philosophical and stylistic differences were noted by all members as central to the conflict, but my suggestion was rejected. At the time I found this refusal extremely frustrating – especially in my double role as teacher and facilitator/mediator. This required me to reassess my own desires as an activist teacher for them to positively experience the process of negotiating differences and the ideally disinterested role of facilitator. This role is about paying attention to the process and helping them to think as a group so that the group can pay attention to the content and goals. My practice as facilitator is to disengage personal identity/investment from any outcome while placing trust in the process of making space for all voices to be heard. This practice comes from realizing that none of us has the complete picture, all of us are implicated in oppressive practices, no one is innocent, so change cannot happen through the process of faulting others to define ourselves as good or right. In over 20 years of facilitating, I have found it relatively easy to decide the importance of my goals and values and either act on them, temporarily suspend them for the sake of hearing a problem out, or let them go altogether. More often than not, once folks in a group feel heard, they will often come back around to what they could not hear in a moment of tension. So my patience for, in a sense, setting myself aside, is substantial. While I worked to set my own goals aside to allow room for their understanding of the situation to develop, what could not be set aside in this situation was my role as teacher in their eyes. In a course designed to create voice, I found myself awkwardly silenced as both facilitator and teacher due to some students' inability to extend liberatory concepts to these roles.

Failing a mediation to address the strong personal and philosophical differences that had arisen, I attempted facilitating the group as a group. I had them all come to see me or email me individually to answer the following questions: What do you see as causing the impasse? What would you suggest for getting through it? What might your part be in creating the impasse and in moving on? In spite of some very creative facilitating on the part of the team teachers, including numerous attempts at role-playing, use of techniques to disengage egos from ideas, rotating our own roles with the class, the failure to mediate the deeper problems created impasses at every turn. Eventually, by scapegoating the faculty most students in the group found enough commonality to move forward with a plan that required the least possible amount of integration of materials they each individually produced. Nevertheless, the problems they articulated in response to the questions I asked offer an interesting outline of common problems to which we often react with whatever our own power/resistance strategies tend to be – a sampling of common stumbling blocks which groups often need to negotiate.

One member of the group summed up the state of affairs: "[We] have sat down three times and gotten absolutely zip zero done other than knowing how to push each others' buttons. With seven people there is going to have to be some give and take and very few people in our group seem to be willing." In the interest of developing tools for addressing these all too common blocks to successful group process, I'd like to offer an analysis of the problems they described. The following were named by at least two members of the group as elements that contributed to a breakdown in agreements or decision-making, most by a majority, roughly in order of importance/emphasis given. Each complaint falls roughly into one of the following three categories: ideals (or principles), feelings, and practices. These three elements inform each other to create harmony or discord: generally, when at least two of the three are in tandem, we are more willing to tolerate differences in the third. But if strong differences exist, in any of the three, or small ones across all three areas, then they tend to inform each other in the direction of discord.

Problem	Category
Conflicting philosophies about collaboration	*ideals*
Differing styles of creative process & decision-making	*ideals/practices*
People not following through on assignments/agreements	*practices*
Feelings of discomfort with making contributions	*feelings*
Discomfort with limited number of contributions – only two proposals polarizes	*feelings*
People not speaking up in group – only behind the scenes	*practices*
Belief that breaking into two groups would be a failure	*ideals*
Personalities in conflict: those two people ought to go work it out	*ideals/practices*
Desire for all perspectives to interplay vs. get-the-job-done focus	*ideals*
Some people's ideas repeatedly dropped, ignored, or not adequately addressed	*practice*
One person trying to direct – feeling time-pressured – ignoring input	*practices*
Lack of trust about honesty of statements made – mixed messages	*feelings*
Disagreement about when to ask for help	*ideals*
Tempers flaring, raised voices	*practices/feelings*

While many of these might generally be coded to be class, race, or gender based, for example, men might be seen as not wanting to ask for help or complaints about raised voices might be seen as related to class differences, the articulations of these issues were far more complex than a simple reading of "differences" could possibly account for. Moreover, in over twenty years of facilitation experience, I have seen people shift positions in different contexts and come to realize that all of us are capable of taking up any of the positions from powerful to powerless, from victim to oppressor, depending on the context.

Developing Cyborg Practices

> The cyborg is a kind of disassembled and reassembled, postmodern collective and personal self. This is the self feminists must code. (Haraway 1991: 163)

The realization that comes after one has "identified" with a group only to find that differences remain and that identity is not static or essential can be devastating, but is absolutely necessary to developing cyborg practices. As Haraway claims: "It is important to note that the effort to construct revolutionary standpoints, epistemologies as achievements of people committed to changing the world, has been part of the process showing the limits of identification" (1991: 157). Realizing that we have choices about each of these elements and that we need not tie our identities to them is central to nurturing alliances. Offering creative ways for people to at least temporarily disengage specific ideals, feelings, and practices from their identities is key. Facilitation and mediation can offer that opportunity if activists are willing to acknowledge their own part in the process. However, as long as differences are engaged as "personal", they are not likely to be negotiable.

Ideals (guiding principles or values) are often articulated as "shoulds". For example: "collaboration *should* integrate everyone's point of view", "decisions *should* be agreed to by everyone", "or we *should not* need to ask for help". Ideals need to be identified, named and evaluated in terms of group goals. I am not suggesting that people let them all go, but that all ideals need to be open to reflection or we tend to revert to oppressive power struggles. We may decide that certain ideals are absolutely the ones we want to guide our work, but they need to hold up to rigorous, ongoing scrutiny. This is where the important work of both personal and group self-reflection comes in.

Feelings often motivate our practices, which too often, under duress, are reactionary rather than responsible. Responsible practices come from assessing our emotional responses to other people's actions and then choosing to respond in a way that is congruent with ideals rather than merely reacting with dominant practices that are likely to recreate all of the power responses that lead groups to deadlock, burnout, and worse. This does not mean ignoring emotion, but rather assessing both its validity and limitations. For example, the lack of trust reported above had validity insofar as members of the group had good reason to think that they were being talked about behind their backs. But counter to this feeling was the shared vulnerability that empowered them all to speak openly in the first semester. Both feelings were accurate. Their choices were to choose one at the expense of the other or to animate the vulnerability to challenge the dishonesty. Challenging the dishonesty while finding creative ways to reconnect to earlier feelings of trust requires a willingness on the part of the group members to see it as in their interests to consider that such a reconnection is both possible and desirable; to discuss what has lead to speaking behind others' backs; decide how to deal with it; and, most difficult of all, set aside identification with the divides that such feelings create. But if people have started to define themselves by making others wrong, such a move will be difficult.

This brings us to practice. The practices named as problematic by the group included: people not following through on assignments/agreements; people not speaking up in group – only behind the scenes; some people's ideas repeatedly dropped, ignored, or not adequately addressed; one person trying to direct – feeling time-pressured – ignoring input; tempers flaring, and raised voices. These practices are hardly uncommon: they are practices of power based upon the assumptions of inequity. Not following through on assignments/agreements could be based on assumptions that others will take the lead or that others are better, have more to say, etc. Not speaking up in a group – only behind the scenes, unless done equally with all group members, is a practice not only based on a belief in insider/outsider groups, it is a practice that creates them. One person trying to direct – feeling time-pressured – ignoring input assumes that others cannot or will not work together unless directed, but that one person must take the lead who will "edit" the group process as he or she sees fit. Tempers flaring and raised voices indicate attempts to seize power and/or a sense of not being heard. While such practices may be quite common, the difference for this group is that they were attempting to negotiate a group project while practicing what they preached – the value of each individual and his or her voice in the process. Unlike the standard group of students facing a project together wherein the unspoken rules of power might operate with little direct critique, this group had come together with the purpose of enacting liberatory practices that engaged them across their differences. Yet, as they attempted to work through their differences, the in/out group behaviors increased and identities became increasingly tied to animosities and divisions. The sense of rights and wrongs increased as common ground disappeared. Individuals grew increasingly unwilling to let go of the identities in relationship to each other that they had formed.

> The cyborg is resolutely committed to partiality, irony, intimacy, and perversity. It is oppositional, utopian, and completely without innocence. (Haraway 1991: 151)

Alliances to create social justice movement will be difficult at best unless the people involved not only realize, but also begin to act with the understanding that defining oneself by making others wrong is at the heart of social injustice. The dehumanization of the othering process is built into our own identity practices and it takes conscious and always fallible practice to change this. The willingness to be fallible and admit such fallibility does not come easily. It is messy and uncomfortable to admit the differences that exist within one's self as well as with those with whom we need to ally. While every individual faces these challenges with different strengths and weaknesses, it has been my experience that the more a person has tasted the privilege of ignorance that the fiction of a cohesive self offers, the more conscious dedication choosing a cyborg consciousness requires. For those who have not had the privilege of living this fiction, the challenge can be one of resisting valorizing a victim role as it seems to offer the most cohesive and mobilizing identity in a world that denies us privileged subjectivity.

Work for social justice requires not only an intellectual critique that calls for realizations about what our critiques of power might mean for our own actions, but also an enactment in personal relations of those realizations. If we all know that we are imperfect, steeped in the very practices we would like to see changed, then we need to leave room – lots of room – not only for ourselves, but for others. Further, we need to define ourselves not through replication of the othering process, but by practicing difference without othering. If corporations can make selective use of cooperative practices to improve their bottom line, certainly activists can learn to transform our personal practices of power into practices that reflect our ideals.

Notes

1   There are far too many to name, but the ones most informative to my own thinking through this piece include Donna Haraway, Monique Wittig, Judith Butler, and Janet Jakobsen.
2   Urvashi Vaid comes to mind as one who works to engage them strategically.

3   For a further development of progressive group process skills, see my workshops, "Roberta's 'Rules': Practical Meeting Practices".

4   Many US universities offer honors programs for students who maintain a high grade point average which allow students special privileges and more advanced instruction and research experiences.

5   Subtleties of class differences were the most distinct lines across which they seemed to split with inflections and intersections with gender and sexual identities (butch/femme and possibly axes of desire). In other groups, some of the othering that went on might well have been articulated through one of the more "standard" categories of difference – race , gender, class, but because this group was very sensitized to most of these differences (though less so with class) and the ways they tend to be articulated, their othering happened in more subtle and diffuse ways. This case dislodges the assumptions that our differences are only or mostly about race, class, gender, sexuality, nationality, etc. to highlight how much the articulation of our differences has to do with our identity production and the uneasiness we face as we attempt to practice power differently.

6   Liberatory practices here refer to techniques meant to help students move in the direction of equitable self-governance with an attention to those social dynamics that militate against social justice.

7   Linda Holtzman, from e-mail discussion, 25 March 1999.

References

Butler, Judith. 1990: *Gender Trouble: Feminism and the Subversion of Identity*. New York: Routledge.

Coover, Virginia, Esser, Charles, Deacon, Ellen, and Moore, Christopher. 1978: *The Resource Manual for a Living Revolution*. New Society Press, Philadelphia.

Haraway, Donna. 1991: *Simians, Cyborgs, and Women: The Reinvention of Nature*. New York: Routledge.

Jakobsen, Janet. 1998: *Working Alliances and the Politics of Difference*. Bloomington/Indianapolis: Indiana University Press.

Urvashi, Vaid. 1995: *Virtual Equality: The Mainstreaming of Gay & Lesbian Liberation*. New York: Anchor Books.

Wittig, Monique. 1992: *The Straight Mind and Other Essays*. Boston: Beacon Press.

Chapter 2

Ivory Towers and Guardians of the Word: Language and Discourse in the Academy

SUSAN JACKSON

Once upon a time, a time that has gone and a time still to come, in a far and distant place, not too far from here, not too far from now, live the Guardians. Who they are and what they guard, no-one can quite remember. We do not know what life was like before the time of the Guardians, and we do not even know if there was such a life before the Guardians, and we do not know if we can imagine what life might look like without the Guardians. They are shining and magnificent, so we are told: dressed in the robes of Righteousness; adorned with the shield of Knowledge; the sword of Power strong and straight at their sides; and on their heads – bright for us all to see, a beacon glowing in the night sky – is the crown of Truth.

In a secret place at the heart of their Ivory Towers, in the midst of the shield of Knowledge, the sword of Power and the crown of Truth, lies the Word. The Guardians hold the key, and it is theirs, and theirs alone. And, if we can find our way in, the Guardians will share their Word with us and it will be ours too.

To reach the Guardians there are different roads. For some, for those molded in their image, the path is smooth and straight. Others of us though struggle and work and toil to climb the rocky tracks. We try to be the Image. The lights shining from the Ivory Towers where the Guardians live are bright. The ivory gleams and glistens in the eternal sky. The light dazzles so it becomes all we can see, blotting out our memories and our dreams; our stories told and untold; our histories and our futures; our lives and our loves. The Word is all there is. We can make their word our own.

I heard tell that one of us reached the Ivory Towers once, shielding her eyes from the crown of Truth, dodging the sword of Power and pushing aside the shield of Knowledge. But the Ivory, so dazzling and full of promises, was just the bleached bones of something long dead, and the Word was ours all the time, waiting to be freed.

Once upon a time, not too far from here, not too far from now, I started to prepare for this chapter on language. It is my aim in this article to scrutinize the language and discourses of the academy by identifying and challenging its patriarchal base. Discourse gives us rules about what it is possible and not possible to speak and therefore, perhaps, to think, showing a clear relationship between social "reality" and language. Discourses, then, are productive of meaning. In the academy, particular academic discourses will privilege certain texts, certain kinds of academic values, and make others unthinkable.

How, though, can I think the unthinkable? I can only mount this challenge in writing, in an academic language which itself limits meaning for me: "This is the oppressor's language / yet I need it to talk to you" (Rich, 1971). It could be argued that there is an analogy between the language and discourses of the academy and those described by George Orwell in the novel *Nineteen Eighty-four*. Like its chief character, Winston Smith, I stare at the blank screen in front of me:

> For some time he had sat gazing stupidly at the paper . . . It was curious that he seemed not merely to have lost the power of expressing himself, but even to have forgotten what it was that he had originally intended to say. For weeks past he had been making ready for this moment, and it had never crossed his mind that anything would be needed except courage. (Orwell 1951: 11)

It is not surprising that Winston could no longer remember what he had originally wanted to say. In the Newspeak of the new society of Ingsoc, thoughts have become limited through language, a language ideologically constructed to only allow expression of the ideas of the dominant class, and to make all other modes of thought impossible. To help the process, all written records, all recorded ideas, have to agree with the orthodoxy. Some memories have to be written out of history, others have to be altered, and yet other memories have to be invented.

And yet even this is not enough. For Winston does still remember something. He remembers that there is another story to tell, that he did once have something to say. The people in this new world have to do more than just rearrange their memories; they also have to forget that they have done so. Winston has not only to learn that there has been a tampering with reality, but also to erase this knowledge from his mind. "In Oldspeak it is called, quite frankly, 'reality control'. In Newspeak it is called *doublethink*" (Orwell 1951: 220). In this chapter, I will explore the "doublethink" required of women in the academy through an

exploration of some of the challenges by "French feminists", Black feminists and other feminist writing. I will ask whether for women to
succeed at university we need to learn to use the language of the
academy, or whether we should be learning to resist, challenge and
reconstruct its discourses and calling for different forms of language,
different ways of being "academic".

The French feminist and philosopher Luce Irigaray argues that
women need to search for a female Imaginary.[1] Language, she says, is
"neither universal, nor neutral, nor intangible" (Irigaray 1993: 31).
Irigaray suggests that the relationship between female, male and
language is an historical phenomenon. When Lacan talks of the univer-
sality of language, he is effectively excluding and silencing women.
Nevertheless, some feminists, including Irigaray, have found Lacan a
useful starting point. The production of language is central for both
Irigaray and Lacan in the formation of subjectivity, although Irigaray
returns to the mother and the maternal through language. By doing so,
Irigaray suggests "a new symbolism so that love among women can
take place . . . instead of collaboration . . . in their own annihilation"
(Brodribb 1992: 107). I find it problematic to discuss women's collaboration in their own annihilation, a view synonymous with blaming the
victim. However, as Irigaray shows, "love among women" is also problematic within patriarchal structures, where primacy is given to the
symbolic phallus and to be female is to signify "lack". The feminine has
still to be created in language.

Irigaray, then, has worked on finding ways in which it is possible to
speak as a woman. In "When our two lips speak together" (1980), she
shows the importance of this task, for "if we speak to each other as men
. . . have taught us to speak, we will fail each other" (Irigaray 1980: 69).
However, "women find it difficult to speak and to be heard as women.
They are excluded and denied by the patriarchal linguistic order"
(Irigaray 1993: 20). What it means to speak as woman is difficult to
define. Irigaray herself says "there is simply no way I can give you an
account of 'speaking (as) woman'; it is spoken" (1974: 32). Speaking (as)
woman is the name for something which does not yet exist, the position
of the female subject in the symbolic order. There is a clear distinction
for Irigaray in speaking *like* a woman and speaking *as* woman. In her
translation of Irigaray's work, Margaret Whitford explains that the term
parler femme has a double meaning. Whilst *parler femme*, then, is "feminine language", *par les femmes* means "by women". This pun is
translated into English as "speaking (as) woman" (Whitford 1991: 49).
Similarly, Irigaray plays with words in her key text "This sex which is
not one" (1977a). A sex which is not One could be considered Other; or
it could instead show women as more than One, multiple. Women, then,

could be nothing, not One; or everything, multiple. For Irigaray, women's place is through the looking glass and beyond: a different conceptual realm, rather than a reflection of masculine realms.

For Irigaray, women's language is the articulation of an unconscious that cannot speak about itself, but can try to make itself heard. Women need to be able to enter language as subject; to speak our own identity; to identify with the mother without objectifying her. Clearly for Irigaray, language is closely linked to sexual difference and to feminine sexuality. A feminine language, then, would be based in pluralities, without trying to find unique meanings, or "proper" meanings of words. Without this, women are condemned to live in a state of madness, shut up in our bodies and in silence, forever in a state of "lack". The future of speaking (as) woman is not yet here. Speaking (as) woman is then difficult and problematic, although it is perhaps not even possible for woman to speak (as) man. Irigaray asks how we deal with this double bind:

> But how could I on the one hand be a woman, and on the other, a writer? . . . I think the effects of repression . . . (are) so powerful that they enable such strange statements to be upheld as "I am a woman" and "I do not write as a woman". (1993: 53)

Yet writing as a woman is lonely, isolating, perhaps even currently impossible. If women within the academy (or elsewhere) want our work to be taken seriously (and that seems to mean by men and within male defined institutions), then we have to write or speak like a man, claiming mastery, truth and objectivity. To speak (as) woman is to allow meaning to be fluid and shifting. Women's written work:

> is often assimilated without a precise indication of who produced it. Culture has taught us to consume the mother's body – natural and spiritual – without being indebted . . . (An) indication of a transformation in the order of the symbolic exchanges would be a proliferation of texts showing a real dialogue between women and men. (Irigaray 1993: 54)

A dialogue between women and men. After discussing the need for women to be seen as other than "lack", of the need for women to be able to become subjective selves in a new symbolic order, it is a pity that Irigaray does not also call for a real exchange of dialogue among *women*. She seems to back away from the "two lips" of women's writing, normalizing heterosexuality, and rejecting a political feminist position.

Like Irigaray, Julia Kristeva rejects the label of feminist, as do other French "feminists" like Hélène Cixous, which in itself is a political decision. Kristeva suggests that liberal feminism demands that women are integrated into the symbolic order, whilst radical feminism celebrates women's marginal position. However, neither of these positions are satisfactory for Kristeva, who says that "feminist practice can only be negative", "one of capitalism's more advanced needs to rationalize" (1974a (1981]:137, 141). This is because there can be no socio-political transformation without a transformation of subjects: in other words, in our relationship to social constraints, to pleasure, and more deeply, to language (Kristeva, 1974a [1981]:141).

In her assertion that "Women can never be defined" (1974a), Kristeva states that the "belief that 'one is a woman' is . . . absurd . . . for a woman cannot 'be'; . . . (she is) something that cannot be represented, something that is not said" (1974a [1981]: 137). Like Irigaray, though, she believes that language positions women as Other, and she moves from the work of Jacques Lacan to consider through semiotic analyses the possibilities of women's writing and speaking. For Kristeva, then, the symbolic – and more valued – level signifies male whilst the lesser valued or recognized semiotic level signifies female. This devaluation occurs through women's identification with the mother in the semiotic stage, an identification which remains in the unconscious, forgotten, but not lost.

Like Lacan, Kristeva describes the infant as having a sense of self linked to the mother. She describes the mirror stage as a metaphor for the change from the semiotic to the symbolic. Language favors the symbolic at the expense of the semiotic. As speaking subjects, then, all we have is a "'phallic' position", so that in "women's writing, language seems to be seen from a foreign land" (Kristeva, 1974b (1981): 165–6). Kristeva argues that what is important is to have a new form of language, which subverts the symbolic and patriarchal order in favour of the more feminine semiotic. The semiotic is more closely linked to the rhythms of the body, to mothering, and to a disruption of linear text – clearly a far cry from the language of the academy.

Like Irigaray and Kristeva, Hélène Cixous is actively engaged in trying to construct a different language. Indeed, we *must* do so, she suggests, for what will become of women if we are forced to use a master-discourse, where only one kind of knowledge is transmitted, a knowledge tied up in male power (Cixous, 1975 [1987]). And what is this discourse of mastery?:

> It is what calls itself the law, but is presented as "the open door" in precisely such a way that you never go to the other side of the door, that you never go to see "what is mastery?". So you will never know that there is no law and no mastery. That there is no master. The paradox of mastery is that it is made up of a sort of complex ideological secretion produced by an infinite quantity of doorkeepers. (Cixous 1975 [1987]: 138)

To find new ideological passages, we need to reject mastery for mystery, in a different, women's language.

In her key text, "The Laugh of the Medusa" (1976), Cixous shows such women's language as lying close to the body and the emotions, all repressed in patriarchal (including academic) writing. Perhaps Cixous' writing could be most closely associated with *ecriture feminine*, or women's writing. What that might mean, though, may not be immediately clear. It remains for the moment elusive, perhaps forever elusive; for once we try to define, to tie down, to put boundaries around, we have destroyed what we want to create. It is real, nevertheless:

> It is impossible to define a feminine practice of writing, and this is an impossibility that will remain, for this practice can never be theorized, enclosed, coded – which doesn't mean that it doesn't exist. (Cixous, 1976 [1981]: 253)

Ecriture feminine is particularly clear in Cixous' imaginative work, "Laugh of the Medusa", which she clearly locates as women's writing:

> Woman must write herself . . . I write this as a woman, towards women
> . . . Write. Writing is for you, you are for you; your body is yours, take it
> . . . Write your self. Your body must be heard. (1976 [1981]: 245)

And making the body heard is a central project within *ecriture feminine*: women need to discover and recreate our own desires, not those based in the phallocentric analyses of a Freud or a Lacan. "I don't want a penis to decorate my body with . . . " says Cixous (1976). "Castration? Let others toy with it. What's a desire originating from lack? A pretty meager desire". Cixous tells us that she has two aims – to break and destroy, and to foresee the unforeseeable.

To write as woman is not merely an exercise in creative writing. It is to reach for, to claim, power and meaning, to refuse to be based within "lack". Cixous tells us "about women's writing: about *what it will do*" (1976). Writing is, she says:

> precisely *the very possibility of change*, the space that can serve as a springboard for subversive thought, the precursory movement of a transformation of social and cultural structures. (Cixous 1976 [1981]: 249)

Dangerous ideas. Perhaps it is not surprising, then, that such a call for a new, a women's, way of writing is so resisted by the academy. This language of the academy is, according to Cixous, "arid" ground. Hard and dry it might be. It is, though, here that writing is grounded, and it is the reserve of men. Women are alienated from this terrain and are unable to write "(b)ecause writing is at once too high, too great for you, it's reserved for the great – that is 'great men'; and it's 'silly'". All women, she says, know how difficult it is to speak in public, "how daring a feat, how great a transgression". We lay ourselves bare, and speak with our bodies, our flesh. Women's words are kept secret and private and silenced. This is distressing. But even if women do find the courage to speak, we will be doubly distressed, for our words will not be heard, falling "upon the deaf male ear, which hears in language only that which speaks in the masculine" (Cixous 1976 [1981]: 246).

However, this does not mean to say that the task of finding a women's language is impossible, nor that it cannot be imagined. French feminists are not alone in imagining such possibilities. In particular, this has been a concern of many Black feminists who, coming from a situated perspective of Otherness combined with a rich cultural heritage, have also considered new ways for women to enter language in recognition of a multiplicity of voices and identities. This is, though, a heritage that is lost, ignored and devalued within the academy, a point taken up by Alice Walker in her creative and re-sourceful[2] prose, *In Search of our Mothers' Gardens*. Like the work of the French feminists discussed above, this is also a search for positive identity with our mothers, our selves, our creativity, our source.

Like the French feminists, too, Walker rejects the label "feminist" for herself: again, a political decision. "Feminist" is a word imposed, a word too closely linked to the white middle-class feminism of the academy. Instead, Walker refers to herself and her prose as "womanist", to relate specifically to Black feminists or feminists of color. It comes, she tells us, from the black folk expression of mothers to daughters: "you acting womanish", and refers to outrageous, audacious, and courageous behavior: words which themselves carry their own poetry and rhythm. However, Walker needs to turn to different perceptions, different ways to think about words, to give her final definition of "womanist": "Womanist is to feminist as purple is to lavender" (1984: pxi/xii).

In searching for her mother's garden, and asking us to search for ours, Walker considers women's writing, women's creativity. She asks:

> How was the creativity of the black woman kept alive, year after year and century after century, when for most of the years black people have been in America, it was a punishable crime for a black person to read or write? (Walker, 1984: 234)

And yet, somehow, it was. All the women have not perished in the wilderness. They have found ways to create their own gardens. One of the ways that this has been done is orally, through the stories and songs of women. What mattered was not what was sung, but keeping alive the notion of song. And, if not the song itself, it is at least this *notion* of song that needs to be created for women to find ourselves in language. What we must do is "fearlessly pull out of ourselves" and identify the living creativity (Walker 1984: 237). We must find ways to bring the color purple into our language.

Like Walker, the Black American feminists bell hooks and Audre Lorde also write as sister outsiders, showing that contemporary feminist thought is often grounded in white racism. And like Walker, they also engage in considering new ways to think about our relationship to language. Lorde was a writer and philosopher who centralized her multiple identities in her work, whilst emphasizing the need for an integrated, holistic and woman-centered approach to such work. In her exciting and influential work, *Sister Outsider* (1984), Lorde shows how "conventional" academic writing leaves women feeling split and alienated, in a constant state of conflict and denial:

> The white western patriarchal ordering of things requires that we believe there is an inherent conflict between what we feel and what we think – between poetry and theory. (1984: 8)

It becomes, in the end, impossible to continue in such a state:

> What are the words you do not yet have? What do you need to say? What are the tyrannies you swallow day by day and attempt to make your own, until you will sicken and die of them, still in silence? (Lorde 1984: 41)

And so, says Lorde, in order to survive women need to re-turn to the poetry within us, for we are not only casualties, but also warriors. We need to reach out to transform silence into language and to share a commitment to reclaiming language that has been made to work against us (Lorde 1984: 41–2). If we do not do so, we will not just lose the poetry, the notion of song: we will not survive. Without poetry, we cannot name the nameless, and so cannot think the nameless. Without poetry, without women's language, "we give up the core – the fountain – of our power" (Lorde 1984: 39). We will have only the perceptions of men, forever speaking in a foreign language. Without poetry we cannot be free, cannot even survive. "For women, then, poetry is not a luxury. It is a vital necessity of our existence" (Lorde 1984: 37).

And yet speaking from and into silence is an act that seems fraught with danger: a revolutionary act (Lorde 1984: 42). This is a point echoed by bell hooks, Black radical feminist theoretician and author. bell hooks searches for a world of woman-talk in her book *Talking Back*. The act of talking back, she says, of "(m)oving from silence into speech" is a "gesture of defiance" (hooks 1989: 9). However, like Lorde, she also recognizes the dangers in this act of talking back: "to speak when one was not spoken to was a courageous act – an act of risk and daring", liable to punishment. And yet talk she must, for the woman-talk she heard around her was "a language so rich, so poetic" that instilled in her was "the craving to speak, to have a voice, and not just any voice but one that could be identified as belonging to me" (hooks 1989: 5).

hooks says it is a mistake to think that women do not have a language of our own, do not share woman-talk together. In black communities, she says, women have not been silent. However, rich as their woman-talk is, it is a private talk, intimate and intense, a talk between mothers and sisters and women friends. It is the right to public speech that is denied to women, the right to be taken seriously, to even be heard (hooks 1989: 6). Like others before her, hooks does not simply call for a creative writing exercise in finding the way for public expression in a form of woman-talk:

> true speaking is not solely an expression of creative power; it is an act of resistance, a political gesture that challenges the politics of domination that would render us nameless and voiceless. As such, it is a courageous act – as such it represents a threat. (1989: 8)

Perhaps because of this threat, hooks demonstrates in later work how language can be – and is – used to oppress and dominate. The oppressors shape language "to become a territory that limits and defines, . . . they make it a weapon that can shame, humiliate, colonize" (hooks 1994: 168). And yet, she says, the oppressed can *use* this language, which needs to be "possessed, taken, claimed as a space of resistance" (hooks 1994: 69). There are, to return for a moment to Lorde, "no new ideas. There are only new ways of making them felt" (Lorde 1984: 39).

Like the Black feminists discussed above, Adrienne Rich – poet, story-teller, writer and philosopher – also writes from a point of Otherness, not just as a woman, but from a multiplicity of identities: as half-Jewish, as a mother, as a lesbian. And from these multiple identities, her writing contains a rich blend of personal experiences. Indeed, "the process of naming and defining is not an intellectual game, but a grasping of our experience" (Rich 1979: 202). In *On Lies, Secrets and Silences* (1979), Rich shows how these experiences and identities can give us different ways of being, of finding ourselves. For instance, she says that it is the lesbian in every woman – by which she means our woman-centered identities with other women – "who drives us to feel imaginatively, render in language, grasp, the full connection between woman and woman" (Rich 1979: 201).

She, too, longs to enrich a woman-centered language by bringing together more poetic forms, for "poems are like dreams: in them you put what you don't know you know" (Rich 1979: 40). They "can break open locked chambers of possibility" (Rich 1993: xiv). And, like the French feminists, she links women's language with the body and emotions. She exhorts us to let into our language "the swirls of your dreamlife, the physical sensations of your ordinary carnal life" (Rich 1993: 32). Indeed, she mourns the split that has occurred between poetic and other writing, other language:

> We might hope to find the three activities – poetry, science, politics – Triangulated . . . Instead they have become separated – poetry from politics, poetic naming from scientific naming. (Rich 1993: 6)

This is not, despite the call for a womanist language located in the possibilities of poetry, an essentialist argument. Instead, it is a realization that the academy currently only recognizes the values of half of ourselves: that based in rationality and objectivity and the linear and hierarchical ordering of theory. It is a realization that such a half is universalized as if it were a whole. It is a realization of how we feel when we look into the mirror and find only half the world reflected back, or no recognizable world at all.

Rich, in considering "Invisibility in Academe", describes it thus:

> when someone with the authority of a teacher, say, describes the world and you are not in it, there is a moment of psychic disequilibrium, as if you looked into a mirror and saw nothing. Yet you know you exist and others like you, that this is a game with mirrors. (1987: 199)

However, some of us do not know even that: we do not know that we exist. We have disappeared into the discourse and language of the male-centered university. With our voices, our own voices, deemed illegitimate in the academy, we do not just disappear for others, we come to doubt our own existence, a point well illustrated by Rich in her collection *The Dream of a Common Language*:

> The scream
> of an illegitimate voice
>
> It has ceased to hear itself, therefore
> it asks itself
>
> How do I exist? (1978: 8)

The dream of a common language is just an illusion. For the common language is built on the symbolic, not the semiotic: it contains no poetry or desires. There is a "lack", and we do not know how or where to search for our mothers' gardens.

The social practices of the university were considered by Rich in her early considerations of moving "Toward a Woman-Centered University" (1979). The universities that we have, she says, are not neutral and objective places of learning, but man-centered universities, "breeding ground(s) . . . of masculine privilege" (Rich 1979: 127). For women to survive in this university, we have to learn to "absorb the masculine adversary style of discourse" (Rich 1979: 138). A woman-centered university, suggests Rich, needs to break down the hierarchical power structures; and to ensure positive role models to renew "the much-distorted mother-daughter relationship" (Rich, 1979: 139). However, she concentrates on meeting the needs of women within two specific categories, which she says would change the nature of the man-centered university towards a woman-centered one. The first is around the issue of child-care; the second considers changing to a more woman-centered curriculum, where "(m)ysogyny should itself become a central subject of inquiry" (Rich 1979: 154).

I do not disagree with her. Some of these issues *would* take us towards a more woman-centered university. But they would not take us all the way there. What is missing from this early work of Rich's is the notion of song and poetry, of considerations of the symbolic nature of language, and of its role in women's entry into the discourse of the academy. Indeed, some writers have felt that it will be very difficult for women to find a place within the academy at all: that the university can never be woman-centered enough. If women currently wish to enter the academy, then it has to be within the confines of a male-centered university.

One such "male-centered university" that has, however, started to consider some of these issues is that elite bastion of power and privilege, Cambridge.[3] Cambridge University discovered that across the university in general, men were more likely to gain first class honors degrees, but that this was particularly marked within the faculty of history, where the gap was large and persistent, even though the subject is studied in equal numbers by women and men. The faculty, then, set up a working party to investigate this, and a BBC2 television documentary, *First Amongst Equals*, reported on some of the findings.

The core of the history degree at Cambridge is a system of writing one essay a week for the whole three year period of the degree. The essay is subject to regular weekly supervision. Jay Winter, Fellow of Pembroke College, Cambridge, explains that taking a risk within these essays to say something original is highly rewarded. There is, he says, a real gender difference in risk taking and risk aversion, and "women bring a deficiency with them" (cited in *First Amongst Equals* 1996). Like Lacan, then, Dr Winter clearly associates women with "lack", as the Other to men's One. Professor Peter Clarke explains that men have a "punchy, aggressive, adversarial style", very different to women's ways of using language:

> They're much more ready to come out with stuff that may be a lot of nonsense, but even if it's bullshit, if it's bullshit of high quality that they feel confident with at that moment, if it makes people look at them, there are an awful lot of men who will do that. (*First Amongst Equals*: 1996)

And no wonder. For in the discourse of the academy, power is clearly linked to constructions of knowledge, and it is the "confident bullshit" of men that wins the prize. Essays are both encouraged and rewarded that are "full of brilliant flair". There may be "lots of facts wrong, but who cares?" (*First Amongst Equals*: 1996).

This position was well demonstrated in the documentary through watching two examiners discuss a script. The script (of a male candidate) had been marked separately by both examiners, a woman and a man. The woman had awarded a low upper second (62%), whilst the man had awarded a first (72%). The male examiner agreed with the woman that there was no theoretical base, "no theories about war", but he liked the allusions to unreferenced sources, and the range of wars discussed of which he had never heard. Confident bullshit in practice?

Jonathan Scott, Director of Studies of History at Downing College, Cambridge, explains that men regard examinations as a game. He tells all students – women and men – that they need to engage in this "game". The rules are not easy to learn, nor indeed are they ones with which women necessarily choose to engage. One of the women students interviewed states that the only way she can write is if she really believes in a topic: "I need a stance I believe" (*First Amongst Equals*, 1996). Indeed, one essay was particularly problematic for her because she rejected the title and found it difficult to write without a personal belief in the issues. Another woman student criticizes the need for a "punchy, aggressive and adversarial style of writing" within a system of having to produce an essay a week, which does not allow any development of, or personal engagement with, ideas. Women have more personal involvement within their essays, and so there is more at stake in receiving criticism on a weekly basis. The women students do not want to heed the advice of Jonathan Scott to play the game and prefer to "say what they deeply think". Although the women have little power to determine what counts as acceptable "knowledge" in their work, they do show some resistance to the dominant discourse. "I like taking a position that backs the underdog", states one woman (*First Amongst Equals*: 1996), a position that perhaps comes from her own oppression within the system.

Of course it is problematic to talk of women's oppression when the women interviewed were part of a privileged few, all white women, and all part of an academic elite. Indeed, Gillian Sutherland, Director of Studies of history at Newnham College, Cambridge, says that considering gender is the easy part. The picture gets much more complicated when we also consider issues of social class and of race, issues which Cambridge has not yet begun to consider. However, whilst I do not agree that "gender is the easy part", their engagement with such issues is a good step forward, and, to consider these in more depth, the working party on gender called in Professor Carol Gilligan of Harvard University to help them examine some of these issues.

Carol Gilligan is perhaps most well known for her work *In a Different Voice* (1982), including her consideration of "Woman's place in man's life cycle". In this work, she shows that our gender socialization leads to women and men developing different "voices", different senses of morality and ethics. In addition, women are more likely to define ourselves within the contexts of human relationships. Indeed, women and men's widely differing perceptions lead them to have different ways of knowing, although it is assumed that they are the same. Women's language, for instance, has a more web like imagery, whilst men's is hierarchical. However, it is men's voices which have dominated for centuries; indeed that have been the only ones heard or valued, especially in the public arena. However, this is also true in the private sphere, with men's theories of psychological development devaluing or ignoring women's voices and experiences. It should not be surprising, then, that women's different voices have not been heard. However, it is only when we start to value the "different voice" of women, built on a "recognition of the differences in women's experience and under- standing", that we can start to expand "our vision" (Gilligan 1982: 174).

Gilligan's role in coming to Cambridge to talk to the working party on gender, then, was to help the faculty to try to find ways to enable women's different voices to take their place in history. She starts by saying that women should be judged by different criteria to those currently in use. Current rules, she says, have been set up by men over centuries, so women are entering into "a set of rules which almost by definition exclude women and women's experiences" (*First Amongst Equals*: 1996). History, she says, is the story that we tell about the past, and women are a group who have not been part of the construction of that story for millennia. Women, therefore, feel at a distance from what they are studying and approach history by asking a different set of ques- tions.

This is well illustrated in an exchange between Jonathan Scott and one of his women students. In a critique of her essay, in which Jonathan Scott feels the student has not properly considered all the issues, he asks: "In the aftermath of civil war, if you asked contemporaries about the bene- fits for the country as a whole, what would they say?". "Peace", replies the student, at which Jonathan Scott is rendered speechless (*First*

Amongst Equals: 1996). Whilst Jonathan Scott wants the student to say that people (men?) on different sides in the civil war would cite different benefits, Carol Gilligan demonstrates that the student is here not giving a *wrong* answer, but one in a different voice.

Following these discussions, Cambridge did bring in some changes within their history faculty. They introduced mock examinations, for instance, so that students can receive feedback before their finals, and are intending to introduce some assessment by coursework. Tutors will discuss some of the issues raised with women students at the start of their first year. Indeed, these changes are making some difference. In 1995, 23 men received first class honors degrees, compared with 8 women; in 1996 the balance changed to 20 men to 12 women. Still not equal numbers, but the faculty is hopeful. However, the question remains: equal to what? There is little evidence so far that there is consideration of the different voices of women and men, and it is certainly hard to imagine Cambridge rewarding any sort of essay written in *parler femme*, ones that consider more poetic forms of writing, when even the word 'peace' appears to be spoken in a foreign language.

In her early, pioneering work, Dale Spender has asked what it means to women to have to speak in a foreign language, a language that is man-made (1980). In later work, she suggests that as women begin to "protest about their absence from encoded knowledge" the only alternative is for women "to invent or construct their own knowledge for themselves" (Spender 1995: 237–8). I would suggest that exactly the same is true of language. In her exciting science fiction book, *Native Tongue*, and its sequel, *The Judas Rose*, Suzette Haden Elgin starts to imagine such an alternative women's language. The book opens in 2179. The women's movement has been crushed, and women are barred from all power. However, power, according to Foucault, is never total, and resistance is always possible, a resistance which is born through oppositional politics and that starts from the bottom and works up. The women start to build and develop their own secret language of resistance, Laadan:

> The linguistic term *lexical encoding* refers to the way that human beings choose a particular chunk of their world, external or internal, and assign that chunk a surface shape that will be its name . . . When we women say "Encoding", with a capital "E", we mean something a little bit different. We mean the making of a name for a chunk of the world that so far as we know has never been chosen for naming before . . . We mean naming a chunk that has been around a long time but has never before impressed anyone as sufficiently important to *deserve* its own name . . . But there is no way at all to search systematically for capital-E Encodings. They come to you out of nowhere and you realize that you have always needed them . . . They are therefore very precious. (Elgin 1985: 22)

41

Whilst women might have a different reality to men's, we have had to encode our perceptions in terms of men's reality.[4] A capital-E Encoding, then, is a *"word for a perception that had never had a word of its own before"* (Elgin 1985: 158) and, whereas before the perception went not only un-named, but also therefore unthought, once encoded in language the perception exists and is shared with other women. Without this, women cannot have the notion of song:

> Now, the only song a woman knows is the song she learns at birth a sorrowin' song, with the words all wrong, in the many tongues of Earth . . . Oh, the tongues of Earth don't lend themselves to the songs a woman sings! There's a whole lot more to a womansong, a whole lot more to learn; but the words aren't there in the tongues of Earth . . . (Elgin 1985: 264)

"Language controls perception" (Elgin 1987: 160), and Laadan is "a language constructed by women in order to express the perceptions of women" (Elgin 1987: 182). Whilst started as a language of resistance by a conquered people, as generations start to use the language more and more it would eventually become their native tongue. This is the wish of the women for the girl children of the future. However, whilst initially the men were unaware of the work of the women, and then dismissed it as trivial, there was still a danger that they would come to realize its power. Deborah Cameron, too, shares a sense of the importance of Encoding. She believes that whilst women have the means to encode their reality, we have been denied the opportunity (Cameron 1992: 144).

The women in these novels make their own opportunities, something which needs all their ingenuity. They have to construct their language in stolen moments, as is true of much of women's relationship to writing:

> *We had to work in scraps of time, five minutes here, ten minutes there, stolen from other work of badly needed sleep . . . sometimes we considered ourselves lucky to find thirty uninterrupted minutes for the language in a whole month.* (Elgin 1987: 258)

However, there was one group of men who started to realize the power of the Word – its Guardians, the Priests – who are "well aware that no more powerful instrument for change exists than language" (Elgin 1987: 352). They, like the women, believe that language can change reality (Elgin 1987: 355). The men considered this a threat to the power of their Word, as indeed it was. However, to borrow a word from Laadan, in the end – for reality to truly change for men as well as for women – men will have to look to women's different voices, and to reach a state of "zhalaad": "the act of relinquishing a cherished/comforting/familiar illusion or frame of perception" (Elgin 1985: appendix).

Moving from *Nineteen Eighty-four* to *The Judas Rose*, I have started and ended this work in the realms of science fiction. For now, though, there seems little chance of us seeing "zhalaad" reached, especially within the language and discourse of the academy. However, challenges can be made. "French feminists" Cixous, Irigaray and Kristeva have considered a women's language, an *ecriture feminine*, showing the relationship between language, identity and subjectivity. They have shown, too, that there are alternatives in writing, alternatives which express women's realities, experiences, sexualities, desires, and alternatives which allow us to look straight at the Medusa (Cixous 1976). Work by Black feminists such as Alice Walker and others have given us the notion of poetry and song and the courage to search for our mothers' gardens. And perhaps, as Astra says in her poem "Woman's Talk" with which Dale Spender opens *Man-Made Language*, women can reach new perceptions so that we come to realize that "what men dub tattle gossip women's talk / is really revolutionary activity" (1980).

> *Once upon a time, a time that has gone and a time still to come, in a far and distant place, not too far from here, not too far from now, was the Word, and the Word is ours after all. And as we look straight at the Word, we see reflected in it a multiplicity of words, dancing, forming and re-forming. No longer separated from ourselves, we find the luxury and the necessity of poetry, and dream of a common language. Together we dismantle the walls of the Ivory Tower, break open the locked chambers of possibility, and start to search for our mothers' gardens, planting the colour purple as we journey on. We stop by the lac, and touch it with our fingers, watching the circles grow as we disrupt the images mirrored back. We look into and through and beyond our reflections. We learn to become resourceful, reaching a state of zhalaad and finding new ways to feel our ideas, reaching new conceptual realms and unimagined perceptions, gossiping our women's talk together. This is our revolutionary activity.*

Notes

1   See Irigaray, 1977b (1990), 84.
2   I stopped at this point for a long time. I could not find the right word. I had intended to use "seminal", but it was not the word I wanted. It was not a *womanist* word. It leads to perceptions based in the masculine, in semen as the source for creativity and productivity. Eventually I found it. Resourceful is new life, new creativity, a new source of ideas, but also a resource which other women can share and learn; and a way for other women to reach new perceptions.
3   See Sutherland 1995 and *First Amongst Equals* (1996).
4   See Cameron 1992: 141.

Susan Jackson

References

Astra. 1980: "Woman's Talk". In Dale Spender, *Man-Made Language*. London: Pandora.

Brodribb, Somer. 1992: Nothing Mat(t)ers: a Feminist Critique of Postmodernism. Melbourne: Spinfex.

Cameron, Deborah. 1982: *Feminism and Linguistic Theory*. Basingstoke: Macmillan.

Cixous, Hélène and Clement, Catherine. 1987: *The Newly Born Woman*, Betsy Wing (trans.), Manchester: Manchester University Press.

Cixous, Hélène. 1981: The Laugh of the Medusa. In Elaine Marks and Isabelle de Courtivron (eds), *New French Feminisms*, Hertfordshire: Harvester Wheatsheaf, 245–64.

Crowley, Helen and Himmelweit, Susan. 1992: Subjectivity and Identity. In Helen Crowley and Susan Himmelweit (eds), *Knowing Women,* Cambridge: Polity Press, 235–9.

Daly, Mary. 1979: *Gyn/Ecology: The Methaethics of Radical Feminism*. London: The Women's Press.

Elgin, Suzette Haden. 1985: *Native Tongue*. London: The Women's Press.

——. 1987: *The Judas Rose: Native Tongue II*. London: The Women's Press.

First Amongst Equals BBC2, 5 November 1996.

Gilligan, Carol. 1982: *In a different Voice: Essays on psychological theory and women's development*. Massachusetts: Harvard University Press.

hooks, bell. 1989: *Talking Back*. Massachusetts: South End Press.

——. 1994: *Teaching to Transgress: education as the practice of freedom*. London: Routledge.

Humm, Maggie. 1989: *The Dictionary of Feminist Theory*. Hertfordshire: Harvester Wheatsheaf.

——. 1995: *Practicing Feminist Criticism: an introduction*. Hertfordshire: Harvester Wheatsheaf.

Irigaray, Luce. [1974] 1985: *Speculum de l'autre femme*. Gillian Gill (trans.), New York: Cornell University Press.

——. [1977a] 1985: *This sex which is not one*. Gillian Gill (trans.), New York: Cornell University Press.

——. [1977b] 1990: Women's Exile: Interview with Luce Irigaray, In Deborah Cameron, Deborah (ed.), *The feminist critique of language: a reader*, London: Routledge, 165–71.

——. 1980: When our two lips speak together. *Signs* 6 1, 69–79.

——. 1993: *je, tu, nous: Towards a Culture of Difference*. New York: Routledge.

Kramarae, Cheris. 1981: *Women and Men Speakin*. Massachusetts: Newbury House.

Kristeva, Julia. [1974a] 1981: Women can never de defined. In Elaine Marks and Isabelle Elaine and de Courtivron (eds), *New French Feminisms*. Hertfordshire: Harvester Wheatsheaf, 137–41.

——. [1974b] 1981: Oscillation between power and denial. In Elaine Marks and Isabelle de Courtivron (eds), *New French Feminisms*. Hertfordshire: Harvester Wheatsheaf, 165–7.

Lorde, Audre. 1984: *Sister Outsider*. California: Crossing Press.

Martin, Biddy. 1992: Feminism, criticism and Foucault. In Helen Crowley and Susan Himmelweit (eds), *Knowing Women*. Cambridge: Polity Press, 275–86.

Orwell, George. 1951: *Nineteen Eighty-four*. London: Secker and Warburg.

Ramazanoglu, Caroline (ed.) 1993: *Up Against Foucault: explorations of some tensions between Foucault and feminism*. London: Routledge.

Rich, Adrienne. 1971: *The Will to Change*. New York: W. W. Norton.

——. 1978: *The Dream of a Common Language*. New York: W. W. Norton.

——. 1979: *On Lies, Secrets and Silence*, New York: W W. Norton.

——. 1987: *Blood, Bread and Poetry*. London: Virago.

——. 1993: *What is Found There: notebook on poetry and politics*. New York: W. W. Norton.

Spender, Dale. 1980: *Man Made Language*. London: Pandora.

——. 1995: The Entry of Women to the Education of Men. In Cheris Kramarae and Dale Spender (eds), *The Knowledge Explosion: Generations of feminist scholarship*. Hertfordshire: Harvester Wheatsheaf, 235–53.

Sutherland, Gillian. 1995: Gender deficit and tradition. *The Times Higher*, 13 October 1996.

Utley, Alison. 1997: Mistress spurns masters. *The Times Higher*, 15 August 1997, 1.

Walker, Alice. 1984: *In Search of Our Mother's Garden: Womanist Prose*. London: Women's Press.

Whitford, Margaret. 1991: *Luce Irigaray: philosophy in the feminine*. London: Routledge.

Chapter 3

TransForm/ando Women's Studies: Latina Theory Re-Imagines América

Margaret A. Villanueva

Introduction

LATINAS IN THE ACADEMY are a rare species, yet have marked out a territory through cutting-edge research, theory, creative production and pedagogical practice. As we enter the new millennium, Latina scholars, along with other women of color in the academy, hold the potential to construct a paradigm shift in Women's Studies and academic feminism. This paper explores both Chicana/Latina critiques of mainstream Women's Studies pedagogy, theory and practice, and the transformational potential of recent Chicana/Latina theorizing for Women's Studies as an academic field.

Few Latina undergraduates are attracted to Women's Studies as a major or minor. The arriving Latina undergraduate may assume that "feminism" is not relevant to her life or social situation because she holds the stereotypical views – common among Anglos as well – that "feminists" are "radical", "anti-family", and/or engaged in "male-bashing". More seriously, Latina college students who turn to Women's Studies from a deeply-felt concern about women's issues often become alienated by introductory courses that fail to take *their* cultural perspectives, social positioning, and history into account.

Despite the growing availability of research and writings by, about, and for Latinas in the US, the Latina student finds little reflection of her life experiences in either traditional Women's Studies or Latino/Chicano Studies courses. Some departments have taken positive steps to incorporate the Latina experience into their curriculum: for example, Latina/Latino or Chicana /Chicano Studies at the University of California campuses of Davis and Santa Barbara, California State campuses of Northridge and San Diego, and the University of Illinois at Urbana. However, while courses on Latinas provide Women's Studies Departments opportunities for cross-listing, such linking may remove the incentive to transform Women's Studies curriculum from within.

Multicultural initiatives across the curriculum seldom deal with emergent Latina critical theory. With Latinas representing less than 2 percent of doctoral recipients per year and rarely over 1 percent of university faculty members (255 Latinas among 57,000 tenured academics according to Pesquera and Segura 1996: 243), how will Chicana/Latina theory and research be effectively integrated into multicultural curricular changes in higher education? Because tenured male faculty of color and Euro-American women set the agenda for multiculturalism, Latina writings receive little attention in curricular transformation workshops and institutes (see also Aparicio 1994: 575–88; Cordova 1998: 24–8; A. Sandoval 2000). "Inclusion" is often limited to a token list of readings on the syllabus.

The processes of *erasure, invisibility, tokenism,* and *denial* that lead to the exclusion of Latina scholars and their work does not rely upon *intentional* exclusionary practices at particular campuses or by individual faculty members – although institutionalized racism and systemic exclusionary practices are far too common in higher education. For a thoroughgoing transformation to occur in Women's Studies, ongoing practices that exclude Latinas and their theoretical production must be changed. Practices change through taking concrete action. Years after Barbara Smith made visible the problematic that "All the women are white, and all the blacks are men", this social construction continues to predominate the contact zones where Ethnic Studies and Women's Studies meet.

Latinas and other women of color have raised critical questions and proposals for change to academic feminism since the 1970s. An impressive record of articles, books, conference papers, and research reports that outline ideas for transforming pedagogy are available to concerned scholars and students in Women's Studies.[1] While Latina and Chicana scholars have worked to disentangle the complex cultural, psychosociological, and historical processes that maintain the marginal status of Latina scholarship, their analyses have not yet moved "from margin to center". When Women's Studies theorizes differences abstractly, adding a few exemplars of Latina (or Black, or Asian, or Native American) scholarship to the canon – while overlooking a proliferation of theory and research in the social sciences and humanities – the status quo is reproduced. Puerto Rican cultural studies scholar Frances

Aparicio points out that this tendency erases "the historical contribu-tions of the various ethnic groups to interdisciplinary studies, cultural studies, and multicultural scholarship and pedagogy" (1994: 582, 579). While the 1990s brought critical scholarship by Anzaldúa, hooks, Patricia Hill Collins, or novels by Toni Morrison, Sandra Cisneros, Alice Walker and Ana Castillo into college curricula, this recent *inclusion*, which Aparicio (1994: 579) termed a "recanonization" of Ethnic Studies, produced hardly a ripple in the theoretical foundations of Women's Studies in the US.

This paper will reflect briefly on critiques of mainstream feminism and established Women's Studies programs. It makes theoretical use of the stories that Latina undergraduate and graduate students related to me over recent years on their educational experiences. Examining reports on the history of Women's Studies and the parallel critiques by women of color over the past three decades, I find a striking correla-tion between the objections raised by local Latina students, and the analyses worked out by Chicana/Latina scholars. Individual students often interpret their own distress as personal and/or emotional responses to Women's Studies course content or faculty attitudes, unaware that their concerns are share and expressed theoretically by Latina scholars.

For example, one Chicana graduate student reported to me, "I raised my hand to ask the professor to 'bracket' the term 'Victorian woman' because as a fourth-generation Chicana with Texas roots, I felt specifi-cally excluded by the focus on upper-class white women." Rather than using this comment as a useful theoretical jumping-off point, the professor asked her to come to her office, where the ensuing conversa-tion was confrontational and unproductive. De-centering the iconic figure of "the Victorian woman",[2] is one key to re-imagining a multi-cultural America, thereby building upon the revisionist, inclusionary history begun by Ronald Takaki (1993) and recently supplemented by Juan González (2000). Envisioning *America* (*las Américas*) as a continent rather than a nation-state provides another alternative: a Latina her-story, as delineated below. To place the Latina critique of Women's Studies in perspective, I juxtapose a brief literature review on the status of Women's Studies in higher education, based on books, reports, and basic college textbooks published from the 1970s through 2000.

Doing Theory: Latina Feminist Critiques

Chicana feminists . . . could not reconcile their needs as feminists and ethnic women to the goals of the broader women's movement because of the latter's insensitivity to and ignorance of the importance of race, class and ethnicity. Del Castillo *Between Borders* (1990: v)

In their efforts to counter the sexism they faced within Chicano and Latino organizations, many Latinas turned their focus on the women's movement in this country. For most, this move was disappointing. Although now women's issues were at the forefront of the political rhetoric, issues of working-class and racialized women were nowhere to be seen. Latina women again faced a wall of silence. Antonia Darder and Rodolfo D. Torres *Latino Studies Reader.* (1998: 13)

Recent publications by Latina historians, literary critics, and social scientists reflect upon the lukewarm curricular reform in Women's Studies, often accompanied by theoretical entrenchment, as noted by Maxine Baca Zinn and Bonnie Thornton Dill (1994: 3):

Since the 1980s, women's studies scholars have increasingly acknowledged that differences among women arise from inequalities of power and privilege . . . While women's studies scholars are now seeking to emphasize the importance of diversity to understanding women's lives, acknowledging diversity is not enough. Today we face the new task of going beyond the mere recognition and inclusion of differences, to permitting them to reshape the basic concepts and theories of the discipline.

Now that most Women's Studies programs have added some readings by Latinas and other women of color to their syllabi, what are the obstacles to further progress and ultimate transformation of the discipline? What foundationalist assumptions underlie notions of what *must* be taught to undergraduate and graduate students in order to properly socialize them into the field? Although the problem of Latina under representation in the academy continues, a solid basis of theory and empirical research has been generated by the "critical mass" of Latina scholars doing gender analysis and empirical research since the 1980s (Pesquera and de la Torre 1993: 2–6). Chicanas and African American women scholars have been prominent in theoretical debates regarding mainstream feminism and Women's Studies over the past two decades, while other Latinas and some Latino scholars have contributed significantly to historical, social science and/or Latin American Studies research with theoretical implications for the current debates.

Theoretical critiques of Western feminism through "Third World Feminism" (Mohanty *et al.* 1991; Bhavnani 1993; C. Sandoval 1991) maintain a fruitful dialogue with Latina scholarship. International perspectives and post-colonial theory inform Latina analyses about the colonializing practices still extant in the academy (Córdova 1998), complemented by scholarly "border crossings" where Latina and Latin American/Caribbean Studies intersect (Marrero 1997: 139–59; Aparicio 1998; Pérez 1993: 57–71, Crummett 1993: 149–67). With increasing globalization, comparative studies on transculturation and transnational migration may bring "Third World Feminism" and Latina Studies into further collaborative dialogues. Critiques by women of color in Europe also share some fundamental concepts: Kum-Kum Bhavnani, for example, identifies many of the same processes informing and structuring Women's Studies in Britain that Latinas have cited for the US: *erasure, denial, invisibility,* and *tokenism* (1997: 30). Bhavnani points out that:

> If woman is not a trans-historical category, and all women's interests do not coincide, then it follows that feminism, the political movement which aims to liberate all women, is also historically and geographically specific. Thus, there are many feminisms – that is, there are many ways of understanding and analyzing women's exploitation and resistances – and therefore there are many ways of transforming this subordination. (1997: 31)

Bhavnani's critique has much in common with the 1993 volume *Building with our Hands: New Directions in Chicana Studies*, when she argues that each component of the exclusionary practices in Women's Studies are linked with the "denial of whiteness as a racialized category". From these linked processes flow the assumption that "all hegemonic feminisms have to do in order to engage with 'race' is to focus simply on the experience of black women" (Bhavnani 1997: 34). In her recent structural-reflexive analysis, psychologist Aída Hurtado (1996) breaks new ground by exploring the sociological and psychological factors that mutually determine the subordinate social location for Latinas and other women of color *vis-à-vis* white women professionals. In *The Color of Privilege: Three Blasphemies on Race and Feminism*, she examines the structural constraints that mitigate against a unification of mainstream Women's Studies and Latina feminism. Expanding upon relational social psychological theory, Hurtado points to the historical, familial logic of sexual relationships and their reproduction over generations. She argues that Euro-American women's relationship to white men are primarily organized around "seduction", while Latina's relationships to the group who hold the most social power in US society is one of "rejection" (1989a: 833–55, 1996: vii–viii, 10–37). That is, historically the white middle- and upper-classes are reproduced by intermarriage among Euro-Americans; hence

women of Color, as a group, have been used primarily as laborers as well

---

as exploited for their sexuality. Women of color are not needed by white men to reproduce biologically pure offspring and therefore have been subordinated through *rejection*, whereas white women have been *seduced* into compliance because they are needed to reproduce biologically the next generation for the power structure . . . Therefore, gender subordination, as imposed by white men, is experienced *differently* by white women and by women of Color. It is in this experiential difference that many of the conflicts around political mobilization occur. (1996: vii–viii)

Hurtado emphasizes that this social reproduction of *economic class* relationships, in the Marxian sense, and of *status-privilege* relationships, in the Weberian sense, means that as a racialized, primarily working-class group, Latina feminists are unlikely to withdraw from their families and communities of origin. Therefore, neither the "liberal" feminist strategy of struggling for individual autonomy and income equality with white men, nor the "radical" feminist strategy of separatism – building a "women's culture" based largely on middle-class counter-culture values inherited from the 1960s – are viable options for Latina feminists.[3] The distinct social locations of Latinas (internally diverse by generation in the US, national origin, and other factors) means that a Latina student in a Women's Studies course cannot relate her own experience to the re-constructed history diligently forged over the past three decades by academic feminists. The "Victorian Woman" who has become a staple in the canon is confined to her ornate home (or, as a recent European immigrant in socialist feminist research, works in an East Coast textile mill).

The ample investigation into women and gender relations during the Victorian era was undertaken to make visible the historical construction of the "housewife" and the middle-class home, and to illustrate that the social division between the public and the private spheres was historically constructed, not natural roles of the human female. Through historical and biographical studies of women who challenged the stereotypical image of Euro-American womanhood, scholars found new role models for girls and women in order to de-naturalize the idea of a private "women's sphere". However, for Latina, African American, Asian and Native American women in the US, state intervention into their private lives has been central to their historical experience. In short, Latinas had no need to unravel the economic and political forces that kept white middle-class women confined to the home:

The differences between the concerns of white feminists and those of feminists of Color are indicative of these distinct political groundings. White feminists' concerns about the unhealthy consequences of standards for feminine beauty, their focus on the unequal division of household labor, and their attention to childhood identity formation stem from a political consciousness that seeks to project private sphere issues into the public arena. . . . Feminists of Color focus instead on public issues such as affirmative action, racism, school desegregation, prison reform, and voter registration – issues that cultivate an awareness of the distinction between public policy and private choice. (Hurtado 1996: 18)

Hurtado further notes that reconstructing "American" history was more crucial for white feminist scholars than women researchers of color for two reasons: first, due to their direct subordination to white men, white women may be "at a greater disadvantage than women of Color in reclaiming . . . or . . . inventing their identity" (1996: 15–16). Secondly, because Latinos and Latinas have maintained the close community ties that stabilize a shared identity, Latina and African American women researchers, teachers, and students already have an awareness about their roots and heritage.

To the extent that Women's Studies theory and practice has left in place a constructed "imagined community" of the nation-state, and has placed "American Women's History" within that already-existing nationalist and Eurocentric framework, it cannot successfully oppose persistent racism, nor expect Latinas and other women of color excluded from the nationalist discourse to share their vision. Unfortunately, the particularist historical trajectory and positionality of white women has been placed at the center of academic feminist theorizing, and, thus, a re-naturalization of that positionality has been constructed. The stories, identities, and knowledges that Latinas or African American women bring with them to the university remain disconnected from the traditional core curriculum. Whether of Mexican, Puerto Rican, Cuban, Central or South American ancestry, Latinas in the US share historical memories distinct from the vision offered in the Euro-American canon. In recuperating their own identities and histories, mainstream Women's Studies scholars generally failed to construct a genuine multicultural perspective on the geo-political construction of "America" and "American". This failure of vision is both understandable and redeemable: Women Studies programs could re-imagine the USA as a multicultural geopolitical and social space. America is not merely a single country or nation-state, but rather a continent with an interlocking history: *Las Américas*.

By re-imagining an already-inhabited continent as it existed during the reign of Queen Victoria (1837–1901), for example, we can begin to write a truly multicultural women's history. To de-construct that iconic figure of the ideally "American" white middle-class and/or working-class woman with European roots, a sister to the "Frontier Woman" who "populated" the West, Latina scholars search for the "other" Victorians: perhaps, a Tejana whose father died at the Alamo fighting against Santa Ana's Mexican soldiers; a Californiana like Teadora Peralta who fought long legal battles to retain her ancestral lands following the Treaty of Guadalupe Hidalgo in 1848 (Luna 2001). Regrettably, for Euro-American Victorians, a 139-year-old Californiana like Eulalia Pérez was not an agent of history, but an exotic object to be placed on display in San Francisco and Philadelphia in 1876! (Padilla 1993: 130–9) To de-center mainstream discourses in our university curricula, the histories of African, Native American, Asian and Latina women of the nineteenth century who lived in that vast geographical expanse now known as the USA must be incorporated into a polyvalent construction of the Victorian-era experience.[4]

Yet, simply "diversifying" the Victorian image will not do. We must ask to what extent the losses suffered by Tejanas and Californianas produced the conditions of possibility for an idealized "Victorian" lifestyle. Asking such questions would require acknowledgment of ongoing conflicts that have resulted in the "unequal distribution of goods, materials, power, and access to knowledge and information" (Aparicio 1994: 578). Neither promoters of academic "multiculturalism" nor mainstream Women's Studies programs wish to create the dis-ease that such analyses engender.

What perhaps the majority of Latina students and faculty bring to the university is a strong sense of commitment to their communities of origin. When these communities and their histories are rendered invis-ible in the social science and humanities classroom, Latinas in the academy may re-live their childhood experience of inhabiting a space where they do not "belong", yet they rely on a strong sense of identity based on family and community ties. In examining the construction of the self in Latina autobiographies, Lourdes Torres (1991) comes to the same conclusion as Hurtado about the Latina sense of self:

> Like black autobiographers . . . , Latina autobiographers do not create a monolithic self, but rather present the construction of the self as a member of multiple oppressed groups, whose political identity can never be divorced from her conditions. The subject created is at once individual and collective . . . (1991: 274)

The cohesiveness of Latino and Latina student groups on US campuses is one outcome of the struggle for a place to call "home". Women's Studies has the potential to be another "space" where Latinas feel welcome, but this will only occur in conjunction with shifts in acad-emic content, approach, and administrative staffing as well. Careful reading of Latina fiction, poetry, literary criticism, urban studies, labor history, cultural studies, ethnomusicology, criminology, politics, etc., points inevitably toward the multiple sense of identity and critical, collective perspectives that Latina scholarship can offer Women's Studies. Published Latina scholarship is available not only across the curriculum, but also within most sub-fields of major disciplines (Medical Sociology, Small Business Administration, Adult Education, Labor Law, etc.). There remains no excuse for limiting information on Latinas to "special" course segments that focus on the diversity of women's lives, or the "race/ethnicity" segment of a social science course. Such constructions treat women of color as marginal to "authentic" histories and social studies dealing with US women.

Latina feminist research has focused on women's contributions to community, local politics, and Latina/Chicana history;[5] on Latinas in the workplace and contradictions between work and family obligations;[6] the immigrant experience for women;[7] and applied social studies on education or aging.[8] Latinas have not only been directly engaged in the arts and other cultural production, but they write historical critiques and analyses regarding Latinos/as in literature, music, visual arts, films and media, and theatre.[9]

If Latinas continue to feel like outsiders in relationship to Women's Studies and academic feminism, the responsibility falls on the successful, institutionalized Women's Studies programs to remedy this situation. The programs were developed by educated, middle-class white women and are discursively structured from the social location specific to that group. The gendered race and class assumptions underlying the discipline systematically marginalize women of color, despite the best intentions of individual white scholars to diversify the canon. Ultimately, the structural contradictions in Women's Studies' discourse and practice can only be overturned through a dialectical reconstruction of the discipline. As Latina scholars have argued for more than two decades, the ongoing processes of erasure, tokenism, and denial that exclude Latinas and other academic women of color from full participation shall only be overcome by a thorough transformation in the theory and practice of Women's Studies itself.

Observations: Women's Studies Across Three Decades

Women's studies programs have been producing successive theories of "correct" women's studies since the 1970s, and as they successively theorize themselves, they do not want to have that construction displaced by the positions of women of color . . . (T)hey are willing to include your article, your book, your novel, your poem, whatever, in their syllabus. What they do not want disrupted are the theoretical underpinnings of that syllabus. Norma Alarcón quoted in de la Torre and Pesquera. (1993: 3–4)

As early as 1968, scholars documented the exclusion of women's history and social experiences from university curricula in the US, leading to program development during the 1970s and 1980s. By 1972, 46 Women's Studies programs existed nation-wide, six offering a BA in the field; by 1984 there were ten times as many programs, including 247 that offered BA's, 55 MA's and 21 doctoral programs. Thus, about one-sixth of US institutions of higher education had feminist-inspired programs by 1984, with seminars and colloquia established by the late 1980s (Schmitz 1983: 1–5; Chamberlain 1988: 298–301). Programs of study and research centers shared the goal of developing a body of knowledge and pedagogy to focus on women and an analysis of gender. Significantly, a second goal was to use these new knowledges to trans-form the male-centered curriculum in higher education (Guy-Sheftall 1995).

Unfortunately, nascent Women's Studies programs lacked texts for or about Latinas because few had been published – and early Chicano Studies programs adopted a primarily male vantage point, taking either a "cultural nationalist" or "political economy" perspective. I recall the efforts of a California community college teacher to incorporate "Chicano Literature" into the innovative course he designed in the 1970s; he managed to obtain a few chapbooks published by poet Lorna Dee Cervantes and the *Mango* collective in San Jose, featuring an early version of her now-classic Chicana feminist poem "In the Shadow of the Freeway". Elsewhere, work by Caribbean and Latin American women was just emerging in "Hispanic-American" literature and the social sciences, such as Edna Costa Belén's 1979 book *The Puertorican Woman* (second edition 1986).

Understandably, the earliest texts to provide course readings, such as McGuigan's (1973 [1975]) *A Sampler of Women's Studies* had little or no access to research or writing by, for or about Latinas in the US. Similarly, *Woman's Place is in the History Books* (1981), a report funded by the Woodrow Wilson National Fellowship and National Endowment for the Humanities, briefly mentions enslaved African women during the early Republic and immigrant women from Europe, but neglects the histories of Mexican, Native American and Asian women. The only early publication that suggests the topic of "Hispanic women" be included in Women's Studies course work was Gerda Lerner's slim 1981 volume *Teaching Women's History*.

However, once research by, for, and about Latinas emerged between

Margaret A. Villanueva

1980 to 1985, it might be expected that significant information about integrating Latina scholarship and Latina women's issues into college and university curricula would appear. Yet, published reports, textbooks, and anthologies after 1984 fall randomly along a continuum: from total neglect of Latina Studies at one extreme to overly optimistic views of an 'already accomplished' multiculturalism in Women's Studies programs at the other. Until the closing years of the twentieth century, there is little evidence of efforts for even a token inclusion of the Latina experience or Latina scholarship into Women's Studies, as indicated by some typical publications in the field:

1   *Gender in the Classroom: Power and Pedagogy* (Gabriel and Smithson 1990) provides no suggestions for incorporating race or ethnic issues into feminist teaching. Relying on European theorists, this text discusses gender bias in reading and writing, raises questions of power relations in the classroom, and deals with confronting sexism but not racism. A subsequent volume that reviews US feminism from a British perspective also neglects Latina scholarship entirely (Robinson and Richardson 1997 ([1993]).

2   *The State of the Art in Women's Studies: Perspectives from Eleven Disciplines* (Hull 1984–5) mentions a number of important books by, for, or about Latinas (e.g., Melville's *Twice a Minority*, 1980; and Moraga and Anzaldúa's *This Bridge Called my Back: Writings by Radical Women of Color*, 1981). A more inclusive strategy appears in *Women Images and Realities: A Multicultural Anthology* (Kesselman *et al.* 1995), presenting reprinted articles by Barbara Smith, Blanca Vazquez and Alma Garcia. However, a lack of guidance for "reading" this rich multicultural buffet limits the transformational potential of this anthology for feminist pedagogy. The effect is merely additive. A problematic form of "inclusion" are social scientific studies that stereotype Latino/a "gender roles" within a *machismo/ marianismo* syndrome while ignoring revisionist scholarship by Latinas themselves, an approach that may also rely on Anglo population research to discuss "fertility rates" and "family size" among Hispanics (Stone and McKee 1999: 102–15). Such a perspective codifies "feminism" as a white middle-class accomplishment that benefits Latinas who reject the feminist label, to wit:

Most Latinas, like most American women of all ethnicities, are reluctant to identify themselves as feminists. But also like most other American women, they have increasingly accepted as their due much of the legacy of feminism: more education, increased access to employment, the right to limit the size of their families, and greater autonomy in general. (Stone and McKee 1999: 115)

3   Focusing on the cutting edge of scholarship and the race/gender debates of the early 1990s, *Women's Studies: A Retrospective* (Guy-Sheftall 1995) writes a report to the Ford Foundation on the "origins and institutionalization of Women's Studies" over the previous two decades, focusing on the diversification of Women's Studies. The introduction states that women scholars of color "virtually transformed the field . . . by insisting that the experiences, roles, and contributions of African-American, Latina, and American Indian women become part of its curriculum", and that a paradigm shift within both Women's Studies and Ethnic Studies is being accomplished "by 'decentering' the experiences of middle-class, Western, white women in the first case, and the experiences of males in the second case . . . " (Guy-Sheftall 1995: 11–12). While usefully outlining transformational possibilities, this report overstates accomplishments; hence, it underestimates the impediments for a transformation in the field proposed by Latinas and other women of color.

4   A few collected volumes intended for use in both Women's Studies and Race/Ethnicity courses have appeared recently, with Latinas or African American scholars as co-editors, such as Gender through the Prism of Difference (Baca Zinn *et al.* 2000) or Race, Class and Gender (Andersen and Collins 2001). The theoretical introductions to each thematic section in these textbook anthologies provide a conceptual framework for instruction on race and ethnic issues, so that college teachers without solid grounding in these fields can adequately use them for introductory courses. However, these texts do not incorporate cutting-edge critiques by Latina scholars who question the foundational underpinnings of Women's Studies itself.

In sum, over the past three decades, Latina/Chicana scholars have continued to write about their ambivalent relationship with feminist and multicultural scholarship. From its beginnings, the goals of Latina scholarship in relation to mainstream and interdisciplinary academic fields were transformational in nature. By the late 1980s, disappointed by the lack of change still apparent in academe, Latinas in higher education turned their energies inward, forming their own scholarly associations, linking professional and community women at conferences and workshops, and publishing in small presses. Commenting on discussions among members of MALCS (*Mujeres Activas en Letras y Cambio Social*), Segura and Pesquera note that "Since they also feel that American feminism has not been sensitive to important race-ethnic or class concerns of Chicana/Latina women, they tend not to join mainstream feminist groups . . . " (1998: 200–1). Latinas are holding on to spaces gained, encouraging young undergraduates and graduate students to achieve their highest academic potentials, and participating in exciting scholarly debate and research. We are not waiting on the sidelines for others to concede that the transformation of Women's Studies is necessary for its own survival.

Theory and Praxis: *Transformando* From a Latina Perspective

one of the greatest obstacles to intellectual development is the academy itself – an academy that has refused to take its mission seriously. If we are to overcome these institutional obstacles, we must engage in widespread institutional reforms and education of traditional mainstream sectors. That is, we must assist the mainstream in leaving behind attitudes, practices, and beliefs that imprison it in the current dynamic of token representation and underrepresentation of ethnic minorities. Angie Chabram-Dernersesian quoted in *Building with our Hands*. (Pesquera and de la Torre 1993: 233)

Several routes exist to escape the ambivalent relationship between Latina feminism and Women's Studies. The inclusion of published works about, for, and by Latinas across the curriculum is well underway. However, this step is only meaningful if accompanied by institutional support for hiring and retaining Latina faculty and empathetic faculty support of Latina undergraduates and graduate students. An institutional barrier to Latina faculty recruitment under affirmative action programs has been the ability of departments to point to national statistics on the numbers of doctorates granted to underrepresented groups in their respective fields; if the available national "pool" is small, the absence of Latinas or other "Others" in a given department is explained, irrespective of whether actual recruiting and retention efforts were undertaken. The vicious cycle of few faculty mentors to encourage Latina undergraduates to enter graduate studies, and the lack of advisers for Latina graduate research will continue until institutional reforms break down the educational barriers that exist at every level, from Kindergarten through high school as well as through graduate school.

A second step recently drawing scholarly attention is to investigate the social structural frameworks that underlie white privilege in the academy and society at large. In addition to Hurtado's 1996 analysis of this question for Latinas, Euro-American scholars such as Roedinger (1991), McIntosh (1992), Frankenberg (1993), and Hurtado and Stewart

(1997) have begun to de-construct the hidden ethnic category of "white-ness", in order to foreground the power relationships that go into this often backgrounded and naturalized social position. The foreseeable danger in this approach is that a study of "whiteness" could become a central focus, while perspectives from women of color could be put on the back burner (a comparative case occurring when "gender" studies overtook and perhaps surpassed "women's studies" research in academic prestige).

In order to dismantle the privilege that comes with assuming the "naturalness" of white identity, Hurtado asserts that ongoing scrutiny will be one of our challenges for the twenty-first century, because "(r)ace privilege has substituted for lineage of royalty in our time . . . (and) countervails class, at times, just like 'royal blood' did in the past" (1996: 158). Unraveling problems within academic feminism in England, Bhavnani (1997) came to a similar conclusion:

> Racial erasure implicates white women. Thus, not only are white women racist or, implicated in institutionalized racism, but there is also a simultaneous *denial* of whiteness as a racialized category. White skin frequently signifies power and privilege – "the rightness of whiteness" – and this is often accompanied by a silence on the part of white women about their privilege as inscribed within political, economic and ideological inequality. This silence can mean denial and this denial can then lead to a lack of focus on examining whiteness, and its role in perpetuating power inequalities . . . However, if whiteness is unpacked, it may then be possible to see more clearly how gender privilege and inequality are expressed through racialized contexts, as well as vice versa . . . (1997: 34)

A third, both necessary and sufficient move for any dialectical repositioning and paradigmatic change (as Hurtado points out, such re-integration must include research and teaching by other women of color), would be accomplished when the underlying premises, assumptions, canonical texts and pedagogy of the field have been transformed.

What would transformed Women's Studies programs look like? Marcus Embry (1999: 94) hints at a canonical re-thinking for the field of American English Literature that could be facilitated by a consideration of the "shadow of *latinidad*". Reminiscent of Edward Said's re-reading of British nineteenth-century classics that uncovered the shadowy expansion of global power through colonial discourses – a reading still resisted by many mainstream English Literature departments – Marcus' analysis explores the shadows and absences in American Literature. Reconsidering Jane Austen's novels, Said (1993) pointed out the barely acknowledged presence of slave plantations in the Caribbean, the political economy of which had created the social structure, wealth, and power upon which the characters, plot, setting, and *existence* of a "Mansfield Park" depended. This search "in the shadows" by Said and Marcus has much to suggest to Latina/o Studies, and to Latina scholars outside literary criticism. Indeed, Latina historians Emma Pérez (1999) and Antonia Castañeda (1990, 1992) have already embarked on such a search, along with Guadalupe Luna (2001) in legal studies.

Latinas challenge Women's Studies to reconsider the historical construction of gender and race in Anglo-America's *spatial expansion* across the North American continent during the past two centuries. Like Hurtado's psychological-structural analysis and Luna's critical legal theory from a Chicana perspective, Latina scholarship uncovers the "naturalized" socio-spatial relations that made possible the imagined community called the United States of America and the (Euro-) American citizen. During the Victorian era, for example, the sexual relations of marriage and reproduction in the Southwest contradicted Hurtado's hypothesis regarding "seduction" and "rejection". The daughters of Mexican landowners were indeed "seduced" into marriage alliances by white settlers in the Southwest, interrupting the reproduction of Tejano and Californio families, and shifting the balance of political and economic power toward Anglo hegemony. Thus adding a spatial, geo-political dimension to the sexual history of Latinas, we see that strategic intermarriages of Anglo emigrants to Tejanas, Californianas, and Nuevomexicanas before 1848 gave the newcomers property rights to Mexican land grants that helped confound later attempts of Mexicans under US rule to defend their rights under the Treaty of Guadalupe Hidalgo (Acuña 1988; Castañeda 1990; Luna: 2001).

Finally, in recuperating their own Euro-American identities and histories, mainstream Women's Studies scholars fail to construct a genuine multicultural perspective questioning the geo-political construction of "America" and "American". This failure of vision is both understandable and redeemable: Women's Studies programs can "reimagine" the USA as a multiple geopolitical and social space. "America" can and should be drawn not as a single country or nation-state, but as a continent with an interlocking history: *Las Américas*.

Complementing the revisionist history proposed by Ronald Takaki (1993), Latino revisionism has refused to follow an East-to-West trajectory for historical research in the humanities. Work by Chicano cultural theorist José David Saldívar (1997), for example, envisions the Americas as a whole. Focusing on intercontinental politics and immigration, Juan Gonzalez (2000) examines how the story of Latinos in the US can not be separated from the story of US intervention in Latin American economies and politics. Chicana scholar Angie Chabram-Dernersesian (1999) likewise insists that making spatial and historical connections across the continent is as relevant to feminist theory as it is crucial for forward-looking Chicana/o discourse:

> Chicana/o studies breaks with the equivalence between the discipline and nation-state, especially insofar as it redraws its object of analysis from competing geopolitical sites and unofficial territories . . . Chicana/o studies can be a border crossing between Chicana/os and other under-represented groups, a way of speaking critically about the internal and transnational connections between Chicana/os and other peoples of the Americas. (1999: 288)

If Women's Studies were to undertake a re-reading of its own canon in the manner illustrated by recent studies cited here – while thoroughly integrating the insights of Latina theory and practice – the result would be a renewed and invigorated discipline that no longer had any "borders" to defend against Latina outsiders. Integrating scholarship by Latinas and other women of color is part of the painful process of recognizing the privileges conferred through the "naturalization" of whiteness. This construction is backgrounded and hidden, just as Caribbean slave plantations were only summarily mentioned in an Austen novel, even though it was the labor of Africans on the plantations which created the possibility for the novel's existence. In order for Women's Studies to develop a broader geographical, socio-economic-cultural, gendered her-story, the scholarship available and forthcoming by Latina scholars is not only salient, but crucial.

Multiple paths could lead Women's Studies and feminists of color toward achieving a paradigm shift, a dialectical renewal. Hurtado brings together some of the principles that characterize Latina theories about gender, subordination, and women's lives. She highlights the interdisciplinarity of Latina thinking:

> Their theorizing and political praxis are not separate . . . Regardless of their diversity, there are some overarching principles that characterize their theorizing about gender subordination. First, (they) resist arranging their derogated group memberships into a hierarchy of oppressions; instead, they insist on deciphering the complexity of their gender, class, and ethnic/racial status simultaneously . . . Second, almost all . . . claim their individual group's history as part of their activist legacy . . . Third, almost all feminists of Color do not make a distinction between theorizing that emerges in the academy and theorizing that emerges from political organizing, everyday interaction, and artistic production. Feminist theorizing by women of Color is trying to build a paradigm that is inclusive in nature, non-elitist, and does not reside exclusively within the academy. Fourth, currently there is an emphasis on attacking head-on the previously taboo subject of heterosexism in their communities . . . (1996: 39–40)

Transforming Women's Studies implies a process that impacts upon other inter-institutional relationships, such as the uneasy linkages of Latin American Studies and Latina/o Studies (or Chicano/a Studies, etc.). Women-oriented scholarship has not yet moved from the margin to the center in these fields, despite the growing recognition of Latina scholarship and creative production on a national and international level. Research and teaching in the areas of gender, sexuality, Gay, Lesbian and Bisexual Studies are necessarily connected to both the Latin American and the US Latino/a disciplines; yet too many program directors fail to incorporate this scholarship into their academic offerings. Recognizing women in established Latino, Chicano, or Ethnic Studies programs means paying attention to the distinct constructions of the intersections between gender, race, and class among the diverse Latino populations. Gender and race/ethnicity can not be separated in research, analysis or teaching if Latino/a Studies, Latin American Studies, Women's Studies and "multicultural education" initiatives are to fulfill their own theoretical and pedagogical potentials.

Notes

Earlier versions of this chapter were published as "Ambivalent Sisterhood: Latina Feminism and Women's Studies", in *Discourse: Journal for Theoretical Studies in Media and Culture*, 21.3 (1999), and presented at the conference "Constructing/Deconstructing Latino/a Studies", University of Illinois-Urbana/ Champaign, 3 April 1998. Special thanks to Rolando Romero at the University of Illinois for useful comments on the manuscript.

1   Examples of critical writings by Latinas and other women of color are Sylvia González (1977); Martha Cotera (1980); Gloria Joseph and Jill Lewis (1981); bell hooks 1981 and 1984; Teresa Córdova and Gloria Cuadraz (1982); Maxine Baca Zinn *et al.* (1986); Patricia Zavella (1988); Aída Hurtado (1989a), (1989b); Alma Garcia (1989); Patricia Hill Collins (1991); Chandra Talpade Mohanty *et al.* (1991); Chela Sandoval (1991); Kum-Kum Bhavnani (1993); Adela de la Torre and Beatriz Pesquera (1993): 1–11; Ana Castillo (1994); Beatriz Pesquera and Denise Segura (1996); Teresa Córdova (1998); Denise Segura and Beatriz Pesquera (1998); Anna Sandoval (2000).
2   Erna Hellerstein *et al.* (1981), for instance, is a founding teaching text on the Victorian era in Women's Studies, providing a history of primarily middle-class white women in Europe and the United States.
3   See Jagger (1983) on second-wave feminist politics and theory.
4   Oral and documentary histories of women of color are included in the works of Genaro Padilla (1993); Arnold Krupat (1994); and Anthony Appiah (1990). Recent oral histories by Latinas are published in the journal *Frontiers*, Vol. 19, nos 1 and 2 (1999).
5   Carole Hardy-Fanta (1993) wrote on Latina grassroots organizing in Boston; Virginia Sanchez-Korrol (1994) on Puerto Rican women's contribution to community-building in New York; Vicky Ruiz (1998) on the

hidden histories of Mexican American women in the Southwest; Mary Pardo (1998) on Mexican American activists in Los Angeles; Josephine Mendez-Negrete (1996, 1999) on Chicana leaders in Northern California; and Chicano historian Jerry Garcia (1999) contributed an oral history of a working-class Chicana in Washington state.

6   Patricia Zavella (1987) studied family change among Chicana factory women in New Mexico; Vicky Ruiz (1987) examined work and union activities of cannery workers in California; Rita Benmayor *et al.* (1988) recorded oral histories of Puerto Rican working women across generations; Irene Campos Carr (1989) interviewed Latina assembly workers in Illinois; Mary Romero (1992) wrote about the gender and class contradictions of waged domestic labor for Latinas who served Anglo women as maids; Altagracia Ortiz (1996) looked at the transnational nature of Puerto Rican factory workers lives.

7   Experiences of migration and immigration among Latinas has been investigated by Karen Garcia (1992); Pierrette Hondagneu-Sotelo (1994); as well as Chicano anthropologist Leo Chavez (1998); and my own Illinois study under review for publication, Villanueva (2000).

8   Teresa McKenna and Flora Ortiz (1989) published an early edited volume on Hispanic women's education; Concha Delgado-Gaita (1997) carried out educational research about women on the US–Mexican border. Sylvia Fuentes (1998) wrote a dissertation on educational experiences of Tejana women in the migrant circuits between Texas and the Midwest; and Elisa Facio (1996, 1993) has done ground-breaking work on Chicanas and aging.

9   Early work on Latina writing was published in an edited volume by Eliana Horno-Delgado *et al.* (1989). Chicana literary and postmodern criticism flourished in the 1990s, such as the work of Roberta Fernández (1994), edited volumes by Norma Alarcón *et al.* (1993, 1999); Gloria Anzaldua (1998: 163-9). Frances Aparicio (1998) examined gendered discourses in Caribbean salsa music, and edited a volume of cultural critiques on representations on the "tropical" in 1999. Gendered dimensions of Latino/Chicano visual/performance, cinema, and theatre arts were analyzed by Coco Fusco (1995), Rosa Linda Fregosa (1993), and Yolanda Broyles (1994) respectively.

References

Acosta-Belén, Edna, and E. H. Christensen (eds). 1979: *The Puertorican Woman*. New York: Praeger.

Acuña, Rodolfo. 1988: *Occupied America: A History of Chicanos*, 3rd edn. New York: Harper and Row.

Alarcón, Norma, R. Castro, M. Melville, E. Perez, T. D. Rebolledo, C. Sierra, and A. Sosa Riddell (eds). 1993: *Critical Issues in Chicana Studies: Temas Críticos en Estudios Chicanas*. Berkeley, CA: Third Woman Press.

——, Caren Kaplan, and Minoo Moallem (eds). 1999: *Between Woman and Nation: Nationalisms, Transnational Feminisms, and the State*. Durham: Duke University Press.

Margaret A. Villanueva

Andersen, Margaret L. and Patricia Hill Collins. 2001: *Race, Class, and Gender: An Anthology*. Fourth Edition. Belmont, CA: Wadsworth/Thomson Learning.
Anzaldúa, Gloria. 1998: Chicana Artists: Exploring *Nepantla, el Lugar de la Frontera*. In A. Darder and R. D. Torres (eds), *The Latino Studies Reader: Culture, Economy and Society*. Oxford: Blackwell, 163–9.
——. 1987: *Borderlands-La Frontera: The New Mestiza*. San Francisco: Spinsters/Aun Lute.
Aparicio, Frances R. 1998: *Listening to Salsa: Gender, Latin Popular Music, and Puerto Rican Cultures*. Hanover, New Hampshire: Wesleyan University Press.
——. 1994: On Multiculturalism and Privilege: A Latina Perspective. *American Quarterly* 46.4, 575–88.
—— and Susana Chavez-Silverman. 1997: *Tropicalizations: Transcultural Representations of Latinidad*. Hanover: Dartmouth College.
Appiah, Anthony (ed.). 1990: *Early African-American Classics*. New York: Bantam.
Aponte, Robert and M. Siles. 1994: *Latinos in the Heartland: The Browning of the Midwest*. Research Report #5. Julian Samora Research Institute Publications, Michigan State University. November.
Baca Zinn, Maxine, Pierrette Hondagneu-Sotelo, and Michael A. Messner. 2000: *Gender through the Prism of Difference*. 2nd edn. Needham Heights, Massachusetts: Allyn & Bacon.
——, and Bonnie Thornton Dill. Difference and Domination. In M. Baca Zinn and B. Thornton Dill (eds), *Women of Color in US Society*, Philadelphia: Temple University Press, 3–12.
——, Lynn Weber Cannon, Elizabeth Higginbotham, and Bonnie Thornton Dill. 1986: The Costs of Exclusionary Practices in Women's Studies. *Signs: Journal of Women in Culture and Society* 11 (21), 290–303.
Benmayor, Rina. 1988: Stories to Live By: Continuity and Change in Three Generations of Puerto Rican Women. *Oral History Review* 16 (2), 1–46.
Bhavnani, Kum-Kum. [1973] 1997: Women's Studies and its Interconnection with 'Race,' Ethnicity and Sexuality. In Diane Richardson and Victoria Robinson (eds), *Introducing Women's Studies*. London: Macmillan.
Bonilla, Frank, Edwin Meléndez, Rebecca Morales, and María de los Angeles Torres. 1998: *Borderless Borders: US Latinos, Latin Americans, and the Paradox of Interdependence*. Philadelphia: Temple University Press.
Broyles, Yolanda Julia. 1994: *El Teatro Campesino: Theater in the Chicano Movement*. Austin: University of Texas Press.
Carr, Irene Campos. 1989: Proyecto la mujer: Latina Women Shaping Consciousness. *Women Studies International Forum* 12 (1), 45–9.
Castañeda, Antonia I. 1992: Women of Color and the Rewriting of Western Women's History: The Discourse, Politics, and Decolonization of History. *Pacific Historical Review* 61, 509–33.
——. 1990: Gender, Race, and Culture: Spanish-Mexican Women in the Historiography of Frontier California. *Frontiers* 11 (1), 8–20.
Castillo, Ana. 1994: *Massacre of the Dreamers: Essays on Xicanisma*. New York: Penguin.

Chabram-Dernersesian, Angie. 1999: 'Chicana! Rican! No, Chicana Riquena!': Refashioning the Transnational Connection. In Alarcón, N. *et al.* (eds), *Between Woman and Nation: Nationalisms, Transnational Feminisms, and the State.* Durham: Duke University Press.

Chamberlain, Mariam K. (ed.) 1988: *Women in Academe: Progress and Prospects.* New York: Russell Sage Foundation.

Chavira, Alicia. 1989: The Social and Political Status of Latino Women in the Midwest. *Conference Proceedings: Structural Changes and Their Impact on Hispanics.* Occasional Paper #1, Julian Samora Research Institute, Michigan State University.

Collins, Patricia Hill. 1991: *Black Feminist Thought: Knowledge, Consciousness, and the Politics of Empowerment.* New York: Routledge.

Córdova, Teresa. 1998: Power and Knowledge: Colonialism in the Academy. In Carla Trujillo (ed.), *Living Chicana Theory.* Berkeley: Third Woman Press, 17–45.

——, Norma Cantú, Gilberto Cardenas, Juan García, and Christine M. Sierra (eds). 1986: *Chicana Voices: Intersections of Class, Race, and Gender.* Austin: University of Texas, CMAS Publications.

—— and Gloria Cuadraz. 1983: *Chicanas in the 80's: Unsettled Issues.* Report from NACS 11th Annual Conference at Tempe, Arizona (1982). Berkeley: Chicano Studies Library Publications Unit, University of California-Berkeley, 31 pages.

Chamberlain, Mariam K. 1988: *Women in Academe: Progress and Prospects.* New York: Russell Sage Foundation.

Chavez, Leo R. 1998: *Shadowed Lives: Undocumented Immigrants in American Society.* Fort Worth, Texas: Hartcourt Brace College Publishers.

Cotera, Martha P. 1980: Feminism: The Chicana and Anglo Versions, A Historical Analysis. In Margarita Melville (ed.), *Twice a Minority: Mexican American Women.* St. Louis: C.V. Mosby, 217–34.

Crummett, Maria de los Angeles. 1993: Gender, Class, and Households: Migration Patterns in Aguascalientes, Mexico. *Building with our Hands: New Directions in Chicana Studies.* Berkeley: University of California Press, 149–67.

Darder, Antonia and Rodolfo D. Torres (eds). 1998: *The Latino Studies Reader: Culture, Economy & Society.* Cambridge, MA: Blackwell Publishers.

de la Torre, Adela and Beatriz M. Pesquera. 1993: *Building with our Hands: New Directions in Chicana Studies.* Berkeley: University of California Press.

Del Castillo, Adelaida R. (ed.). 1990: *Between Borders: Essays on Mexicana/Chicana History.* Encino, California: Floricanto Press.

Delgado-Gaita, Concha. 1997: Dismantling Borders. In Anna Neumann and Penelope L. Peterson (eds), *Learning from Our Lives: Women, Research, and Autobiography in Education.* New York: Teachers College Press, 37–51.

Embry, Marcus. 1999: The Shadow of Latinidad in US Literature. *Discourse: Journal for Theoretical Studies in Media and Culture.* Issue on Latina/o Discourses in Academe 23 (3), (Fall).

Facio, Elisa. 1996: *Understanding Older Chicanas.* Thousand Oaks: Sage Publications.

——. Gender and the Life Course: A Case Study of Chicana Elderly. In A. de la

Torre and B. M. Pesquera (eds), *Building with our Hands*. Berkeley: University of California Press, 1993, 217–31.

Fernández, Roberta. 1994: Abriendo Caminos in the Brotherland: Chicana Writers Respond to the Ideology of Literary Nationalism. *Frontiers – A Journal of Women's Studies* 14 (2), 23–50.

Frankenberg, Ruth. 1993: *White Women, Race Matters: The Social Construction of Whiteness*. Minneapolis: University of Minnesota Press.

Fregosa, Rosa Linda. 1993: *The Bronze Screen: Chicana and Chicano Film Culture*. Minneapolis: University of Minnesota Press.

Fuentes, Sylvia. 1998: *La Pizca, La Familia, y Las Schools*: Personal Narratives of Tejana Women in the Midwest and the Nature of Adult Education. Doctoral Diss., Leadership and Education Policy Studies, Northern Illinois University.

Fusco, Coco. 1995: *English is Broken Here: Notes on Cultural Fusion in the Americas*. New York: The New Press.

Gabriel, Susana L. and Isaiah Smithson (eds). 1990: *Gender in the Classroom: Power and Pedagogy*. Urbana: University of Illinois Press.

Garcia, Alma M. 1989: The Development of Chicana Feminist Discourse, 1970–1980. *Gender and Society* 3, 217–38.

Garcia, Jerry. 1999: A Chicana in Northern Aztlán: An Oral History of Dora Sánchez Treviño. *Frontiers* 19 (1), 16–36.

Garcia, Karen. 1992: Gender and Ethnicity in the Emerging Identity of Puerto Rican Migrant Women. *Latino Studies Journal* 3 (1), 3–8.

González, Deena J. Speaking Secrets: Living Chicana Theory. In Carla Trujillo (ed.), *Living Chicana Theory*. Berkeley: Third Woman Press, 46–77.

González, Juan. 2000: *Harvest of Empire: A History of Latinos in America*. New York: Viking Press.

González, Sylvia. 1997: The White Feminist Movement: The Chicana Perspective". *Social Science Journal* 14, 67–76.

Guy-Sheftall, Beverly. 1995: *Women's Studies: A Retrospective*. A Report to the Ford Foundation.

Hardy-Fanta, Carole. 1993: *Latina Politics, Latino Politics: Gender, Culture and Political Participation in Boston*. Philadelphia: Temple University Press.

Hellerstein, Erna O, Leslie P. Hume, and Karen M. Offen. 1981: *Victorian Women: A Documentary Account of Women's Lives in Nineteenth-Century England, France, and the United States*. Palo Alto: Stanford University Press.

Hondagneu-Sotelo, Pierrette. 1994: *Gendered Transitions: Mexican Experiences of Immigration*. Berkeley: University of California Press.

hooks, bell. 1994: *Outlaw Culture: Resisting Representations*. New York: Routledge.

_____. 1984: *Feminist Theory from Margin to Center*. Boston: South End Press.

_____. 1981: *Ain't I a Woman? Black Women and Feminism*. Boston: South End Press.

Horno-Delgado, Eliana Ortega, Nina M. Scott, and Nancy Saporta Sternback (eds). 1989: *Breaking Boundaries: Latina Writing and Critical Readings*. Amherst: University of Massachusetts Press.

Hull, Suzanne W. (ed.). 1984–5: *The State of the Art in Women's Studies: Perspectives from Eleven Disciplines*. Reports presented at The Huntington Library Seminar in Women's Studies, Los Angeles.

Hurtado, Aída. 1996: *The Color of Privilege: Three Blasphemies on Race and Feminism*. Ann Arbor: University of Michigan Press.

——. 1989a: Relating to Privilege: Seduction and Rejection in the Subordination of White Women and Women of Color. *Signs: Journal of Women in Culture and Society* 41, 833–55.

——. 1989b: Reflections on White Feminism: A Perspective from a Woman of Color. In Sucheng Chan (ed.). *Social Gender Boundaries in the United States*. Lewiston: Edwin Mellen Press, 155–86.

——. and Abigail Stewart. 1997: Through the Looking Glass: Implications of Studying Whiteness for Feminist Methods". In Michelle Fine, Linda Powell, Lois Weis, and Mun Wong (eds), *Off White: Readings on Society, Race and Culture*. New York: Routledge.

Jaggar, Alison. 1983: *Feminist Politics and Human Nature*. Totowa, New Jersey: Rowman and Allanheld.

Joseph, Gloria I., and Jill Lewis (eds). 1981: *Common Differences: Conflicts in Black and White Feminists' Perspectives*. New York: Anchor Books.

Kesselman, Amy, Lily D. McNair and Nancy Schniedewind. 1995: *Women Images and Realities: A Multicultural Anthology*. MountainView, California: Mayfield Publishing.

Krupat, Arnold. 1994: *Native American Autobiography: An Anthology*. Madison: University of Wisconsin Press.

Lerner, Gerda. 1981: *Teaching Women's History*. Washington, D.C.: American Historical Association.

Luna, Guadalupe T. (Forthcoming 2001): Chicanas, Land Grant Adjudication and the Treaty of Guadalupe Hidalgo: "This Land Belongs To Me". *Harvard Latino Law Review*.

Marrero, Maria Teresa. 1997: Historical and Literary *Santeria*: Unveiling Gender and Identity in U.S. Cuban Literature. *Tropicalizations: Transcultural Representations of Latinidad*. Hanover: Dartmouth College, 139–59.

McGuigan, Dorothy Gies (ed.) [1973] 1975: *A Sampler of Women's Studies*. Center for Continuing Education of Women. Ann Arbor: The University of Michigan.

McKenna, Teresa, and Flora I. Ortiz (eds). 1989: *Broken Webs: The Educational Experience of Hispanic American Women*. Encino, CA: Floricanto Press.

McIntosh, Peggy. 1992: White Privilege and Male Privilege: A Personal Account of Coming to See Correspondences through Work in Women's Studies. In M. L. Andersen and P. Hill Collins (eds), *Race, Class, and Gender*. Belmont, California: Wadsworth, 70–81.

Melville, Margarita B. 1980: *Twice a Minority: Mexican American Women*. St. Louis: Mosby.

Mendez-Negrete, Josephine. 1996: "*No es lo que dices, es lo que haces!*": Grassroots Leadership and Chicana Notions of Feminism. Paper presented at invited panel on "Indigenous Feminisms", Annual Meeting of the American Anthropology Association, San Francisco.

——. 2000: Awareness, Consciousness, and Resistance: Raced, Classed, and Gendered Leadership Interactions in Milagro County, California". *Frontiers* 20 (1), 25–44.

Mohanty, Chandra Talpade, Ann Russo, and Lourdes Torres (eds). 1991: *Third*

World Women and the Politics of Feminism. Bloomington: Indiana University Press.

Moraga, Cherríe and Gloria Anzaldúa (eds) 1983: *This Bridge Called my Back: Writings by Radical Women of Color*. New York: Kitchen Table.

Morales, Rebecca and Frank Bonilla. 1993: *Latinos in a Changing US Economy: Comparative Perspectives on Growing Inequality*. Newbury Park, California: Sage Publications.

National Endowment for the Humanities and Woodrow Wilson National Fellowship Foundation. 1981: *Woman's Place is in the History Books: Her Story 1620–1980, A Curriculum Guide for American History Teachers*. Washington, D.C.

Ortiz, Altagracia (ed.). 1996: *Puerto Rican Women and Work: Bridges in Transnational Labor*. Philadelphia: Temple University Press.

Padilla, Genaro M. 1993: *My History, Not Yours: The Formation of Mexican American Autobiography*. Madison: University of Wisconsin Press.

Pardo, Mary S. 1998: *Mexican American Women Activists: Identity and Resistance in two Los Angeles Communities*. Philadelphia: Temple University Press.

Pérez, Emma. 1999: *The Decolonial Imaginary: Writing Chicanas into History*. Bloomington: Indiana University Press.

——. 1993: Speaking from the Margin: Uninvited Discourse on Sexuality and Power. In A. de la Torre and B. M. Pesquera (eds), *Building with our Hands: New Directions in Chicana Studies*. Berkeley: University of California, 57–71.

Pesquera, Beatriz and Adela de la Torre. 1993: Introduction. *Building with our Hands: New Directions in Chicana Studies*. Berkeley: University of California, 1–11.

Pesquera, Beatriz M. and Denise A. Segura. 1996: With Quill and Torch: A Chicana Perspective on the American Women's Movement and Feminist Theories". In David R. Maciel and Isidro D. Ortiz (eds), *Chicanas/Chicanos at the Crossroads: Social, Economic, and Political Change*. Tucson: The University of Arizona Press, 231–47.

Robinson, Victoria and Diane Richardson (eds). [1993] 1997: *Introducing Women's Studies*. New York: Macmillan.

Roediger, D. R. 1991: *The Wages of Whiteness: Race and the Making of the American Working Class*. London/New York: Verso.

Romero, Mary. 1992: *Maid in the USA*. New York: Routledge.

Ruiz, Vicky L. 1998: *From Out Of The Shadows: Mexican Women in Twentieth-Century America*. Oxford: Oxford University Press.

——. 1987: *Cannery Women, Cannery Lives: Mexican Women, Unionization, and the California Food Processing Industry, 1930–1950*. Albuquerque: University of New Mexico Press.

Said, Edward W. 1993: *Culture and Imperialism*. New York: Alfred A. Knopf.

Sánchez-Korrol, Virginia E. 1994: *From Colonia to Community: The History of Puerto Ricans in New York City*. Berkeley: University of California Press.

Saldívar, José David. 1997: *Border Matters: Remapping American Cultural Studies*. Berkeley: University of California Press.

Sandoval, Anna. 2000: Building Up Our Resistance: Chicanas in Academia. *Frontiers* 20 (1), 86–92.

Sandoval, Chela. 1991: US Third World Feminism: The Theory and Method of Oppositional Consciousness in the Postmodern World. *Genders* 10, 1–24.

Schmitz, Betty. 1983: *Integrating Women's Studies into the Curriculum: A Guide and Bibliography*. Old Westbury, New York: The Feminist Press.

Segura, Denise A. and Beatriz M. Pesquera. 1998: Chicana Feminisms: Their Political Content and Contemporary Expressions. In A. Darder and R. D. Torres (eds), *The Latino Studies Reader: Culture, Economy and Society*. Oxford: Blackwell Publishers, 193–205.

Stone, Linda and Nancy P. McKee. 1999: *Gender and Culture in America*, Upper Saddle River, New Jersey: Prentice-Hall.

Takaki, Ronald. 1993: *A Different Mirror: A History of Multicultural America*. Boston: Little Brown and Company.

Torres, Lourdes. 1991: The Construction of the Self in US Latina Autobiographies. In C. T. Mohanty, A. Russo, L. Torres (eds), *Third World Women and the Politics of Feminism*. Bloomington: Indiana University Press, 271–87.

Treviño, F., D. B. Treviño, C. A. Stroup, and L. Ray. 1989: *The Feminization of Poverty among Hispanic Households*. San Antonio, Texas: The Tomás Rivera Center.

Trujillo, Carla (ed.). 1998: *Living Chicana Theory*. Berkeley: Third Woman Press.

Villanueva, Margaret A. 1996: Ethnic Slurs or Free Speech? Politics of Representation in a Student Newspaper. *Anthropology & Education Quarterly* 27 (2), 168–85.

——. 2000: Reproducing Households, Building Communities, Claiming a Place Latina Newcomers and Settlers in the Heartland. Under submission to *Feminist Economics*.

Zavella, Patricia. 1988: The Problematic Relationship of Feminism and Chicana Studies. *Women's Studies* 17, 123–34.

——. 1987: *Women's Work and Chicano Families*. Ithaca, New York: Cornell University Press.

Part II

Representation and Resistance

MARY Brewer's essay, *Violating the Seal of Race: The Politics of (Post)Identity in the Theatre of Adrienne Kennedy*, explores the way in which Kennedy's plays contest the exclusionary force of white discourse by pointing to the material hybridity of whiteness. This essay analyzes how Kennedy's theatre provides a voice for the subjective and cultural experiences of African-American women, and, in so doing, complicates the way that both the black and white female self is constructed in dominant culture and mainstream feminist discourse. Brewer demonstrates how Kennedy deconstructs the myth of the white subject as unitary and transcendental, revealing the instabilities of white race-gender identities, and she discusses the potential afforded by this critical move for dislodging the white female subject from the center of feminist theory and practice.

Melissa Chinchillo's *(Post)Colonial (Dis)orders: Female Embodiment as Chaos in Tsitsi Dangarembga's Nervous Conditions and Bharati Mukherjee's Jasmine* considers the promise afforded by chaos theory for pushing the theoretical and disciplinary boundaries in thinking about womanhood. Sketching the parallels between scientific perceptions of disorder as "monstrous" and patriarchal and colonial discursive constructions of women and natives as threatening, Chinchillo puts forth a triangulated conceptual model of feminist-postcolonial-chaos theories as a means to considering how women's bodies – particularly those of "minorities" – may function as sites disruptive to established social orders. In particular, the essay explores how the representation of Native women in Dangarembga's and Mukherjee's novels challenge oppressive ideological constructions of womanhood by revealing order and disorder as commingled, and as giving rise to a third system of "orderly disorder". By allowing a move away from binary thinking, Chinchillo demonstrates how feminism can make chaos meaningful and useful in avoiding exclusionary discourse and thought.

Kathleen Iudicello's *"See, I've got my tit out!": Women's Performance Art and Punk Rock* explores the feminist meanings that may be produced through the exposed bodies of women on stage in performance art and punk rock. The essay examines first the ways in which a certain type of naked female body operated as a site of struggle for agency in women's performance art in the 1960s and 1970s, one of the places where its radical potential was first explored. Iudicello goes on to consider how the exposed body in performance has been incorporated into other forms of women's cultural production such as punk rock in the 1990s. The essay reveals that, despite punk's coding as a male art form, some female performers have been able to use punk to re-present women as desiring, aggressive subjects, rather than sightless objects-to-be-taken. While always cognizant that their success has been linked to the relative power afforded by the women's particular race-sex-gendered locations in culture, the paper gestures toward a way for more women to develop the kind of public presence needed in the struggle against the physical and non-physical violence characteristic of patriarchal society.

In *Leaving Las Vegas: Reading the Prostitute as a Voice of Abjection*, Doreen Piano looks at how the prostitute functions as an ambiguous and compelling figure in contemporary culture, so compelling that she has become a site of conflicting powerful discourses, both hegemonic and counter-hegemonic. Against the "othering" of the prostitute by mainstream society and anti-sex feminists alike, sex workers and pro-sex feminists have begun theorizing a space that contests both discourses through the production of a prostitute politico-sexual identity. While pro-sex feminists and activists agree that prostitution, as it is situated within patriarchal discourse, contributes to the victimization and exploitation of women, they also claim that eliminating prostitution will not alleviate discrimination or acts of violence against women. Rather, prostitutes need a legitimate political identity. Piano argues that it is through the disavowal of prostitutes and other sexual minorities as legitimate identities that mainstream feminism has maintained its own structure of power within dominant culture. Thus, the dichotomies that result from the prostitute's exclusion – madonna /whore, reproductive/unproductive, pure/impure – are still part of the discursive baggage that the prostitute, and feminist theory, carries into the twenty-first century.

Chapter 4

Violating the Seal of Race: The Politics of (Post)Identity and the Theatre of Adrienne Kennedy

MARY BREWER

The White man is sealed in his whiteness.
The black man in his blackness.
> *Frantz Fanon (1952: 11)*

I'm always fighting not to be diminished by the so-called majority culture.
Whatever that is.
> *Adrienne Kennedy (quoted in Diamond 1996: 137)*

You must learn to know your enemy so well that you borrow the
very structures of his discourse.
> *Gayatri Spivak (1989: 214)*

The Subject of Post-Identity Politics

The black subject, declares Stuart Hall, has reached the "end of innocence", meaning that one can no longer assume any essence to blackness
(1997: 224). Hence, progressive critics must relinquish the politically/
theoretically youthful belief that a movement or discourse centered on
"race" will necessarily lead to effective cultural practices. Instead, if we
are to forge productive social movements, we must accept the plurality
of subject positions, experiences, and cultural and political identities
that make up the category of race. However, for many blacks, and
others, who have fought on the anti-racist front, by mobilizing community action or resisting prejudice on a day-to-day basis, decentering the
subject and abandoning the secure notion of race is a high-risk and

daunting task; because it threatens to remove what is perhaps the last unifying feature from an always threatened and fragile alliance of subordinated peoples.

Anglo-American black feminism in particular has expressed strong skepticism toward postmodern (de)constructions of subjectivity. Audre Lorde expressed unease concerning the "fractured metaphors and ambiguous subjecthood" to which postmodernism would assign black people, pointing out that "assaults on human bodies demand unambiguous collective responses" (quoted in Rabine 1988). The influential critic bell hooks criticizes the academic elitism of much poststructuralist/postmodern feminist theory. Increasingly, she argues, "only one type of theory is seen as valuable by academic writers – that which is Euro-centric, linguistically convoluted, and rooted in Western white male sexist and racially biased philosophical frameworks" (1989: 36). hooks reminds us that the way women use postmodern theory to write the female self may exacerbate barriers among us, especially divisions of race and class, by making it more difficult for different social groups of women to communicate with each other or collectively organize.

Historically, black feminism has demonstrated a strong commitment to a politics of identity premised on the notion of a coherent black female subjectivity. One early manifesto, *The Combahee River Collective Statement*, expressed the belief that black women's oppression is embodied in the concept of identity politics, and that "the most profound and potentially radical politics come directly out of our own identity . . . " (1983: 275). A more recent attempt to shore up the black female subject was made by Alice Walker, who introduced the term "womanist" into the lexicon of black feminists' theoretical vocabulary, which, she suggested, might offer a universal space/identity from which black women could articulate their lived experiences and strategically assert their political aims. Patricia Hill Collins' influential account of black feminism, *Black Feminist Thought: Knowledge, Consciousness, and the Politics of Empowerment*, names the primary guiding principle of black feminism through the 1980s as a "recurring humanist vision". She too posits a fundamental link between the black female subject and black feminist politics by defining black feminist theory as discourse "produced by black women intellectuals designed to express a Black woman's standpoint" (1991: 31, 43).

For anyone who belongs to a group whose interests are opposed to that of the dominant, and, who, as a result, has endured stigma resulting from stereotypical and derogatory depictions of their lives, it can seem self-evident that a principal strategy of resistance to social marginalization and oppression must entail offering an unequivocal corrective to dominant misrepresentations. Yet, we must acknowledge also that women from many different social groups have been engaged for several decades now in promulgating "authentic" representations of femininity. While these versions of what it means to be a woman in contemporary Anglo-American society have assisted some groups of women in building self-esteem and greater levels of self-awareness – an important dimension of feminist practice – identity politics have just as often assisted in the privileging of one groups' account of womanhood (that group which has more access to the structures of power) over other versions.

Despite the potential drawbacks to progressive feminist movement that taking up wholesale the ideas of poststructuralism could present, I would argue that the idea of a radically decentered subject can be translated into feminist theoretical frameworks in ways that might furnish certain enabling conditions for a multicultural feminist movement. I want to argue here that if the female subject, black and white, were to violate successfully the seal of race, feminism could be presented with two critical opportunities: (1) to dislocate the racialized hierarchy of subject relations; that is, those developmental models of subjectivity whereby the existence of black subjectivity is either completely denied, or blackness is constructed as derivative of whiteness, with black signifying the "not-white" object of white psychical identity formation; and (2) to effectively challenge the ideological power and exclusionary practices of white discourse by pointing to the material hybridity of whiteness, deconstructing the myth of white subjectivity as unmediated, transparent, transcendental consciousness.

To fracture the seal of race and force the white female subject to cede the center of feminist discourse requires, paradoxically, a feminist theory divested of identity as ground or center of its politics. What feminism needs, Diana Fuss argues, is a theory and politics of identification (1995). Whereas the goal of identity politics is the discovery of an authentic self-consciousness capable of transforming the material boundaries of race and gender, a politics based on identification distinguishes itself first by its disavowal of this binary notion of an in/valid female self. Within the context of identity politics, the feminist subject would emerge as the result of a linear sequence of stages through which one progressively peels off the layers of false consciousness resulting from institutional racism and sexism. To the contrary, in what I am calling post-identity politics, identification would enable women to exchange the notion of the self as the purified product of a forward trajectory for an understanding of the self as configured through its relation to others in a single continuum of action.

Fuss' *Identification Papers* suggests how such a reconfigured female subjectivity might be successfully mobilized for a radical politics. Via a re-reading of Fanon, she sheds new light on how the psychical, the unconscious processes by which the subject is constituted in language, operates as a political formation, as that which fundamentally presupposes politics. She uses Fanon to locate the historical and social conditions of identification, drawing attention to the way in which identification is never outside or prior to politics. Identification, like language, "is always inscribed within a certain history: identification names not only the history of the subject but the subject in history" (1995: 165).

Therefore, to say that the black subject has lost her innocence is not to bear witness to her annihilation, but rather her metamorphosis, her replacement in language and history. In this re-conceptualization of the subject, identity arises from a fictionalized narrativization of the self, a narrative produced in the interstices between the real and the symbolic.[1] Within a material space of language and fantasy, Hall explains, identity no longer "signals an irreducible core of the individual or group collective self" (1996: 2-4).[2] Because it is no longer thought of in terms of something that can be "won" or "lost", far from being a politically impotent construction, this concept of identity offers a materially effective subject position that may allow us to move beyond the limitations of identity politics, what Jonathan Dollimore terms "wishful theory" (1996).

Theatres of Identification

Elin Diamond proposes a compelling account of identification and its relation to the theatrical representation of identity, one that challenges the classic hypothesis of identity based on a hierarchical structure of mimesis, with identity understood as the "real" foundation of the subject. She defines identification as "a passionate mimesis, a fantasy assimilation not locatable in time or responsive to political ethics" (1997: 106). Identification involves "drawing another into one-self, projecting oneself onto another", and, thus, it *"creates* sameness not with the self but with another: you are (like) me" (Diamond 1997: 109). While her theory of identification accepts that it cannot offer the same secure anchorage for political struggle as essentialist concepts of identity, at the same time it recognizes that a "private psychic act" can afford an opening into "cultural and political meanings". Taking into account that identification is only a partially conscious project, Diamond underscores how it is not necessarily politically correct given that it involves unconscious fantasies of desirable or powerful imagoes. In other words, "a black woman can identify with Marlon Brando, can *be* Marlon Brando in fantasy and therefore love white women or homoerotically other white men. In conscious life, few black women would find it politically desirable to take up such positions" (Diamond 2000 email correspondence). The bridge Diamond lays between conscious and unconscious processes of identification demonstrates that the psychical as multiple and even self-contradictory construct in no way precludes the "you" and the "me" whom you are (like) from remaining historically and socially rooted.

Diamond illustrates the logic and operations of identification through an analysis of Adrienne Kennedy's theatre. She suggests that Kennedy's theatre is one of identification, not identity, and, for this reason, her plays offer women a promising invitation to political self-consciousness. Briefly, Diamond argues that Kennedy's plays underscore the imbrication of identity and identification; theatricalize identification's disturbances; offer up characters that belie the representational apparatus which functions to construct the myth of a unitary ego or self; interrogate the fixities of racism precisely by avoiding positivities of form or ideation; and serve to repudiate the charge of political vapidity and ahistoricism often directed at postmodernism (1997: 107, 114, 117).

I want to use Diamond's reading of Kennedy's work, her observations regarding how the plays interrogate the fixities of race and stage the instabilities of race-gendered identifications, as a jumping off point for a further interrogation of how Kennedy's theatre may point to new strategies for transforming power relations among women. In particular, I explore how the plays elucidation of subjectivity not only give a language to the intra-subjective structures of black American women, but, in doing so, problematize the way in which both the black and the white female self has been written in feminist discourse. In other words, finally I want to shift the analysis of Kennedy's theatre onto the terrain of white psychical identity formation, in order to demonstrate how the plays complicate the gendered and racialized material contexts in which the white female subject is located. I am aware that in attempting to narrativize subjectivity in this way one must be careful to avoid simply inverting the direction of the schema, which can only result in the power of the white subject being revalorized through its capability of recuperating black as otherness. However, by working within the scene of the subject's constitutive processes, I hope to reveal how the shifting psychic terrains of Kennedy's hybrid subjects may present feminists with an opening into a political theory capable of dislodging the white female subject as the fixed center of feminist discourse, while avoiding the re-colonization of black female subjectivity.

Mary Brewer

The Dynamics of Conflict in Kennedy's Black Female Subjects

Within the context of an analysis of how three black women artists stage the self, Gabriele Griffin writes that, whereas naming belongs to the symbolic order and constitutes a socializing move, "not naming" is one way for black women to refuse the symbolic order and thus the categorizations that dominate society (1993: 37).[3] Although a refusal to name goes against the thinking embodied in the popular feminist catchphrase "to define is to empower", Kennedy's theatre shows the strategy of refusing essentialist conceptions of the subject to be especially apposite for revealing the ideational and material contexts of black women's experiences.

Kennedy's female characters are highly syncretic entities. That they support the hybrid nature of psychic formation has been well documented by critics.[4] Neither black, nor white, woman or female, African or American or European, but striding all of these categories, they occupy, both at the level of the conscious or visible and the unconscious, the in-between spaces of race, gender and culture. The characters' psychological as well as physical make-up, like the author's own autobiographical self-representation, point to the theatricalized nature of a voice which speaks from the borders of subjecthood.[5] By this, I mean that the subject is represented as an effect of an inherently mimetic and, thus, artificial structure. Diamond calls this mimesis-mimicry – "in which the production of objects, shadows, and voices is excessive to the truth/illusion structure of mimesis, spilling into mimicry, multiple 'fake offspring'" (1989: 65).

Negro Sarah in *Funnyhouse of a Negro* (Kennedy 1962) and Clara Passmore as well as Bastard's Black Mother from *The Owl Answers* (Kennedy 1963) are prime examples of the theatricalized self.[6] Sarah, born of rape – the rape by a black man, "the blackest of them all", of a black woman who "looked like a white woman", repeatedly attempts to disguise the dis-eased location of her race-gendered origins by inscribing her self in a number of alternative cultural and autobiographical narratives. Unable to insert securely any of her various selves – the Duchess of Hapsburg, Queen Victoria, Jesus and Patrice Lumumba – into a coherent and stable discursive mode, she can only slip between fictive, provisional discursive modes of race-gender. Sarah's inability to recognize a self not distorted by the mirrors of the funhouse (the values and discursive structures of white patriarchy) results in a traumatic splaying of her personality. Moreover, her failed attempts at psychic wholeness foreground the fictive position of white authored blackness

78

and, more important, the mythic status of race-gendered categories themselves.

Homi Bhabha suggests that what emerges between mimesis and mimicry is a mode of representation that is a kind of writing. And this figurative writing serves to marginalize the power, the monumentality, of historical models, that which supposedly makes these models imitable and worth imitating (1994: 87–8). The representational narration works similarly in *The Owl Answers*. Clara changes back and forth between the Virgin Mary, the Bastard and the Owl while Black Mother moves in and out of characterizations of Anne Boleyn and the Reverend's Wife. The women's transmogrifications never result in a sense of belonging, bodily or psychic integrity, nor does Kennedy allow them to even effectively *pass* as a unified subject. Her stage directions make clear that each is always already marked as a cultural exile; for evident on the body of each incarnation is the trace of a previous self in the form of a fragment of some garment, which functions to remind the spectator of their plural natures. Their shape-shifting reveals that identity is not closed or static or any whole thing available for a straight-forward re-presentation. *The Owl Answers*, like *Funnyhouse*, exposes all constructs of identity, dominant and subcultural, as existing on the margins of various interpellating systems, for example, race, gender, religion, colonialism, etc. The characters' borderline negotiations of race, gender and cultural difference, enacted through language spoken and signed on the body, reveal the historical and psycho-social signifying practices that shape these women. This revelation of an absence of essence gestures toward the political possibilities that could follow if feminist theory conditionally abandoned the notion of a unified female subject as a model for feminist movement; for this refusal of identity impoverishes the representational authority of models of White patriarchal discourse.

Re-plotting Race and Gender

Kennedy's theatre embodies the same possibilities and limits of positionality in American culture that May Joseph recognizes in black British women's theatre, where positionality implies "locating oneself as a subject already overdetermined by various contingent narratives, and self-consciously engaging in foregrounding those narratives that become crucial in demarcating the boundary one has chosen to occupy . . . ". Positionality becomes important for an understanding of subjectivity, Joseph suggests, as it is through the realization of a certain series of identifications that one comes into voice" (1997: 205). For instance, in *Funnyhouse,* Sarah's struggle for the sign of whiteness is partly waged in terms of a locational epistemology. This is reflected in the play's use of stage space, which is divided into Sarah's room, a room in an English Castle, the Duchess' Chamber, the hotel where Sarah believes she killed her father, and the jungle. Her movement back and forth between these spaces reflects not only her fragmented psychic space, but also the fact that she premises her validation of selfhood on her relative closeness to whiteness: the degree to which Negro Sarah can inhabit white psychical perspectives and approximate white cultural practices.

Ultimately, it proves impossible for Sarah to find a voice in any of her diverse rooms:

> I find there are no places only my funnyhouse. I try to create a space for myselves in cities, New York, the Midwest, a southern town, but it becomes a lie. I try to give myselves a logical relationship but that too is a lie . . . I clung loyally to the lie of relationships, again and again seeking to establish a connection between my characters. Jesus is Victoria's son . . . A loving relationship exists between myself and Queen Victoria, a love between myself and Jesus but they are lies. (Kennedy 1962: 7)

None of the places Sarah tries to occupy can accommodate her desire for socio-psychic plenitude, such plenitude being itself a mythic construct of desire. Further, her status as a racial hybrid, a "pallid", "yellow" Negro who inhabits the "in-between" spaces of culture means that she bears a disjointed relation to each of the stories she tells and to each of the figures and places through whom she attempts to come into a fullness of being. The statue of Victoria, which dominates the stage-space designating Sarah's room, serves, Janet Winston points out, as "a monument to an Anglo-European supremacy erected upon the foundation of racism" (1997: 246). In the world of Sarah/Victoria, "everything is white and everyone is white and there are no unfortunate black ones" (Kennedy 1962: 5). Therefore, Sarah-as-Victoria represents the repository of white civilization: she exists to police the borders of whiteness, both in physical terms, by outlawing the production of and/or keeping out "mixed breeds" like Sarah, and by preserving the hegemony of dominant white cultural practices, most notably in the play muscular Christianity.

Just as Sarah cannot accommodate herself within White cultural narratives, she can find no secure homeplace in tales of her patrilineal origin in Africa; for she has, through her desire to "maintain recognition against myself", internalized the imperial colonizing gaze. In various guises, Sarah repeatedly constructs for the audience a visual representation of her father's black appearance, his alien origins, and primitive behavior; he is: an African who lives in the jungle, who has always lived in the jungle, a nigger, a black man, the man's dark, he is the darkest, he who is the darkest one, the darkest one of them all (Kennedy 1962: 9, 11, 20). Sarah's jungle-room functions as a site for the production and dramatization of powerful distinctions between self and "other": here normative categories of physical bodies, psychic attributes and cultural practices are opposed to those of others constructed as deviant in the play. For example, the persona of White Jesus, the figure who brings the gift of salvation to the jungle inhabitants, contrasts with that of the Black Father – the destructive beast who is driven solely by savage (sexual) desire. Because the duty of taming the black beast falls to Sarah/Jesus, ably assisted by his Mother, Sarah/Victoria, obviously Negro Sarah cannot identify with an historical, socio-psychic space that justifies the West's colonial project in Black Africa.

Ironically, Sarah's paternal origin in the jungle displaces her also from anti-colonialist narratives. Rather than reconciling her to black psychic and cultural space, the fact that she is also Patrice Lumumba, "a nigger of two generations", further alienates her from herself. To the part of herself that would inhabit the royal world of Victoria and the Duchess, that world which knows that "black is evil and has been from the beginning", blackness can only ever signify ugliness and horror (Kennedy 1962: 5). Sarah's failure to cope with herselves' alienation from her Black Father, either by physically fleeing his influence or through imaginatively killing him, ultimately lead to her suicide. In a classic instance of the return of the repressed, at the end of the play Sarah's selves form a chorus to remind her that she will always remain "the black shadow" that haunts her own conception: "He keeps returning forever, keeps returning and returning and he is my father. He is a black Negro" (Kennedy 1962: 12, 21).

In *Funnyhouse*, the violent echoes of colonial narratives are played out via Sarah's imaginative murder of her father, both her own and her mother's physical deterioration and gradual descent into emotional despair, and finally by Sarah's suicide. However, Kennedy's violently fragmented portrait of the black female self is not simply a residue of historical processes, but applies equally to present-day American black/white race-gender relations. Rosemary Curb describes Kennedy's characters as "battlegrounds for wars of race, class and gender" in contemporary US culture (1992: 142). This link between the violence at the center of old and new world racist and sexist regimes is further evidenced in *The Owl Answers*. Clara, an almost-white school-teacher in Savannah, the bastard product of an illicit relationship between a white man and his black cook, tries to flee the pain of non-acceptance in the American South through an imaginative journey to the land of her white ancestors: the England of William the Conqueror, Chaucer, Shakespeare, Dickens, and Eliot. But her dream of belonging in her white father's world proves as illusory as Sarah's dream of fitting into Victoria's world. Clara's adored white icons, animated in her mind, end up imprisoning her in The Tower of London, effectively barring her access to the place of the White father and reconfirming it as a space reserved for an idealized white womanhood.

Clara is no more able than Sarah to "know places". Acts of identification for both characters can take place only across the hazy borders that mark the differences within and between whiteness and blackness and race and gender. Yet, both women insist on walking a tightrope of race, and, it is this quest for an unadulterated racialized identity that precludes them from ever specifying what their relation to their various selves, the relation of each to her other(s), might be. Moreover, it prohibits them from negotiating some foothold along the boundaries of social and psychic space, some room of their own capable of accommodating them in all of their differences.

Staging AnOther Race

In an interview with Elin Diamond, Kennedy states that one reason her plays are not staged very often is because they "make people uncomfortable" (1996: 137). Kennedy's dramatic world is bleak, saturated with violence, and, on the surface at least, it seems to offer women scant hope for successful resistance. Nevertheless, I suggest that the key to the political promise of Kennedy's theatre lies in its very ability to provoke audience/reader anxiety, whatever side or place on the margins of the race-gender divide one positions oneself. I want to explore further exactly how the plays evoke discomfort, this time focusing particularly on the potential of Kennedy's theatre for unsettling the foundations of white identity.

For this, I turn to Bakhtin's concept of language and hybridization. According to Bakhtin, language represents the co-existence of socio-ideological contradictions between the present and the past and between different socio-ideological groups in the present. "As a living, socio-ideological concrete thing, as heteroglot opinion, language, for the individual consciousness, lies on the borderline between oneself and the other. The word in language is half someone else's" (1981: 293). One of the most important things that Kennedy's theatre achieves is to reveal how subcultural groups may be part owners of discourses that emerge from within dominant structural paradigms. I have discussed above how the plays transliterate postmodern concepts, situating them within black philosophical and cultural parameters, a necessary step, I suggest, if the notion of a radically decentered female subject is to enable the cause of black female empowerment and open up the possibility of a multicultural progressive women's movement. When read in terms of Bakhtin's theory of hybridized language, it becomes clear how Kennedy's theatre also illustrates the ability of the black female voice to unmask and ironize white cultural discourse and identificatory processes.

That this unmasking can be effected within the same utterance and often relying upon the same vocabulary is foregrounded in *A Lesson in Dead Language* (Kennedy 1968). In this brief play, a large White Dog delivers a Latin lesson to a group of black girls. Surrounding the class-room where the lesson takes place are larger-than-life statues of Jesus, Mary, Joseph, the Biblical Wise Men, and a number of Roman figures. In addition to the White Dog, the play contains another white dog belonging to one of the pupils, which Kennedy describes as "great, white, stiff" and positioned as if it were begging. Both actors playing the dogs are masked. The face of the White Dog is concealed, while the whole upper body of the actor playing the white dog is costumed as an animal. Only the White Dog and the pupils speak.

A central question of the lesson is who killed the White Dog. To expect an answer to this question appears to be a logical impossibility given that it is being posed by the White Dog itself. On one level, it seems that the only thing the plays allows the girls and the audience to know for sure is that who killed the White Dog killed Caesar too. However, if we agree with Rosemary Curb's reading of the teacher-Dog as a symbol of the "world of elders and ancestors from Christianity and classical antiq-uity", then the White Dog, like Caesar, both *has* and *has not* been killed (1987: 55). The White Dog remains able to speak, in the same way that Latin, the language of the assassinated Caesar, continues to circulate in White Western culture by virtue of its status as one of the founding languages of White Western thought. Once again, we see that history and ideology remain stubbornly alive in Kennedy's theatre.

In *The Dialogic Imagination*, Bakhtin writes that at any one moment languages of different epochs and periods of socio-ideological life cohabit with one another. As a result, at any one moment of its histor-ical existence, language is "heteroglot from top to bottom" (1981: 291). If we unpack what Latin represents in the play, the heteroglot character of White discourse, as well as some of its material effects, become more apparent. *A Lesson in Dead Language* assumes the same the historical resonance of former symbolic and material racist and sexist structures in contemporary Anglo-America's race–gender system as do *Funnyhouse* and *The Owl*. For instance, as the language of Imperial

Rome, Latin is analogous to English, the language of Imperial Britain and now the language expressive of US economic, military, and cultural dominance. Both Latin and English represent the historical intellectual property of elite social groups, whose class, race, and sex-gender privileges bear a reciprocal relation to nationalist colonialist and neo-colonialist economic enterprises. And one need only think of Colonial Shakespeare to realize how English has been constructed as the new, natural language of Culture, superimposing itself upon the artistic values of "beauty and truth", those values that once resided within the province of classical languages.

Yet, in the play, neither of these languages of the ruling classes possesses the power of providing truthful, comforting, or even logical answers to the questions surrounding race-gendered identity. The subject of the girls' lesson is "I BLEED", which refers to their emergence from childhood into puberty being marked through the onset of menstruation: "Teacher, the white dog died, I started to bleed," states one of the pupils. However, the White Dog bleeds as well: "The day the white dog died, I started to bleed. Blood came out of me" (Kennedy 1968: 48). Hence, the emergence of a black womanhood is tied in the play to the White Dog, to its apocryphal death and to knowledge concerning its quasi-demise. That the black female subject comes into being, indeed awakens sexually, through an identification with the White Dog, that is, the White voice, again renders the formation of black female psychical identity as hybrid, fragmented, and alienated from any one location in language or culture.

The girls' alienation is expressed in the play by their inability to perceive sensibly the world in words; for example:

> Who killed the white dog and why do I bleed? I killed the white dog and that is why I must bleed. And the lemons and the grass and the sun. It was at the Ides of March. (Kennedy 1968: 49)

In the play, Latin, typically praised for the logic and elegance of its structure, here simply cannot be made to make sense. And English proves just as futile for interpreting character's personal or social realities. Significantly, the White Dog's speech is unaccompanied by any movement of the actor's mouth. The mask Kennedy places on the actor could work dramatically to diminish the force of the White Dog's voice and to conceal the place from which its speech originates. In the context of a discussion of how masks function in *Funnyhouse*, Deborah Thompson writes that "the characters' masks, and the characters-as-masks, complicate any notion of what is mask, what is real" (1997: 20). Therefore, in theoretical terms, by concealing the movements of the White Dog's mouth, the mask also denies the possibility of determining with any sense of accuracy either the validity or the univocality of dominant White discourse.

The uncertainty surrounding whether the voice giving the lesson arises from the place occupied by the White Dog has the effect of placing this character within the representational structure that Bhabha calls the "not quite/not white". Here, discourse can only be uttered between the lines and, as such, both *within* and *against* the rules structuring dominant discourse. This scenario, Bhabha argues, reveals the founding objects of Western culture to be erratic, eccentric and accidental (1994: 89). In a moment of incongruity typical of Kennedy's theatre, masking the White Dog ironically serves to unmask as myth the authority of white discourse. This bears the potential to push the spectator, black and white, toward the same ambivalent stance expressed by Kennedy in the keynote above concerning what constitutes whiteness, blackness, or race itself. To append the tag, *so-called majority, whatever that is*, to white culture, is profoundly disruptive to white identity's presumed ontological supremacy; for it stages the category of whiteness in terms of just AnOther race.

Furthermore, this textual strategy subverts the processes of white identification. If language is that register that locates us and within whose confines we look at each other, that is, one locates "oneself" and the "other", then, in the case of *A Lesson*, it is no longer a question of the white subject always looking at the black object. The border between subject and object, outer and inner, superior and inferior, shifts, and that between whiteness and blackness expands. For this reason, exactly *who is* the white dog may perhaps be a more pertinent question than who killed it. To turn the questioner into the question itself suggests that there is no "real" face behind the White Dog's mask, and this strategy bears the potential to unsettle white psychical identity formation by disrupting the internalized authority of white discourse; in other words, the play dissociates white speech from the intact white body, the site identified by Bhabha as that where its priority is naturalized onto the skin. In this way, Kennedy's theatre carries the potential to shake the foundation of those psycho-social props relied upon to instantiate identity, to produce the white subject's self-recognition. Returning to Fuss' sense of identification, as that which signifies the play of difference and similitude in self-other relations (1995: 2), Kennedy's *Lesson* demonstrates how white race-gendered identities signify *by virtue of* and *not despite* their hybridity. At the end of the play, the audience cannot be sure who inhabits which site on a now expanded border zone of race-gender, and this moment of indeterminacy further problematizes the notion of an undefiled whiteness, one that may be defined over and against a blackness firmly identified as "other".

Mary Brewer

Decentering the White Female Subject

Jacques Derrida's work on white mythology identifies how White Western metaphysics takes Indo-European mythology as its own logos – the mythos of its idiom. "White Mythology – metaphysics has erased within itself the fabulous scene that has produced it, the scene that nevertheless remains active and stirring, inscribed in white ink, an invisible design covered over in the palimpsest" (1982: 213). Fuss reiterates Derrida's assertion that White identity draws its ideological power from its proclaimed transparency, from its self-elevation over the category of race (1995: 144). The work of Richard Dyer, Ruth Frankenberg, Matthew Frye Jacobson, and Vron Ware has also contributed valuable insights into the apparent emptiness of whiteness as a signifier: how it is represented in dominant cultural terms as formless and unnamable, as opposed to a range of "other" identities marked by race, ethnicity, and nation.

Above, I began to address how Kennedy's theatrical discourse denies whiteness its self-proclaimed position as transcendental signifier. I want to conclude by examining further how the plays uncover the remains of Whiteness' "fabulous scene", that site where the white subject defines itself through a fantasy of escaping the matrix of historical and social conditions that form it. To quote Dyer: "The point is to see the specificity of whiteness, even when the text [or discourse] itself is not trying to show it to you, doesn't even know it is there to be shown" (1997: 13–14).

A Movie Star Has to Star in Black and White (1976) proves exemplary among Kennedy's plays for revealing the exclusionary practices of white psychical identity formation. Diamond contends that in *Movie Star* the imbrication of identification and identity displayed in Kennedy's earlier plays becomes full-scale collision (1997: 128). The play makes Whiteness visible not only to those it excludes, but, more important, to those it includes within its boarders – those who by virtue of their secure housing within this category can rarely perceive its material effects.

Movie Star features a leading cast of actors who closely resemble the actual film stars Bette Davis, Paul Henreid, Jean Peters, Marlon Brando, Montgomery Clift, and Shelley Winters, figures with whom Kennedy relates she has been fascinated since childhood. The supporting roles are taken by Clara, a 33 year-old black woman, her husband and parents. The play is densely inter-textual: the play-life of Clara elides with the playwright's own experiences. The action consists of events related to those recalled by Kennedy in her autobiography combined with moments and dialogue from her earlier plays. The movie stars, framed

86

within a set of film narratives – *Now Voyager, Viva Zapata,* and *A Place In The Sun* – play out scenes featuring Clara and her family.

Clara, like so many of Kennedy's other black women characters, desires continuity of self. Her strategy for attaining this resembles that of Clara in *Owl* and Sarah in *Funnyhouse,* namely to cement a proximity to a dominant ideal of race-gender identity, in this case by placing herself within a trio of classic Hollywood film narratives. Clara experiences reality in and through her fantasy identification with a set of white-authored feminine images. She presents herself as obsessed with recording her life: "my diaries make me a spectator watching my life like watching a black and white movie" (Kennedy 1976: 99). In fact, we are told that her life *is* for her one of her black and white movies, with Clara playing a bit part. Thus, her relation to her self plays itself out in spectatorial terms, as the desire to become the image that captures her own gaze. However, in a neat twist, she does not simply inhabit the images of Davis or Peters. Rather, these white-authored representations are made to voice her subjective reality. Although Clara's position in the socio-symbolic contract is mediated through these iconic images of white womanhood, she is only partly colonized by the white gaze; for the female film characters serve as the source of enunciation for Clara's black femininity. In other words, each figure occupies a part-presence in relation to the other.

One reason Kennedy's movie stars have to star in black and white is because psychical processes of identification involve a detour through the "other", and it is this detour, Fuss argues, that defines the self (1995:2). For example, the movie stars, as seeing and desiring female subjects, only enter the narrative as a result of having traversed blackness; likewise, Clara/Kennedy can effectively resist some of the structures of family and social oppression only by virtue of refusing binary divisions between self and other, which allows her to comment on what she watches in her life, to say what might otherwise have to remain unconscious, unspeakable.

When Clara maps herself onto the terrain of fantasy, she makes race-gender identity an effect of a theatricalized-cum-filmic discourse, altering both the way she sees herself and the ways in which the spectator might see her. The ordinary point-of-view structures in narrative regarding race-gender are destabilized, and, given that ways of looking at self and others are intimately connected to ways of theorizing self and others, ontologies of race-gender are also disturbed. Diamond explains how Clara sees whiteness and blackness as images, not origins, and this produces a crucial alienation effect. In *Movie Star,* "the political is marked in spectatorial consciousness when identification-as-*racial* resemblance breaks down. Clara's movie stars are proximate and continuous with her psychical life but their mimetic relation creates, rather than mystifies, cultural, social, and racial difference" (Diamond 1997: 128). Staging the white female subject at the enunciative level of theatrical discourse reveals it to be an effect of the discursive production of its others. In the same way that Whiteness discursively generates, via its operations of identification, a range of racialized and gendered others, now it too appears to be produced as an effect of language.

A similar exposure of Whiteness as mythos of its own idiom occurs in *A Lesson*. Recall the link identified by Curb between classical historical personae and the White Dog; then conjoin this with the image of the girls' blood and its association with that of the bleeding Caesar (whose own bridge to the production of Western hegemonic discourse is amplified, via Shakespeare's *Julius Caesar*, in the play's reference to Calpurnia's dream), and this inter-textual chain of images suggests that Whiteness too is hemorrhaging. The white ink that writes the scene of white psychical identity formation not only becomes visible here, but also is revealed as prone to bleed, perhaps even, like Caesar, to be at risk of bleeding away into a state of non-recognizability. Consequently, a stable white self and the continued stability of White cultural hegemony can no longer be comfortably assumed.

To return to this theme in *Movie Star*, when Davis-as-Clara or Winters-as-Clara speak Clara's blackness, they do so of course with a difference, and, under these circumstances, *la differance* is whiteness. Firstly, to make the white female subject voice a black woman's experience displaces Whiteness from its normative narrative structural position. Whiteness as self-identical sign is deferred, and, in the moment of its deferral, it is (dis)placed onto an alternative psycho-social space. Secondly, by making Whiteness as a sign corporeally visible, Whiteness as the place of the seeing subject shifts to the same level of blackness – that of the seen object. Diamond makes a similar point when she says that the whiteness of the performers in *Movie Star* is revealed when, and only when, they speak the life of the *visible* black woman. (1997: 128). Usually, where the subject is part of a dominant cultural group, it does not have to name itself. If we accept that white power reproduces itself through its invisibility, then to name Whiteness as *Movie Star* does works to reveal the constitutive processes of White authority and to delimit its material effects.

Decentering the white female subject by making visible the design of whiteness, its historicity, could provide the best means for solving what Elizabeth Spelman terms the ampersand problem in feminist thought: where the terms of feminist theory require that a person be either a black female or a white woman, and there exists no language with which to describe those who are both (1988: 120). To reveal the plural character of white female subjectivity may offer a materially powerful way of resisting exclusionary practices in feminist discourse, by enabling women to think what it could mean to occupy the position of *either/and* in the race-gender system, rather than *either/or*, or *both/and* – positions that are bound within binary, hierarchical thinking. The subject of what I've called post-identity feminist politics, whose outline we glimpse in Kennedy's theatre, would exchange binary operations of naming and counter-naming for a schema in which the race-gendered subject draws its agency and meaning by its implication in the relations of power which constitute it – the same relations of power it may seek to oppose.

Through staging the interconnections among history, politics, philosophical discourse, cultural production and identity, the plays discussed here illustrate how the operations of identification that configure the subject are constructed through independent though interrelated economies of production and intervention. Kennedy's theatre repeatedly re-stages the subject's constitutive moment in the place where, Kristeva posits, it operates with the maximum intransigence, that is, in personal psycho-sexual identity itself (1986:209). In this way, the status of the white subject as self-producing term may be made to disintegrate in its very nucleus. This opens up the possibility of effectively challenging traditional ways of conceptualizing race-gender and thereby, the place of the white female subject at the center of feminist discourse. In turn, this may provide a new space in feminist discourse for black women to articulate their psychic reality and cultural practices that remain largely absent from the theoretical foundations upon which both dominant female and feminist identity have hitherto rested.

Acknowledgment

I am indebted to Steve Bottoms, Carl Muckley, Laura Salisbury, and David Roberts for their cogent suggestions on earlier versions of this paper.

Notes

1   I use the terms real and symbolic in a Lacanian sense, with the real referring to that which cannot be represented at a particular historical moment and the symbolic designating the order of language and sexual difference.

2   See also Hall 1995.

3   Griffin's notion of the symbolic order follows that of Lacan. In Lacanian terms, the symbolic order refers to the order of culture and language into which the subject is inserted as a result of the Oedipus Complex.

4   See, for example, Barnett (1996); Oha (1997); Patsalidis (1995).

5   See Kennedy 1987.

6   All references to Kennedy's plays are from the collection *Adrienne Kennedy: In One Act*. Minneapolis: University of Minnesota Press, 1988 – dates referenced in the body of the text refer to the original publication date for each play.

References

Bakhtin, M. M. 1981: *The Dialogic Imagination*. Michael Holquist (ed.) Caryl Emerson and Michael Holquist (trans.). Austin: University of Texas Press.
Barnett, Claudia. 1996: This Fundamental Challenge to Identity: Reproduction and Representation in the Drama of Adrienne Kennedy. *Theatre Journal* 48, 141–55.
Bhabha, Homi. 1994: *The Location of Culture*. London: Routledge.
Collins, Patricia Hill. 1991: *Black Feminist Thought: Knowledge, Consciousness, and the Politics of Empowerment*. New York: Routledge.
Combahee River Collective Statement. 1983: In Barbara Smith (ed.), *Home Girls: A Black Feminist Anthology*. New York: Kitchen Table Press, 272–82.
Curb, Rosemary. 1992: (Hetero)Sexual Terrors in Kennedy's Plays. In Paul K. Bryant and Lois More Overbeck (eds), *Intersecting Boundaries: The Theatre of Adrienne Kennedy*. Minneapolis: University of Minnesota Press, 142–56.
——. 1987: "Lesson I Bleed": Adrienne Kennedy's Blood Rites. In Helen Krich Chinoy and Linda Walsh Jenkins (eds), *Women in American Theatre*. New York: Theatre Communications Group, 50–6.
Derrida, Jacques. 1982: White Mythology: Metaphor in the Text of Philosophy. In *The Margins of Philosophy*, Alan Bass (trans.). Hemel Hempstead: Harvester Wheatsheaf.
Diamond, Elin. 1989: Mimesis, Mimicry and the 'True-Real'. *Modern Drama* 32, 58–72.
——. 1996: Adrienne Kennedy. In Philip C. Kolin and Colby H. Kullman (eds), *Interviews with Contemporary American Playwrights*. Tuscaloosa: The University of Alabama Press, 125–37.
——. 1997: *Unmaking Mimesis: Essays on Feminism and Theatre*. Routledge.
Dollimore, Jonathan. 1996: Bisexuality, heterosexuality, and wishful theory. *Textual Practice* 10 (3) 523–39.
Dyer, Richard. 1997: *White*. London: Routledge.
Fanon, Frantz. 1952 [1986]: *Black Skin, White Masks*. London: Pluto Press.
Frankenberg, Ruth R. 1993: *The Social Construction of Whiteness: White Women, Race Matters*. London: Routledge.
Fuss, Diana. 1995: *Identification Papers*. London: Routledge.
Griffin, Gabriele. 1993: "Writing the Body": Reading Joan Riley, Grace Nichols and Ntozake Shange. In Gina Wisker (ed.), *Black Women's Writing*. Houndmills: Macmillan, 19–42.
Hall, Stuart. 1997 [1995]: New Ethnicities. In Bill Ashcroft, Gareth Griffiths, and Helen Tiffin (eds), *The Post-Colonial Studies Reader*. Routledge, 223–7.
——. 1995: Fantasy, Identity, Politics. In E. Carter, J. Donald, and J. Squires (eds), *Cultural Remix: Theories of Politics and the Popular*. London: Lawrence Wishart, 63–9.

——. 1996: Introduction: Who Needs Identity? In David Morey and Kuan-Hsing Chen (eds), *Stuart Hall: Critical Dialogues in Cultural Studies*. London: Routledge, 1–17.

hooks, bell. 1989: *Talking Back: Thinking Feminist, Thinking Black*. Boston: South End.

Jacobson, Matthew Frye. 1998: *Whiteness of a Different Color: European Immigrants and the Alchemy of Race*. Cambridge, MA: Harvard University Press.

Joseph, May. 1997: Bodies Outside the State: Black British Women Playwrights and the Limits of Citizenship. In Peggy Phelan and Jill Lane (eds), *The Ends of Performance*. New York: New York University Press, 197–213.

Kennedy, Adrienne. 1987: *People Who Led To My Plays*. New York: Theatre Communications Group.

——. 1988 [1963]: The Owl Answers. In *Adrienne Kennedy: In One Act*. Minneapolis: University of Minnesota Press.

——. 1988 [1962]: Funnyhouse of a Negro. In *Adrienne Kennedy: In One Act*. Minneapolis: University of Minnesota Press.

——. 1988 [1968]: A Lesson in Dead Language. In *Adrienne Kennedy: In One Act*. Minneapolis: University of Minnesota Press.

——. 1988 [1976]: A Movie Star Has To Star in Black and White. In *Adrienne Kennedy: In One Act*. Minneapolis: University of Minnesota Press.

Kristeva, Julia. 1986: Women's Time. In Toril Moi (ed.), *The Kristeva Reader*. Oxford: Basil Blackwell, 187–213.

Oha, Obododimma. 1997: Her Dissonant Selves: The Semiotics of Plurality and Bisexuality in Adrienne Kennedy's *Funnyhouse of a Negro*. *American Drama* 6 (2), 67–80.

Patsalidis, Savas. 1995: Adrienne Kennedy's Heterotopias and the (Im)possibilities of the (Black) Female Self. In Marc Maufort (ed.), *Staging Difference: Cultural Pluralism in American Theatre and Drama*, 300–21.

Rabine, Leslie Wahl. 1988: A Feminist Politics of Non-Identity. *Feminist Studies* 14 (1), 11–32.

Spelman, Elizabeth V. 1988: *Inessential Woman: Problems of exclusion in feminist thought*. London: The Women's Press.

Spivak, Gayatri Chakravorty. 1989: A Response to "The Difference Within: Feminism and Critical Theory". In Elizabeth Meese and Alice Parker (eds), *The Difference Within: Feminism and Critical Theory*. Philadelphia: John Benjamin, 207–20.

Thompson, Deborah. 1997 (Fall): Reversing Blackface Minstrelsy: Improvising Racial Identity: Adrienne Kennedy's Funnyhouse of a Negro. *Post-Identity*, 13–38.

Walker, Alice. 1984: *In Search of Our Mother's Gardens*. London: The Women's Press.

Ware, Vron. 1991: *Beyond the Pale*. London: Verso.

Winston, Janet. 1997: Queen Victoria in the Funnyhouse: Adrienne Kennedy and the Rituals of Colonial Possession. In Margaret Homans and Adrienne Munich (eds), *Remaking Queen Victoria*. Cambridge: Cambridge University Press, 235–57.

Chapter 5

(Post)Colonial (Dis)Orders: Female Embodiment as Chaos in Tsitsi Dangarembga's Nervous Conditions and Bharati Mukherjee's Jasmine

MELISSA CHINCHILLO

The new geometry mirrors a universe that is rough, not rounded, scabrous, not smooth. It is a geometry of the pitted, pocked, and broken up, the twisted, tangled, and intertwined.

James Gleick, Chaos: Making a New Science

THE ABOVE LINES from James Gleick's seminal work on the evolution of chaos theory appear as the epigraph of Bharati Mukherjee's novel *Jasmine*, prompting the reader to draw connections between chaos and the story of a young Indian woman fleeing from postcolonial India to America. In *Jasmine*, the protagonist's body and subjectivity are represented as chaotic, disordered by the conflicting tensions of adolescence, gender, race, class, and national politics. Choosing an epigraph from Gleick's *Chaos*, then, Mukherjee alerts us to the "pitted, pocked, and broken up" nature of the "new geometry" structuring her novel: the threatening and threatened boundaries of women's corporeality and identity, complicated by India's transition from a colonial to postcolonial government and the protagonist's eventual assimilation into American culture.

The epigraph of Tsitsi Dangarembga's novel *Nervous Conditions* is taken from Jean-Paul Sartre – "The condition of the native is a nervous condition" – and even more specifically highlights the ruptured *embodiment* of colonial subjects.[1] Oppressed by British imperial and Shona patriarchal systems, the "condition" of "native" women in *Nervous Conditions* is often hysterical and disorderly, figured through the body in the form of nervous habits, eating disorders, and mental instabilities. The epigraphs of both novels emphasize nervous, broken up, and disordered bodies and spaces, which may benefit from methodologies of *chaos*, more so than those deploying *otherness*.[2] Unlike "the other" – a concept invoked in relatively closed, elite, academic circles – "chaos" has mythic, historical, religious, and scientific implications, enabling it to function as a "matrix where various cultural associations interact and converge" (Hawkins 1995: xi). Chaos, as such a cultural meeting ground, lends itself to being an apt trope for thinking about the interactions between cultures in (post)colonial environments.[3] Furthermore, in religion and mythology, chaos is often gendered as female like Pandora or Eve, which makes it easier to understand the genealogy of the stereotype that female sexuality is disorderly and threatening – a myth that cuts across cultural boundaries – because it arouses male heterosexual desire that cannot be controlled. It is important to note here that chaos science moves away from such binary thinking (male as order; female as disorder) because it positions order and disorder as co-mingled, each giving rise to the other and to a third system that N. Katherine Hayles calls "orderly disorder". The aforementioned gendering and stereotyping of chaos remain a significant backdrop to this analysis, however, for the novels' protagonists are both characterized by and rebel against these connotations of disorder.

Several scholars, N. Katherine Hayles in particular, have used chaos science to bridge gaps between technology, nature, and culture, so it should come as no surprise that writers like Dangarembga and Mukherjee seize upon the implications of chaos to represent challenges to womanhood and women's challenges to patriarchal and imperial ideologies. The similarities among feminist, postcolonial, and chaos theories are no mere coincidence, according to Hayles: "Different disciplines are drawn to similar problems because the concerns underlying them are highly charged within a prevailing cultural context" (Hayles 1990: xi). The "similar problems" upon which feminist, postcolonial, and chaos paradigms converge is the effort to recuperate the marginal and absent – whether it be disorder found in nature or women subordinated by colonization and patriarchy – as central and present. Gleick's endeavor to recuperate chaos, "making a new science" (the subtitle of his book) that values disorder as worthy of scientific study was published in 1987. In the years immediately following, Dangarembga's and Mukherjee's novels were published in 1988 and 1989 respectively. The timeliness of these three publications suggests that postcolonial novelists and chaos theorists are drawn to similar problems, which, in this case, are "highly charged" by the potential subversion of hegemonic systems of belief like the dominant paradigms of science, gender, and race.

In physics, for example, nonlinear differential equations – which generally do not have explicit solutions – were usually relegated to the margins of discussion, thus reinforcing the implicit assumption that linearity (order) is the rule of nature, nonlinearity (disorder) the exception. Benoit Mandelbrot corroborates the existence of this "rule" in *The Fractal Geometry of Nature*, where he recounts how nonlinear geometry was described by mathematicians as "monstrous", "counter-intuitive", "pathological", and "psychopathic" (Hayles 1990: 164). Suggestive of *human* deformity, disease, and disorder, these descriptions resonate with the nineteenth-century imperialist invention of the "native" as "savage", "dirty", and "diseased". In late twentieth century postcolonial and feminist theories, the "native" came to be conceptualized as one of the many kinds of others. The other – marginalized often to the point of erasure – occupies a "site of differences", since s/he differs from the hegemonic norm due to race, ethnicity, sexual orientation, class position, gender, age, etc.

One of the problems with "other" thinking is its tendency to group all others together as the other, sometimes collapsing differences and erasing the specificities of otherness.[4] Such erasure occurs not only at the level of language – of homogenizing myriad cultures as the other – but also at the level of ideology under-girding the deployment of the term. Ideologically, terms like "other" or "differences" are frequently invoked as part of a larger project to privilege and prioritize the "agency" and "resistance" of the othered subject, over that which the other resists: the "domination" of political, social, and cultural institutions. On the one hand, bringing the other from the margins to the center of discussion is a critically important strategy, if only for its insistence that individuals and cultures not part of Western tradition are important in their own right. On the other hand, however, emphasizing local concerns – the other's agency and resistance, for instance – without considering their interaction with global structures of oppression like colonization, capitalism, and patriarchy paints a lopsided, and usually populist, picture of the other. Such a perspective, biased toward local specificities, may present the other in a vacuum that seems to transcend historical structures of economic domination and political power. Marxist and materialist thinkers would remind us to consider the other's position in class structures and how the other's differences are material products of labor and power relations, not merely immaterial, discursive effects of language.

Discourse remains an effective strategy of domination, however, and it should not be ignored in any analysis of class, race, or gender relations. As an example, Mandelbrot's anecdote above demonstrates how language – words like "monstrous" and "pathological" – marginalized studies of chaos and positioned it as the pathological monster of "real" (orderly) science. This essay draws a parallel between the "scientific" perception of nonlinearity and disorder as "monstrous" (the stuff of physics' freak shows) and patriarchal and colonial perceptions of women and "natives" as disorderly threats to established social orders. As the evolution of chaos science brought entropy out of the wings of side-show freakery and into center stage for meaningful analysis, so too have feminist and postcolonial studies made women and "natives" present, powerful agents, rather than invisible, insignificant victims.

In focusing on how this parallel manifests itself in *Nervous Conditions* and *Jasmine*, this analysis will consider challenges to womanhood and women's challenges to oppressive ideologies on three levels: (1) within the novels, female protagonists challenge the limits of the body, subjectivity, and established social orders; (2) positioning the novels within chaos theory, the female protagonists' bodies disrupt hegemonic ideologies about what constitutes order and disorder; (3) situating the entire argument at the intersection of feminist, postcolonial, and chaos paradigms pushes theoretical, disciplinary limits in thinking about womanhood, in particular how it is consumed, embodied, and produced by minority women in colonial and postcolonial environments. Drastically oversimplifying the principles of chaos theory is inevitable for this literary analysis, and in order to do so, I employ a few specific elements of nonlinear dynamics (chaos theory) as tropes: strange attractors, feedback mechanisms, and Hayles's conceptualization of "orderly disorder" (deterministic chaos).[5] By using dynamical systems methods here, I aim to elucidate the complexities of (post)colonial corporeality in the two novels under consideration, and to foreground the materiality of the "disorderly" body, whose threatening effects can be traced back not only to class struggle and power relations, but also to the ideology of "order" that structures these systems and against which those deemed "disorderly" must struggle.

The protagonists of *Nervous Conditions* and *Jasmine* – Tambu, Nyasha, and Jasmine – are forced into acute consciousness of their own and other women's bodies by the colonial and patriarchal systems oppressing them.[6] In both texts, systems of domination control women's bodies often by marking them as dirty and disordered – as sites of chaos that pose threats to political, cultural, and economic orders. The young women's realizations of the disordered status of their embodiment prompts not only an awareness of corporeality, but also of their positions in a larger matrix of "ordered" social institutions, which posit their bodies as "disordered".

On the first page of *Nervous Conditions*, for example, the body is foregrounded as unhealthy, dirty, contagious, and disordered as Tambu recounts why her brother Nhamo didn't like to take the bus: "the women smelt of unhealthy reproductive odours, the children were inclined to relieve their upset bowels on the floor, and the men gave off strong aromas of productive labor" (Dangarembga 1988: 1). While both men and women exude scents, the different effects of their (female) "odours" and (male) "aromas" reveal how women's bodies are constructed as dirty, disorderly threats to the patriarchal system. That female bodily scents should be *unhealthy odours* derived from *reproductive* systems, whereas male scents are *strong aromas* derived from *productive labor* signals that the diseased entropy of female embodiment is an effect of the materiality of labor and production. As Nhamo perceives it, men's "labor" is "productive"; they work in the hot Utmali sun and perspire as a result of their work. Women, however, threaten this orderly system because they are not "working" in the same way: they simply "smelt" (seemingly without producing anything) as a result of their unhealthy reproductive systems. Nhamo de-values women's (re)production, labels it "unhealthy", and does not consider that women on the bus may also be engaged in some form of "productive labor" – perhaps getting food for their families, going to a job, or transporting their children to and from school. These activities, and "reproductive" ones, do not constitute "labor" in Nhamo's patriarchal ideology, and, therefore, female odors challenge the order of this system. To contain this threat, women's scent must be constructed as unhealthy, dirty, and smelly (as opposed to aromatic) in order to render it inferior.

Steeped in this patriarchal thinking, Tambu perpetuates her brother's perceptions of bodily uncleanliness:

> I knew, had known all my life, that living was dirty . . . I knew, for instance that rooms where people slept exuded peculiarly human smells . . . I knew, too, that the fact of menstruation was a shamefully unclean secret. (Dangarembga 1988: 70)

Living on the Shona communal lands is a dirty business, but the fact of menstruation is a dirtier one: it is shameful, unclean, and should be kept secret. Other peculiarly human smells are acceptable, however, just as male smells are strong "aromas" produced by labor. Women, as threats to what counts as "acceptable" dirt and odor, occupy a position of chaos which patriarchal ideology cannot order, and thus must deem unclean, unhealthy, and shameful as a means of implementing its domination.

Dangarembga's representation of the Shona lifestyle as dirty, as opposed to the cleanliness of the "Anglicised" mission, may seem to co-exist in problematic relation to the European construction of "the savage natives" as "the very embodiment of dirt and disorder" (Comaroff 1993: 306). As Jean Comaroff describes in "The Diseased Heart of Africa", controlling and curing the disordered native body was the centerpiece of the colonizing mission since the late eighteenth century, through which the imperialist enterprise in Africa found its alibi. This positioning of the "native" masked colonization as a mission to relieve suffering and bring "progress" to the "poor, diseased heart of Africa", as Reverend Willoughby describes in *Native Life on the Transvaal Border* (Comaroff 1993: 305).

In stark opposition to the filth of life on the communal lands in *Nervous Conditions* stands the clean, modern lifestyle found at the mission house of Tambu's uncle Babamukuru, a member of the black colonial elite and a Shona patriarch. Tambu contrasts the uncleanliness of her mother Mainini, who lives on the communal lands, with the cleanliness of her aunt Maiguru who lives on the mission. Tambu's aunt

> looked well-kempt and fresh, clean all the time. She was an altogether different kind of woman from my mother. I decided it was better to be like Maiguru, who was not poor and had not been crushed by the weight of womanhood. (Dangarembga 1988: 16)

Here, the "disorder" of "native" Shona corporeality (embodied in Tambu's mother) is made visible by its contrast to the cleanliness of Westernized Maiguru. A clean female body becomes the sign of cultural affiliation, class standing, and the ability to bear "the weight of womanhood" – a burden, which for Maiguru "who was not poor", is relieved by economic position. More importantly, Tambu's cognizance of Maiguru's economic position (detected through her well-kemptness) privileges her over Tambu's mother, creating a hierarchy which makes Tambu's later realization that Maiguru is just as much weighted down by her womanhood as is her mother (but in non-economic terms) all the more powerful.

After she moves to Babamukuru's home to attend the mission school, Tambu's first discoveries are the lack of dirt in their house and that she is "clean now, not only on special occasions but every day of the week" (Dangarembga 1988: 93). Bathed bodies and good housekeeping, however, cannot order the hysterical disorder of this space, for as Nyasha reveals, the mission house is a hysterical site: "I need to relax with all this hysteria in this house" (Dangarembga 1988: 48). The reader begins to see that wiping away the dirt on the surface of Shona culture does not order things; instead it uncovers the more deep-seated disorders in patriarchal and imperial "orders", in which Babamukuru participates as the headmaster of the mission school and academic director of the Church's Manicaland Region.

Everyone living in the house – which straddles Shona and English cultures – exhibits some form of nervous condition: Nyasha's "exam nerves", Tambu's "ennerved experience of transplanting herself at the mission", her "nerve-wracking" exposure to Nyasha's eating habits, and the "ennervating vagueness" of her life, Chido's "nervous" reaction to Nyasha's smoking, Maiguru's "muttering . . . about her nerves", and Babamukuru's "nerves were bad" (Dangarembga 1988: 108, 91, 151, 117, 113, 102). As symptoms of their cultural hybridity and their struggles against patriarchy, "the condition of the [female] native" is vexed not only because of colonization, but also because of male hegemony. Because these conflicts are inscribed on the body in the form of nervous behavior, embodiment is marked as a critical site of instability as its subjects try to resist sexist and colonizing domination.

The body, as such a vexed site, can be thought of in terms of chaos theory, as a *strange attractor* within the larger systems of patriarchy and imperialism. In chaos theory, a strange attractor is a point of instability within a dynamic system (like the weather systems of thunder-storms, or, to the extreme, tornadoes). This instability *provides information* as it *provokes disorder*, a dynamical process that we could compare to the effects produced by the apple in the garden of Eden (Hawkins 1995: 20). While the apple brings knowledge and experience (usually associated with order), it also incites chaos when God banishes Adam and Eve from paradise. We need only look as far as Dangarembga's and Mukherjee's novels to find examples of strange attractors represented in non-Western literature. Like the apple in the earlier example, women's bodies in *Nervous Conditions* and *Jasmine* unleash chaos in male and European paradigms of order. Lucia, in *Nervous Conditions*, is characterized as a "thunderstorm" that Jeremiah wishes to "make . . . crackle and thunder and lightning at [his] command" (Dangarembga 1988: 127). And Jasmine is likened to a tornado, "a rubble-maker" who provokes "confusion and destruction" wherever she goes, but this disorder also provides information about the relationship between the marginalized "exotic" and the hegemonically "normal" (Mukherjee 1989: 214, 190). In both cases, women represented as weather systems (potentially chaotic structures) embody the violent potential to disrupt and challenge patriarchal and (post)colonial boundaries of order.

The term "attractor" refers to the system's behavior after it is in motion. After moving a glass of water, for instance, the water will slosh around and eventually return to its still state because the attractor of a moving water system is a fixed point. An attractor becomes "strange" when it takes on a seemingly random and unpredictable path, and this path charted in space is the strange attractor. As an example, think of the way smoke might lift off a cigarette on a breezy day, swirl through the air haphazardly, and then disappear. Taking the cigarette smoke as our dynamic system, we could map its movements to present it as a strange attractor.[7] Smoke appears to waft about in unpredictable, erratic ways, but we may find a deeply encoded structure of order within the movement of its particles.

By mapping out strange attractors, one finds that some forms of chaos (called deterministic chaos) are not truly random because a chaotic system can "generate patterns of extreme complexity, in which areas of symmetry are intermixed with areas of asymmetry down through scales of magnification" (Hayles 1990: 10). Strange attractors reveal that deterministic chaos possesses a deep structure of order, a phenomenon which Hayles calls "orderly disorder". We may detect, for instance, complicated patterns in the seemingly random cigarette smoke, and, thus, it would be a "deterministic" form of "orderly disorder" rather than pure randomness. *Jasmine*'s narrator makes a similar detection of order within chaos in the novel's opening scene, when she discovers a star-shaped pattern in the scar on her forehead. When she comes to think of the scar as her "third eye", thus making herself over into sage, the scar/eye stands in as a site/sight of orderly disorder, the strange attractor (Mukherjee 1989: 2). The scar may disorder the skin's surface, but it is also patterned into an orderly shape that, like the strange attractor, enables a new way of seeing (as Jyoti's third eye), as the discovery of strange attractors changed the way scientists see chaos.

While Dangarembga foregrounds the dirty disorder of corporeality in the opening of *Nervous Conditions*, Mukherjee emphasizes the body's "scabrous", "scarred", "rotten", and "broken" nature in the first chapter of *Jasmine*. The adjectives applied to Jyoti's body, her "scabrous" arms and "scarred" forehead, and the "rotten", "broken" body of a dog carcass she brushes against in the river, allude to the "new geometry" Gleick describes in the novel's epigraph. The chaos of the body's new geometry is inscribed on its surfaces through scars, scabs, and rough skin, but, ultimately, flesh is insignificant according to Hindu religion because the body is a mere shell lent to the individual by "the Lord" (1989: 51). In *Jasmine*, Mary Webb leaves her body and crosses boundaries of gender, race, and nation, but the narrator crosses these same boundaries by staying in her body and leaving behind her identity.

Throughout Jasmine's meteoric transformations in identity, there is no simultaneity or continuity between her various conceptions of self and embodiment. The narrator illustrates the chaos of these often violent metamorphoses when she distinguishes one persona from another:

> Jyoti of Hanaspur was not Jasmine, Duff's day mummy and Taylor and Wylie's au pair in Manhattan; that Jasmine isn't this Jane Ripplemeyer having lunch with Mary Webb at the University Club today. And which of us is the undetected murder of a half-faced monster, which of us had held a dying husband, which of us was raped and raped in boats and cars and motel rooms? (Mukherjee 1989: 114)

> Jyoti was not a sati-goddess; she had burned herself in a trash-can-funeral pyre behind a boarded-up motel in Florida. Jasmine lived for the future, for Vijh & Wife. Jase went to movies and lived for today. (Mukherjee 1989: 156)

In the narrator's cataloguing of her multiple selves, there is no connection between the identities; rather each subject is *murdered* by its successor: "We murder who we are so we can birth ourselves in the images of dreams" (Mukherjee 1989: 25). The ambiguity of *whose* dreams Jasmine's identity is modeled to fit and the difficulty of locating *agency* in her transformations mark subjectivity and embodiment as disorderly sites.[8] But as we will see later, these chaotic systems (corporeality and identity) are not without a deep structure of order, and, thus, they resemble the strange attractor's intermixing of order and disorder.

This chaotic "violence of identity", as Kristin Carter-Sanborn calls it, is enacted on and mediated through the body because the narrator's prior sense of *embodiment* is "murdered" with the birth of each new *identity* (1994: 573). From Jyoti to Jasmine, Kali, Jazzy, Jase, and Jane, the new geometry of subjectivity is inscribed on the body's surface, giving each subject a different embodied style, for example, Kali's monstrousness, Jazzy's jazziness, Jase's vampishness, and Jane's glamour. When Jyoti's husband Prakash re-names her "Jasmine" (the narrator's first identity transformation), he does so to make her into a "new kind of city woman" (Mukherjee 1989: 70). Jasmine, according to Prakash, will leave behind Jyoti's "feudal compliance", which "kept India an unhealthy and backward nation. It was up to women to resist [getting pregnant] because men were generally too greedy and too stupid to recognize their own best interests" (Mukherjee 1989: 70). The protagonist's new name may seem to mark her liberation from forced reproduction, but it also reveals that Prakash places the burden of an "unhealthy" and "backward" India on female sexuality and reproduction, much like Nhamo's perception of female reproductive embodiment as "unhealthy". Again we see women's corporeality as dangerous disorders jeopardizing the health of the nation: men are too aroused ("too greedy and too stupid") by women's sexuality, and they shouldn't be expected to curb their desires or use contraceptives. Therefore, "it was up to women" to keep their sexuality and reproductive systems in check in order to save the nation from disease and backwardness. Linking the state of the nation with the state of female embodiment, Prakash reveals the interconnections between the local, women's bodies, and the global, multinational power structures: female corporeality is positioned as a local manifestation of "disorder" that threatens the "orderly" national system. But women's embodiment is also a manifestation of the disorder inherent in a national system that uses sexism as an organizing principle.

The Facts of Blackness and Embodied Resistance to Order

Thinking of bodies in relation to disorder and characterizing them as "chaotic" does not imply they are lacking in some way, since one of the major accomplishments of chaos theory was the revisioning of disorder from an absence lacking order to a positive presence of information. In this transvaluation of chaos, a crucial move was to separate information from meaning: chaotic systems are "rich in information", rather than "poor in order" (Hayles 1990: 6). Having made this distinction, scientists now conceive of chaos as sending messages (information) independent of whether they actually hold any meaning for the receiver. As an example of this definition of chaos, imagine that someone calls you on the telephone and begins speaking, but you cannot understand a word they are saying. Or if you have access to the internet, imagine that someone sends you an e-mail message, but you receive garbled computer language in place of the words you are accustomed to reading. In both instances, you receive information, but, because you cannot understand it, the interaction *provokes disorder as it provides information.*

In "The Fact of Blackness", Frantz Fanon's discussion of the "certain uncertainty" sometimes produced by embodiment illustrates this point in terms that are useful to our discussion: the experience of embodiment often inspires disorder while yielding information, especially when the experience includes interactions with different races, ethnicities, and/or cultures. If we think of embodiment as the sending and receiving of information through one's body – like the exchange of information via telephone or computer as described above – we can look more closely at the disorder occasionally produced by interactions between people of varying race, ethnicity and culture. Senders and receivers in these situations may be incapable of understanding each other's messages due to cultural, linguistic, or racial differences. But if we position these differences within the paradigm of chaos theory, we see that they mark the presence of information (for example, that person speaks a different language than I do) separated from meaning (I do not understand that person's language). It is crucial to note, however, that such an experience of embodiment is not devoid of all meaning because it is usually heavily loaded with political and economic signification, as Fanon describes:

> And then the occasion arose when I had to meet the white man's eyes. An unfamiliar weight burdened me. The real world challenged my claims. In the white world the man of color encounters difficulties in the development of his bodily schema. Consciousness of the body is a solely negating activity. It is a third-person consciousness. The body is surrounded by an atmosphere of *certain uncertainty*. (Fanon 1967: 110, my italics)

This "certain uncertainty" is a manifestation of the orderly disorder of embodiment when one's body is "challenged" and "burdened" by the "unfamiliar weight" of the "white man's eyes". As a visible sign of difference, the colonial subject's body, namely its racial "differences", is the most direct and immediate way in which s/he can be constructed as subaltern. In recounting his experience of bodily self-consciousness under the white gaze, Fanon reconfigures his disrupted embodiment as the presence of information, though its meaning is "uncertain". His claim that "Consciousness of the body is a solely negating activity" is not necessarily valid from the perspective of chaos theory if we think of this "negating activity" as not only negating order, but also positing information: that a racial challenge is posed to Fanon's "bodily schema".

Dangarembga represents similar threats to the bodily schema in *Nervous Conditions*, when, for example, Tambu calls Nyasha's Westernized preference for slimness and angles, rather than voluptuousness and curves, "things that did not make sense" (1988: 92). While Tambu is conscious of her body – she often scrutinizes herself in the mirror to confirm her beauty – she cannot make meaning out of her cousin's desire to be thin because the Shona ideal of beauty is more rounded than the European valuation of slenderness. Nyasha's fanatic preference for slimness, then, represents the presence of information divorced from meaning. For Nyasha as well, the chaos of anorexia nervosa is entangled with an over-saturated presence of *information*, historical "facts" she consumes as study for exams designed by a British education system.[9] This information provokes disorder (an eating disorder) through Nyasha's act of self-induced vomiting, "I did it myself. With my toothbrush. *Don't ask me why. I don't know*" (1988: 190, my italics).

A similar "certain uncertainty" occurs when Tambu first encounters the white missionaries at her new school, describing them as holy, special, and self-sacrificing because they have given up the comforts of their more advanced homes to "lighten our darkness" in "darkest Africa" (Dangarembga 1988: 103). Invoking Joseph Conrad's and generations of rhetoric about Africa as "the heart of darkness", Dangarembga constructs the mission and its "deified" whites as perpetuating colonial ideology and effectively brainwashing students like Tambu who come to believe that Europeans "were in fact more beautiful". Young Tambu erases her own fact of blackness as she privileges the position of white missionaries as superior, more beautiful, and deified. Until she learns to "love the Whites", Tambu feels "guilty and unnatural" (Dangarembga 1988: 104). Her sense of guilt and unnaturalness is symptomatic of the chaos of colonial embodiment: the struggle for self-presence in the face of a culture that attempts to "tame", "cure", "lighten", and ultimately erase the indigenous African.

Tambu's struggle is complicated by the difficulty she has in trying to make meaning out of the messages she receives from the missionaries, especially when Europeans speak in Shona:

> Because there were so many Whites on the mission I had a lot to do with them, but their behavior remained difficult to understand. What I noticed, early on, was that some of the missionaries were definitely *strange, strange* in the way that Nyasha and Chido were strange when they came back from England. These missionaries, the *strange* ones, liked to speak Shona much more than they liked to speak English. And when you, wanting to practice your English, spoke to them in English, they always answered in Shona. It was disappointing, and confusing too for people like me who were bilingual, since we had developed a kind of reflex which made us speak English when we spoke to white skins and reserved our own language for talking to each other. (1988: 104, my italics)

In response to the paradox of "white skins" speaking in black tongues, Tambu's repetition of "strange" highlights this contradiction between race and language and its "difficult", "disappointing", and "confusing" implications. The Shona-speaking Europeans appear to the African as the embodiment of chaos, of behavior that is difficult to understand because it is information dislocated from meaning. As reverse-images of Nyasha and Chido, the strange missionaries' duality (white skin/black language) is entropic for Tambu, but not necessarily so for the deified whites who occupy positions of power.

When the "white skins" speak Shona, they participate in a colonizing discourse, "Orientalism", which Edward Said describes as "a certain *will* or *intention* to understand, in some cases to control, manipulate, even to incorporate, what is a manifestly different (or alternative and

103

novel) world; it [Orientalism] is, above all, a discourse that is . . . produced and exists in an uneven exchange with various kinds of power" (1995: 90).

It is precisely the will and intention of the missionaries that makes them "strange"; for Tambu can't understand *why* they speak Shona. By describing the missionaries as strange and confusing, Tambu may recognize the uneven exchange of power occurring in the discourse between them, but she bends to it rather than resists it. However, young Tambu's seemingly naive complicity in colonization cannot mask the adult Tambu's rebellion against it, when the older narrator enters and disrupts the narrative to remind readers: "you must remember that I was very young then, very young and correct in my desire to admire and defer to all the superior people I found at the mission" (Dangarembga 1988: 103). Since Tambu "refuse[s] to be brainwashed" at the end of the novel, the sarcastic irony of her "correct" desire to defer to "superior" missionaries reveals the insidious colonizing subtext by concealing it (Dangarembga 1988: 204, 103).

The racial-linguistic contradiction illustrated by the strange missionaries is embodied, in *Jasmine*, in the character of Mary Webb. In Mary's out-of-body experiences, the white American woman becomes a black male Australian Aborigine, and through her "visceral revelations", Mary problematizes the conception of the body as a sign of difference (Mukherjee 1989: 110). After she/he experiences corporeality as both a white American woman and a black Australian man, Mary begins speaking an Aboriginal tribal language and has nostalgia for kangaroo flesh. Jane claims that "Her face *is* transformed as she tells me. Her voice drops, there is a slight Australian diction to her description" (Mukherjee 1989: 112). Like the strange missionaries in *Nervous Conditions*, Mary Webb disrupts the notion that one's body stands metonymically for visible signs of difference as her white female body adopts the voice, diction, and cravings of a black male Aborigine. This paradox presents Jane with an "incongruity" that she tries desperately to process, just as Tambu is confused by the missionaries' behavior. Once again, we see that embodiment is the site of chaos, perhaps even more so for Jane who *receives* the corporeal messages than for Mary who *sends* them. Jane must try to decipher Mary's/the Aborigine's incongruous messages, but this information, as chaos, is independent of meaning.

Mary's description of the body as a "revolving door" illuminates the strange attractor quality of corporeality, functioning as it does according to the principles of deterministic chaos. Because the door lets one soul in and another out in a sequence, it is orderly, but the very action is chaotic since it disrupts the idea of "original" identity. When Jasmine first sees a revolving door, she wonders, "How could something be always open and at the same time always closed?" (Mukherjee 1989: 119). The ability of the entrance to be always open suggests the distribution of information, but this data is closed in so far as its receivers have difficulty comprehending or believing it: when Mary speaks the language of the Australian Aborigine, no one understands her.

Jyoti herself is such a revolving door, having been "reborn several times" and shuttling between identities within the same life, and like Mary Webb, the narrator presents incongruous messages to those she encounters in America as she repeatedly forges new identities and body images. When Jasmine violently transforms into Kali, for example, the body becomes a vehicle of power, as well as a vision of monstrosity, both of which are symptoms of patriarchal and racial domination.[10] Rescued by Lilly Gordon, Kali is renamed Jazzy, a variation of Jasmine which captures her new, jazzy American style and marks the beginning of her assimilation into American culture. Jazzy's body is one that walks and dresses American: She "lost her shy sidle" and looked "Jazzy in a t-shirt, tight cords, and running shoes" (Mukherjee 1989: 118, 119). Jase, the day mummy for Taylor and Wylie, is more exotic than Jazzy as she lives "for today" and buys lingerie and "blouses with vampish necklines" (Mukherjee 1989: 156). She describes how Taylor "didn't want to scour and sanitize the foreignness", but rather he exoticizes it when he admits that he began to fall in love with Jase the moment she "came in afraid to talk, not knowing much English" (Mukherjee 1989: 166).

Jase's exotic foreignness crystallizes into "mystery" and "inscrutability" – the Orientalizing epitome of Eastern otherness – which Bud attempts to contain and normalize by renaming her Jane: "You *were* glamour, something unattainable" (Mukherjee 1989: 177, my italics). The protagonist *was* glamorous and unattainable, but now Bud has attained her as Jane (albeit not with too tight a leash as she's also "Calamity Jane") (Mukherjee 1989: 22). Early in the novel, Jane states that her "genuine foreignness frightens" Bud, and thus his calling her Jane is both a patriarchal and imperial move to incorporate and tame her exotic, calamitous nature: "Me Bud, you Jane. I didn't get it at first. He kids. Calamity Jane. Jane as in Jane Russell, not as in Plain Jane. But Plain Jane is all I want to be. Plain Jane is a role, like any other" (Mukherjee 1989: 22). Jane wants to be Plain Jane, "a role like any other", because she does not occupy a role, or at least not one that can be easily categorized. Rather, she exists on the edge of chaos, capable of enacting catastrophic violence, but also endowed with the creative power of bringing Bud "back from the dead" (Mukherjee 1989: 178).

Even as Jane, the narrator occupies various positions: as Tarzan's Jane, as Rochester's Jane (in *Jane Eyre*), and as Calamity Jane. Collapsing their relationship with that of Tarzan and Jane, Bud's renaming both tames Jane and makes Bud a wild and powerful Tarzan, more capable of meeting the challenge of Jane's sexuality than his wheelchair allows. On the other hand, Mukherjee's allusion to *Jane Eyre* returns Bud to a handicapped position as he becomes the crippled Rochester and Jane becomes Jane Eyre, as the narrator ponders, "I think maybe I am Jane with my very own Rochester" (Mukherjee 1989: 210). As Calamity Jane, she is described by Karin as a tornado, a metaphor that captures the cataclysmic disorder Jane's exotic embodiment poses to the whiteness of Baden, Iowa. The very foreignness that can cause tornado-like destruction, however, can also order such catastrophe by its ability to rejuvenate Bud, thus positioning Jane within the realm of deterministic chaos on the frontiers of order and disorder.

What is especially disconcerting about Taylor's and Bud's exoticizing of Jase and Jane is the narrator's acquiescence to their othering discourse. The act of naming functions as colonizing rhetoric that seeks to control the Eastern native other, and by accepting their constructions of her, the narrator perpetuates the Orientalizing discourse: "I am darkness, mystery, inscrutability" (Mukherjee 1989: 178). By proclaiming that she is alien and inscrutable, Jane locates herself at the site of the subaltern, abdicating her agency by allowing men to rename and re-invent her.

Although *Jasmine*'s protagonist does not resist discourses that subordinate her (in the above instances), other forms of resistance to systematized oppression are found in both novels. Each protagonist's resistance is embodied as a *physical* "system failure" – like an eating disorder or temporary paralysis – through which she protests against *ideological* "system failures": the disorderly oppression of patriarchal and colonial institutions. In *Nervous Conditions*, for example, both Tambu and Nyasha articulate, through their bodies, the resistance that they don't have permission to speak with their tongues; as Sally McWilliams explains:

> [Nyasha] and Tambu individually *embody* the *disruptive forces* that both natives and women come to have from within the constraints of their social worlds. These young women may not have permission to speak against the man in charge of their upbringing [Babamukuru], but their bodies *"talk"* in that they are physical disturbances to the status quo of that society's cultural codes. (1991: 110, my italics)

As embodied "physical disturbances", the two cousins use their corporeality to threaten the order of the status quo, and, thus, we can think of them as chaotic systems that disrupt the organization of power relations in patriarchy and imperialism.[11] In examining the young women's system failures, however, we find a deep structure of order patterning their apparently chaotic behavior, and, in this sense, women's embodiment is once again positioned as a strange attractor that exhibits both orderly and disorderly behavior.

Tambu disorders the power structure that subordinates her to her uncle Babamukuru, the Shona patriarch, through a bodily resistance to his orders. When Baba plans Tambu's parent's wedding, the "plot which made such a joke" of her parents, home, and self, her "body reacted in a very alarming way" (Dangarembga 1988: 149). She describes how her skin crawled, her chest contracted, and her bowels threatened movement whenever she thought about the wedding (Dangarembga 1988: 149). What is so "alarming" about Tambu's reaction is the instability of embodiment, when bodily boundaries challenge their orderly limits by crawling (skin), contracting (chest), and threatening movement (bowels). Tambu is caught between, on the one hand, her uncle's authority as Shona patriarch and as figurehead of the black colonial elite, and, on the other hand, her own sense of dignity and respect for her home and family. As her body becomes the voice of this conflict, Tambu orchestrates a self-induced breakdown on the morning of the wedding, during which her body remains paralyzed in bed, while her spirit hovers "somewhere near the foot of the bed, watching [Nyasha's] efforts" to coax her out of bed (Dangarembga 1988: 166). Tambu's "act of internal distancing" effects a failure of physical functions: her muscles refuse to obey, her heart races, and her voice is high and thin (McWilliams 1991: 109). But, like in strange attractors, there is an order in this disorderly bodily malfunction: "I knew I could not get out of bed because *I did not want to . . . I had gone somewhere where he could not reach me*, and I congratulated myself for being so clever" (Dangarembga 1988: 166, my italics). Because Tambu does "not want to" participate in the wedding that marks her family as inferior to her uncle's family, she chooses not to get out of bed. Instead, she produces an "extraordinary drama", rupturing the Shona and imperial systems because she does not bend to the rule of Baba, who demands her presence at the wedding (Dangarembga 1988: 166). Tambu's paralysis – a bodily disorder that disorders the mission house and thwarts her uncle's orders – produces for her a sense of order, in that she can take control of her actions rather than submit to Baba's will.

Like Tambu, Nyasha is also a physical disturbance to the status quo. She is painfully cognizant of the political and patriarchal histories constricting her life through her experience with her patriarchal father, her stay in England, and her education – especially her avid consumption of historical texts. And like Tambu's resistance through paralysis, Nyasha's refusal to eat is an act of agency and self-control: "I did it

107

myself. With my toothbrush" (Dangarembga 1988: 190). Her purging, though clearly an eating *disorder*, is also an effort to *order* her body, to "do it herself", rather than be manipulated by the colonial mission. Because food functions as a sign of maternal, paternal, and cultural affiliation in the novel, Nyasha's refusal to eat is, symbolically, an attempt to reject certain affiliations, namely her father's patriarchal domination and the British colonizing ideology being force-fed to her as a student at the missionary school. She protests her father's author- itarian hold by purging the dinner he demands her to eat: "he ought to look at things from my point of view and be considerate and patient with me, so I start fighting back", she tells Tambu after she vomits (Dangarembga 1988: 190). Nyasha "fights back" against Shona patri- archy by rejecting the father's food, an act which aims to expurgate the colonizer's "food" as well. When she does not eat the Western food her mother prepares, Nyasha resists the European ideology she is forced to consume at school, and Mainini corroborates the significance of her actions, saying, "you couldn't expect the ancestors to *stomach* so much Englishness" (Dangarembga 1988: 203, my italics). By not stomaching English food, Nyasha tries to purge herself of the English education, "Their history . . . Their bloody lies", that she crams while studying for examinations (Dangarembga 1988: 201). She "binges" on Englishness while studying and then "purges" European culture by vomiting, and, in this figural sense, her eating disorder is symbolically more bulimic than anorexic.

Whether it is bulimia or anorexia, Nyasha's eating disorder is both orderly and disorderly, propelled by a desire for control that degener- ates to disorder when she can't "stomach" the flux of cultural, political, and racial information she consumes (1988: 203). Ironically, the disorder's resulting weight loss parodies a Western ideal of beauty that is part of the colonizing ideology Nyasha wants to purge: "her anorexic body is a parody of a Western ideal of slim, feminine, sexual desir- ability" (Thomas 1992: 31). As such a parody, her emaciated physique is a sign of the burden of femininity (virtually unachievable Western ideals of beauty), and, at the same time, it represents an attempt to lose the "weight of womanhood" imposed on her by European imperial and Shona patriarchal systems (Dangarembga 1988: 16). As both parodic compliance with and an embodied rebellion against Western culture, her eating disorder is a symptom of her dis-ease and her protest against the structures causing these conditions – finally culminating in her tortured revelation: "I'm not one of them but I'm not one of you" (Dangarembga 1988: 201). This negation of both her Shona and European associations seals her hybridity, but more importantly, it locates her identity and corporeality in a chaotic space which separates information (knowing where one does *not* fit) from meaning (not knowing where she *does* fit in).

Nyasha's body, as a strange attractor, enacts disorder as it attempts to order the chaos of domination inscribed upon it, and both her eating *disorder* and struggle for *order* are tangled up in the processes of *consumption* and *production* (culturally, politically, and nutritionally). Her consumption and production cycles manifest what chaologists call a *feedback mechanism*, a process in which the output of a system feeds back into the system as input. Consider, for example, James Gleick's use of the human population and sound from a loudspeaker to illustrate the process of feedback:

> [F]ollowing a population through time is a matter of taking a starting figure and applying the same function again and again . . . The whole history of the population becomes available through this process of functional iteration – a feedback loop, each year's output serving as the next year's input. Feedback can get out of hand, as it does when sound from a loudspeaker feeds back through a microphone and is rapidly amplified to an unbearable shriek. (1987: 61)

If we think of Nyasha's input and output as such a feedback loop, we see the complex interactions between culture, politics, and gender playing on and through her body. This feedback does "get out of hand" by the end of the novel and is "amplified to an unbearable shriek", symbolically taking the form of Nyasha's bodily failure due to anorexia.

As a self-proclaimed "hybrid" poised precariously between the Shona and the European, Nyasha consumes the products of both Shona and Western culture: she speaks both languages, wears clothing from both traditions, smokes Western cigarettes, reads examples of British colonizing rhetoric, and studies her father as an "historical artefact", all the while living in a country colonized by England and under the rule of a father who is part of the black colonial elite. As a result of this conflicted consumption, her production is also a site of contestation, a heteroglot of Shona and Western signs, along with signs of anti-colonial and anti-patriarchal struggle. She is, as her father Baba perceives her, "an obstinate budget which ought to balance but wouldn't" (Dangarembga 1988: 112). Nyasha's body is like a budget in so far as it is the receptacle for incoming and outgoing cultural "funds", and a complex set of biological systems that usually function according to orderly, "budgeted" rhythms. The budget doesn't balance physically because her anorexia causes several bodily functions to fail (like periodic menstruation), nor does it balance intellectually because the hybridized messages she sends are often misunderstood. For example, other girls at the mission think she is "proud", "loose", and acts like she's "white"; and even her own father "did not recognise her" when Nyasha dresses up (in Western clothes) to go to a school dance (Dangarembga 1988: 109). Her hybridity disrupts the status quo of the Shona "budget", and therefore, according to Baba's "math", Nyasha's budget won't balance.

Hayles's explanation of how an orderly feedback mechanism can produce disorder highlights this point:

> The irony is that the more the liberating play of the intellect works on its material, the more power relations are exposed, and consequently the more helpless the subject is made to feel. One could imagine a feedback loop in which the critic writes in order to feel empowered; but the result of her writing is to identify her as a deconstructed subject whose "self" is only the inscription of anonymous forces. Realizing this, she returns to her writing, for now she needs more desperately than ever the feeling of empowerment that comes from writing. But her writing only tells the same story in other ways, and the only relief is to write some more . . . (1990: 287)

Positioning Nyasha as the "critic" who, instead of "writing", starves herself in order to feel empowered, we see that her efforts toward empowerment also uncover the power relations subordinating her. The more she refuses to eat, the more helpless and nervous she becomes. Therefore, input and output loop into one another in an orderly process, but produce entropic results: an eating disorder and other nervous conditions.

Like Nyasha's refusal to eat and Tambu's refusal to get out of bed, *Jasmine*'s protagonist refuses her identity to forge new ones throughout the novel. Most of the times "Jasmine" takes on a new identity, she does so to suit the desires of men and assimilate into American culture; thus, to some degree, she participates in sexist and colonialist ideology. Her transformation into Kali, however, is the one time Jasmine's identity springs from within and is not given to her from beyond. Kali is the reflection of the narrator, since Jasmine sees Kali's "dark shadow" and "murkiness" in the bathroom mirror at the Flamingo Motel, thus enabling her to re-vision herself as Kali and mark this new subjectivity by slashing her tongue, instead of her throat. This rite of initiation challenges bodily limits by slashing them and collapses the protagonist's humanity as she becomes "monstrous" (Mukherjee 1989: 106). Monstrous Kali is the personification of chaos, but also of creation as the narrator's adoption of this identity incites the protagonist toward self-preservation and self-organization. In this sense, the murder is a productive act (in addition to its obvious destruction), since it effectively removes the narrator from an abusive situation, frees her from old ways of thinking, that she must "balance [her] defilement with death", for example, and forces her on the journey to New York (Mukherjee 1989: 105). The murder scene is entropic in more than its violence, though, because it reverses Kali's and Half-Face's roles as hero and monster, as the rape victim becomes the monster, who "stabbing wildly", commits a "monstrous" act, and, in saving her own life, becomes "walking death. Death incarnate" (Mukherjee 1989: 106). As death incarnate, Kali epitomizes the paradox of chaos; she is death brought to life, human turned monster, whereas the former monster Half-Face becomes a "human form" after Kali stabs him to death.

Prior to the moment she slashes her tongue and becomes Kali, Jasmine almost commits suicide to cleanse herself of her body's "defilement" after she is repeatedly raped by Half-Face. This system failure, when the body self-destructs, marks the system failure of patriarchal Hinduism: that a woman is only as valuable as her body, and, therefore, if her body is defiled, she is better off dead than a live threat to the patriarchal system. The raped woman's challenge to patriarchy materializes when the narrator opts to kill her rapist instead of herself. Evading the law of the father that condemns her to death, the protagonist saves herself. As an act of self-preservation, the murder does constitute a "system failure" of the sort Tambu and Nyasha experience, in which the narrator's embodied disorder threatens the order of the status quo and reveals its inherent disorders, in this case, rape.

Conclusion: Local and Global "Geometries"

> The image never resolves itself to either order or chaos, continuing to show infinitely fine-grained complexity for as long as the magnification proceeds. Is not this an apt image for the interplay between the local and the global?[12]
>
> N. Katherine Hayles, Chaos Bound

Examining (post)colonial embodiment as chaos should make clear that chaos matters as a physical materiality and theoretical issue: *"Issues become energized in theories because they are replicated from and reproduced in the social"* (Hayles 1990: 285). Issues concerning female corporeality have been energized in both feminist and postcolonial theories because they are replicated from and reproduced in a social matrix that is structured by globally-reaching strategies of domination. With the creation of a global economy, interactions between institutions of domination and local embodiment become all the more important. This significance is made visible in representations of "Third World" women and "natives" to a global audience, as they sometimes tread dangerously close to neocolonialism or cultural imperialism, of which several scholars have criticized Mukherjee's portrayal of the exoticized and eventually Americanized Jasmine.[13]

Chaos theory's concern with the local and global – how localized orderly systems can be found within globally disordered systems, and conversely, how globally ordered systems can spawn offshoots of localized chaos – provides a useful methodology for considering the relationships between local bodies and global power relations. The *representation* of localized embodiment to a global audience is an important facet of these interactions, as Kwame Appiah's summary of postcolonial representation reveals:

> Postcoloniality is the condition of what we might ungenerously call a *comprador* intelligentsia: a relatively small, Western-style, Western-trained group of writers and thinkers, who mediate the trade in cultural commodities of world capitalism at the periphery. In the West, they are known through the Africa [or India] they offer; their compatriots know them both through the West they present to Africa and through an Africa they have invented for the world, for each other, and for Africa. (1991: 348)

What Appiah describes as the "mediation" of representation is also a feedback loop circulating among local and global sites: the postcolonial intelligentsia, their compatriots and audience, the Africa they have invented for the world (via artistic production, for example), Africa (the nation, its people, and their cultures), and world capitalism. Each element of the mechanism is a vexed and complicated system – politically, culturally, and physically – particularly the producers and consumers whose work is inflected by myriad factors (like race, ethnicity, gender, class, etc.), thus yielding a mechanism, which, though ordered, is open to disorder at every turn.

As Jasmine, Tambu, and Nyasha have demonstrated, this entropy is articulated through the body, which is both shaped by and rebels against global structures of domination. The "new geometry" of (post)colonial women's corporeality, then, is intermixed with the new geometry of global power relations produced by (post)colonialism. In both novels, the co-mingling of the local and global is seen through the intersection of corporeal, national, and ideological boundaries. Such intersections destabilize the binary ideology of order/disorder that under girds "first" and "third" world relations, as well as the interaction between local corporeality and global institutions of oppression. Dangarembga and Mukherjee disrupt the dichotomy between "disordered" third worlds and bodies and "ordered" first worlds and bodies by positioning both local and national bodies within a site that Hayles calls "orderly disorder" (deterministic chaos).

At the beginning of *Jasmine,* for example, India is caricatured as a place of rebellious disorder and backwardness, and the narrator's perception of India as a site of political chaos suggests that her passage to America is not only an escape from chaos, but also an attempt to order the disorderly forces acting upon her body. Jyoti describes how the partition of India rendered Lahore "chaos", and the "whole country was a bloody mess" in which men talked "vengeful, catastrophic politics . . . . Sikh nationalists had gotten out of hand . . . Punjab would explode in months" (Mukherjee 1989: 36, 56). Though in a disorderly state of political rebellion, India is ordered, to some degree at least, by Hinduism, and the chaotic turn of events Jyoti encounters in Punjab and during her passage to America are also patterned by order: "all acts are connected" (Mukherjee 1989: 102).

Like this orderly disorder that structures India, America is also situated at the borders of order and disorder: "The first thing I saw were the two cones of a nuclear plant, and smoke spreading from them in complicated but seemingly purposeful patterns, edges lit by the rising sun, like a gray, intricate map of an unexplored island continent" (Mukherjee 1989: 95). Comparing the patterns of smoke to an intricate map of an unexplored America, Mukherjee presents the first world country as foreign and unexplored, but there is an order to it, a map, which will lead Jasmine on her journey. The diction of these initial descriptions of America mimic nineteenth-century colonial rhetoric which constructed Africa as the "unexplored continent". From this perspective, Mukherjee enacts a parodic reverse-imperialism in which Jasmine, the "native", sets out to explore and map America. Jazzy discovers that the country is "humiliating", "disappointing", "perverted", and not unlike the Punjab she left behind. This representation of America could be read as both a parody of the Western construction of the "Third World" and as a critique of America's violence and degradation. As Jase's exploration progresses, she discovers that there is "so much trash in America", that it's rare to see "an 'American' face", and that "New York was an archipelago of ghettos seething with aliens" (Mukherjee 1989: 115, 124). Not only is America dirty and disordered, but the very idea of what an 'American' face looks like is problematized by the influx of immigrants. In short, the country is the epitome of chaos and transformation, described by the narrator as "the fluidity of the American character and the American landscape" (Mukherjee 1989: 123). But just as Punjab's chaos retains vestiges of order, so too does America's fluidity have a "crazy kind of logic". Even the disorderly ugliness of American poverty contains an ordered structure of "beauty", as Stuart argues: "poverty had shape, clarity, its own crystalline beauty" (Mukherjee 1989: 161). While measuring poverty obviously does not erase its debasement, it does reveal orderly patterns in disorderly failures of the socio-economic system, in the same way that, as we saw earlier, the three protagonists' bodily disorders contain deep structures of order.

In *Nervous Conditions*, Dangarembga also disrupts the order/disorder opposition in her portrayal of Tambu's Shona homestead and Nyasha's European mission house. The homestead appears, on the surface, to be far more dirty and chaotic than Babamukuru's modern house at the mission. As the novel progresses, however, we learn that the European mission is disrupted by its inhabitants' hysteria and nervous conditions and that the Shona hierarchy can be "complicated and confusing", as Tambu discovers when she must carry the water-dish at a family gathering (Dangarembga 1988: 40). The same Shona traditions that disorder Baba's Anglicized home order Jeremiah's home, giving meaning to his family's poor existence. Therefore, both Shona and Western structures of order can give way to disorder, revealing Dangarembga's subversion of the imperial construction that European culture and "progress" are orderly, whereas African culture is dirty, primitive, and disorderly.

The two novels illustrate that chaos cannot be entirely subsumed into the familiar, and as Hayles argues, some residue of disorder's liberating function remains:

> By finding within [chaos] structures of order, these scientists have in effect subsumed chaos in the familiar. But if this incorporation were entirely successful, *chaos* could no longer function in its liberating role as representation of *the other*. Perhaps this is why Mandelbrot goes out of his way to argue against the complete rationalization of chaos; he believes that some residue of the untamable and nonrational should always remain. (Hayles 1990: 173, my italics)

If we conceptualize the conflicted nature of local embodiment and its interplay with global power relations as chaotic, rather than othered, we can recuperate this experience from global fetishization, familiarization, and annihilation. For like Tambu's refusal to be brainwashed by colonial and patriarchal ideology, entropy resists rationalization and containment by orderly systems. As such a form of resistance, chaos is a liberating tool for women's (post)colonial embodiment, especially in relation to global power structures.

Notes

1 The sentence is borrowed from Sartre's introduction to Frantz Fanon's *The Wretched of the Earth*.
2 There is also something troubling about these epigraphs: Why do

Dangarembga and Mukherjee borrow from white men of philosophy and science when their novels are positioned against the very paradigms of which these men are emblematic? As an answer to this question, I refer to Kwame Appiah's argument in "Is the Post- in Postcolonial the Post- in Postmodernism?":

> *Man With a Bicycle* is produced by someone who does not care that the bicycle is the white man's invention: it is not there to be Other to the Yoruba Self; it is there because someone cared for its solidarity; it is there because it will take us further than our feet will take us; it is there because machines are now as African as novelists. (357)

Like the artist who created *Man with a Bicycle*, Dangarembga and Mukherjee seem not to care that they use the work of white men to advance their projects. Furthermore, chaos and nervous conditions are "now as African" or Indian as the writers are themselves. On this point, Bharati Mukherjee is often criticized for relinquishing her Indian heritage as she proclaims herself an American writer and is now a naturalized American citizen. This issue, while an interesting area of inquiry, is not the subject of my work here.

3 I use "(post)colonial" here to refer to both the colonial context of Southern Rhodesia in *Nervous Conditions* and the postcolonial situation of India in *Jasmine*.

4 Feminist women of color (like Chandra Mohanty) have argued that Western feminists are trapped within a white middle-class brand of feminism which ignores or flattens the specificity of differences. However, even within discussions of difference and otherness, one risks the criticism of what Edward Said has described as, "the fetishizing and relentless celebration of difference and otherness", or as treating a marginalized subject as what Sara Suleri calls an "otherness machine" (Said 1995, 213; Suleri 1989, 105).

5 In the scientific community, chaos theory is referred to as nonlinear dynamics, dynamical systems theory, or dynamical systems methods.

6 *Jasmine*'s protagonist adopts several identities throughout the novel, and each one is marked by a different name or nickname: Jyoti, Jasmine, Kali, Jazzy, Jase, and Jane.

7 Harriet Hawkins describes the strange attractor as follows:

> [A] particle may settle down in a periodic cycle, going back and forth like the pendulum of a clock, and thus its motions can be predicted . . . The phenomenon that signals chaos . . . is conceptually far stranger: while remaining in some bounded region of space, the particle will continue to move wildly and erratically. Thus, although the motion is specified by precise laws, the particle behaves as if it were moving randomly, and there is no way to predict its future path. The regions of space traced out by such motions are called strange attractors and the space they occupy is called "phase space". (126–7)

8 Kristin Carter-Sanborn effectively analyzes the problem of agency in *Jasmine* in her article "'We Murder Who We Were': *Jasmine* and the Violence of Identity", and, therefore, I do not discuss it at length here.
9 Nyasha's eating disorder has been called both anorexia and bulimia by critics, but in this instance, I use "anorexia nervosa" because of its resonance with the title *Nervous Conditions*.
10 Kali often appears as a black, laughing, naked hag-looking woman wearing only a garland of human skulls. She usually has four arms, two of which hold a sword and a human head; the other two arms are believed to remove fear and grant bliss. Kali is capable of devouring all that exists and represents absolute night. She is also creative, however, because she protects her devotees.
11 In *Nervous Conditions*, the mothers of Tambu and Nyasha also experience system failures: Mainini's "chronic lethargy" taking the form of a slowly decaying physical entropy, and Maiguru's rebellion against her husband (and the systems of oppression he represents) appearing as a more abrupt and ephemeral manifestation of bodily disorder.
12 The "image" to which Hayles refers is the Mandelbrot set, shown in figure 1.2.
13 See, for example, Kristin Carter-Sanborn's "'We Murder Who We Were': *Jasmine* and the Violence of Identity".

References

Appiah, Kwame Anthony. 1991: Is the Post- in Postmodernism the Post- in Postcolonial? *Critical Inquiry* 17, 336–57.
Carter-Sanborn, Kristin. 1994: "We Murder Who We Were": *Jasmine* and the Violence of Identity. *American Literature* 66 (3), 573–93.
Comaroff, Jean. 1993: The Diseased Heart of Africa: Medicine, Colonialism, and the Black Body. In Shirley Lindenbaum and Margaret Lock (eds), *Knowledge, Power, Practice: The Anthropology of Medicine and Everyday Life.* Berkeley: University of California Press, 305–29.
Dangarembga, Tsitsi. 1988: *Nervous Conditions.* Seattle: Seal Press.
Fanon, Frantz. 1967: *Black Skin, White Masks.* New York: Grove Press.
——. 1963: *The Wretched of the Earth.* New York: Grove Press.
Gleick, James. 1987: *Chaos: Making a New Science.* New York: Viking Penguin.
Hawkins, Harriet. 1995: *Strange Attractors: Literature, Culture, and Chaos Theory.* New York: Prentice Hall.
Hayles, N. Katherine. 1990: *Chaos Bound: Orderly Disorder in Contemporary Literature and Science.* Ithaca: Cornell University Press.
McWilliams, Sally. 1991: Tsitsi Dangarembga's *Nervous Conditions*: At the Crossroads of Feminism and Post-colonialism. *World Literature Written in English* 31 (1), 103–12.
Mukherjee, Bharati. 1989: *Jasmine.* New York: Ballantine Books.
Said, Edward. 1995: Orientalism. In Bill Ashcroft, Gareth Griffiths, and Helen Tiffin (eds), *The Post-Colonial Studies Reader.* New York: Routledge, 87–91.

——. 1989: Representing the Colonized: Anthropology's Interlocuters. *Critical Inquiry* 15 (2), 205–25.

Suleri, Sara. 1989: *Meatless Days*. Chicago: University of Chicago Press.

Thomas, Sue. 1992: Killing the Hysteric in the Colonized's House: Tsitsi Dangarembga's *Nervous Conditions*. *Journal of Commonwealth Literature* 27 (1), 26–36.

Chapter 6

"See, I've got my tit out": Women's Performance Art and Punk Rock

KATHLEEN IUDICELLO

Performance Art

WOMEN'S EXPLICIT performance art of the 1960s and 1970s introduced the naked, in part or in full, female body as an essential part of the struggle for agency. The exposed (unclothed) female bodies on stage in punk rock in the early to mid-1990s updated this work within a different cultural milieu, asserting, through overtly political or spectacular gestures, various and diverse interpretations of the female body as a social and sexual agent in a male-dominated area of performance. Read as a political gesture, as an assertion of power and gender, as a reconstituted twist on expected feminine behavior, or as a site of resistance through the pleasure of amusement, the action is transgressive. I argue here for the potentially transformative power of nakedness for female performers in two cultural realms. Within this context, I suggest that nakedness is a strategy for female performers to take control of their sexuality, as it were, in defiance of patriarchal norms that have defined female sexuality in terms of a virgin/whore dichotomy.

These performances provide a site through which to view alternative representations of certain women's bodies on stage, not as objects to be viewed but as desiring subjects with sight that cannot be readily contained within archaic and repressive structures. Women's explicit performance art of the 1960s and 1970s evokes the importance and power of the female body in the struggle for subjectivity. In this struggle, the "activity and agency, the mobility and social space, accorded to women" is at stake, as Elizabeth Grosz argues, and "[f]ar from being an inert, passive, noncultural and ahistorical term, the body may be seen as the crucial term, the site of contestation, in a series of economic, political, sexual, and intellectual struggles" (1994: 19).

There is tension within such interference, however. Some of the female performers discussed here are located in heterosexual (straight) and particularly white spaces. In fact, out of respect to the various identities that women embody, I cannot and so do not position all women against patriarchy here, as being equally able to intervene, in the same way, with the same effects, in the male-dominated genres of performance art in the 1960s and 1970s and punk rock in the early to mid-1990s. These genres are also racially marked genres, and many of their radical female participants embody their dominant racial marker – whiteness. Of the punk bands under discussion here, only Tribe 8 features a woman of color. The traditional invisibility of whiteness in punk in the early to mid-1990s is a state similar to that of the feminist movement of the 1960s and 1970s. Straight white privilege damaged and disempowered the feminist movement of this time period to various and significant degrees. Performance art reflected this state of feminism: "In that body's first reincarnation in feminist representation . . . she was universalized as Anglo-American, heterosexual, able-bodied, and middle class" (Harris, in Bennet *et al.* 1993: 260). White performers such as Carolee Schneemann received most of the attention, but even this attention was due largely to what was read as the scandalous use of their bodies.[1] Regardless, no matter how activist any interference in institutional ways of knowing and seeing may be, it is only as effective as it is inclusive. In "Toward a Lesbian Theory of Performance", Hilary Harris writes: "a refunctioned notion of gender, coupled with a race- and class-inflected theory of sexuality, may come closer to dismantling that configuration of (hetero)gendering and (hetero)sexuality that is narrativized in Western political economies as the social contract" (in Bennet *et al.* 1993: 262). This invisibility of whiteness in many discussions of women and performance must be marked as readily as bodies are marked "woman" if traditional patriarchal ways of viewing women's bodies on stage are ever to be permanently disrupted.

What potential cultural exchange can occur in the space between performer and audience? What sort of meanings may be produced/reproduced in that space through the exposed bodies of women on stage in performance art and punk rock? These spaces are sites of resistance where women's bodies on stage may be re-viewed as desiring, aggressive subjects. Within these public spaces, performing women are viewing subjects and not sightless objects to be taken, as Jill

Kathleen Iudicello

Dolan's work points out.[2] Such a theoretical take may be viewed by some critics as banal. However, the bodily presence that evokes this perspective here is significant in its potential to aid in the struggle against the violent patriarchal oppression that women still fight daily in forms of both non-physical and physical violence. Such an approach is necessary in the year 2001 where women are still seen as objects and so raped and beaten by men on a daily basis – crimes all but hidden and so seemingly denied in the mainstream American press. Therefore, I am arguing that in the early to mid-1990s, women in punk rock, similar to performance artists of the 1960s and 1970s, were activists, in a new definition of the term "activist art", in which women see themselves and others see them as subjects and not objects to be taken. This activist art is any performance that interferes with patriarchal, heterosexual, and white institutions of viewing through radical gestures. This intervention occurs, for example, when women aggressively play instruments on stage in a genre dominated by men. While doing so, they create, to varying degrees, feminist subjectivities, empowered images of women in a public space, through moments of charged physical rhetoric.

How were women performance artists changing perceptions of female bodies in the 1960s and 1970s? At this point in America's cultural history, performance art was dominated by male performance artists. In fact, certain female performers were forced out of Fluxus, a group of artists who shared specific concerns that they expressed through their art (O'Dell 1997: 43).[3] Carolee Schneemann, Shigeko Kubota, and Yoko Ono are a few of the female performance artists who were associated with Fluxus. As Kathy O'Dell notes in her article "Fluxus Feminus", a significant number of female artists were removed from this shifting collective because their work posed a threat to dominant forms of patriarchal power by creating a relationship between "body, as the actual physical entity of the artist . . . [and] text, as the words the artist uses or produces" (1997: 45). During this time, in terms of art, the naked female body on stage was considered pornographic or an object of art if painted and then displayed by a male artist. Female sexuality was for straight male appreciation only, regardless of the context.

Such dominant perceptions of women as objects without voices within American society incited women activists to storm male-controlled spaces in protest. As the women's movement started in America in the 1960s, stages and art spaces became places of radical protest against gender inequity. New York Radical Women organized the first major demonstration of the Women's Liberation Movement (WLM) at the 1968 Miss America pageant in Atlantic City, disposing of "feminine products" such as dish towels, girdles, steno pads, and bras in a "Freedom Trash Can". Reflecting upon the media response to this

120

protest, its co-organizer Robin Morgan believes that this protest "was translated by the male-controlled media into the totally invented act of 'bra-burning', a non-event upon which they have fixated constantly ever since, in order to avoid presenting the real reasons for the growing discontent of women" (quoted in Koebel 1998: 53). Mainstream society attempted to create a collective specter of leftist female extremists out of such protesters, hoping to make invisible the reasons for such public demonstrations of activism so that what were considered reasonable roles and behaviors for women could be maintained and patriarchy could rest undisturbed.

The media itself was attacked for supporting gender inequity in America by fetishizing the rape and murder of women. The 1977 performance *In Mourning and In Rage* was a direct response to the sensational media coverage of the Hillside Strangler's series of brutal rape-murders (Roth 1983: 31). Not only were popular spaces such as beauty pageants and mainstream news reports under fire but so were monuments to high culture. The elite display spaces of New York City's Whitney Museum became a target of feminist art circles. Raw eggs and sanitary napkins were used to protest the low percentage of female artists in the Whitney Museum's 1970 Bicentennial Exhibition (Roth 1983: 16).

The subjective use of the female body by female performance artists that emerged from these times is an activist form of art. The process of performance art, which is often never the same twice, like a live punk rock show, gives voice to political demands for equity. It is a configuration of art and politics, which is similar to punk rock music's origin as an anti-establishment form of artistic expression. In the performance art featured here, the creators are the performers and the subjects of their art. Within their performances, these artists demand a re-examination of the sexuality of their bodies and the subjectivities that their bodies represent.

In 1963 Carolee Schneemann performed *Eye Body* for the first time. In an interview with Andrea Juno for the issue of *Re/Search* entitled *Angry Women*, Schneemann discusses the physical construction of this particular work:

> *Eye Body* was a performance in my New York loft which I had transformed into an "environment" – with 4x9 panels, broken mirrors and glass, lights, photographs and motorized umbrellas. Then in a kind of Shamanic ritual I incorporated my own naked body into the constructions – putting paint, grease and chalk on myself. (1991: 68)

Through this performance, Schneemann adapted an object (a naked, female body) that already always exists within a set of meanings (passive female body as object) and placed it in a different context (within broken glass and inanimate objects), bestowing an entirely new contradictory meaning: woman as aggressively, physically, painfully, and dangerously framed. However, she is the subject of her own framing. Therefore, within this performance, Schneemann's body can be viewed in its societal status as material object. It can also simultaneously be seen as a viewing subject who is intentionally, dangerously, and painfully categorizing herself among these objects in recognition of how patriarchal society categorizes her body. In this piece, Schneemann transgresses the boundaries of how a woman's body is supposed to be viewed by re-creating the dangerous elements in which she moves in the world. She is making viewers see this representational reality that she has created and in which she is the subject.

Ana Mendieta also worked with glass and, like Schneemann, as viewing subject and creator of her own performance, blurs the boundaries between object and subject. Her work offers alternate views of her body, distorted images not associated with normal spectatorship, window and lens-framed images that are not beautiful-body-to-be-viewed but violent distortions of such viewing. In "Tracing Mendieta", Michael Duncan presents and discusses these recorded photographed 1972 performances, entitled *Glass on Face Imprints* and *Glass on Body Imprints*, respectively:

> she seemingly lifts a square pane of glass . . . pressing it against her flesh. The six photos of Mendieta's face [depict] . . . her features as variously contorted by the glass . . . The glass seems to smash into Mendieta's face from a variety of angles . . .

> In her *Glass on Body Imprints*, Mendieta presses her buttocks and stomach against a pane of glass as if to emphasize the key sections of female anatomy that define a "good figure". Mendieta perversely flaunts these parts as she flattens them. The glass reduces bodily curves to flesh circles . . . (1999: 110)

This seemingly grotesque performed bodily display is actually transformative, smashing the lens of the camera against a female body so viewers can see how media images contort a woman's body and turn it into a distorted fetish for viewing.

In 1964, Shigeko Kubota performed her *Vagina Painting* at the Perpetual Fluxfest in New York City. This performance consisted of Kubota squatting over white paper and, with a brush extending from her vagina, executing a painting. Kubota, like Schneemann and Mendieta, is the subject and creator of her performance, utilizing her specific body, demanding a re-viewing of what George Bataille (in)famously claimed to be a site of horror in *Story of the Eye*. Bataille wrote: "Now I stood up and, with Simone on her side, I drew her thighs apart, and found myself facing something I imagine I had been waiting for in the same way that a guillotine waits for a neck to slice. I even felt as if my eyes were bulging from my head, erectile with horror" (Bataille [1928] 1967: 84). Unlike Bataille's text, an object of terror is not waiting to be pried open and examined; the vagina in Kubota's performance is the subject of her performance, the sex-specific, unnerving part of her female body with sight. What is transgressive about this piece is the uncloaking of the vagina as something under the body's control, the artist's control, under the control of the woman of whom it is a part. Here, the vagina is real and not monstrous. It is within the subjective control of the female performance artist and the pleasure she actively takes in her sexuality.

Yoko Ono also destabilizes traditional practices of sight in terms of the female body with her performance art piece entitled *Cut Piece*. In "Fluxus Feminus", O'Dell describes the performance, which was presented at Carnegie Recital Hall in New York in 1965:

> Ono knelt, placed a pair of scissors in front of her and invited audience members to come up on stage and cut the clothing from her body. Throughout most of the piece she sat completely still, training an icy stare on the audience, past those who took her up on her offer. (1997: 47)

Here Ono watches the audience, which is forced to view the disrobed woman in a skewed perspective, through the violence of cloth being cut away from her body and under her observation. Within this performance, Ono takes on the voyeuristic position that patriarchal institutions of viewing take for granted.

Though these performances by Schneemann, Mendieta, Kubota, and Ono present moments of subjectivity, it is within these moments that performed bodily display is actually transformative. Addressing the disruptive potential of women's performance art in "Women's Performance Art: Feminism and Postmodernism", Jeanie Forte writes that this mode of performance

> poses an actual woman as a speaking subject, throwing [her position of other in relation to a socially-dominant male subject] into process, into doubt . . . The female body as subject clashes in dissonance with its patriarchal text, challenging the very fabric of representation by refusing that text and posing new, multiple texts grounded in real women's experience and sexuality. (1988: 20–1)

Punk Rock

Punk rock in the 1970s in London did not require polish, skill, or instruments. Bands such as the Sex Pistols and The Clash often borrowed or stole the instruments and recording places they used to get their music out. Punk rock for the Sex Pistols emerged out of an active protest against the glam and polish of the 1970s. That is why punk rockers wore ripped up clothes and came from members of the working or out of work class within Britain's youth culture. Siouxsie Sioux was one woman who took the stage with a microphone at this time. She and her band, The Banshees, opened for and went to shows with the Sex Pistols, using their studio while the band was on tour (Stevenson 1999: 68). Like most performance art, the punk rock shows that the Sex Pistols and the Banshees played were in small, intimate venues. In punk, though, members of the audience danced and often got on stage. In fact, audience participation in a live punk show, especially for women in bands at this time, was often violent. In *Vacant: A Diary of the Punk Years, 1976–1979*, Nils Stevenson writes: "I don't know how Siouxsie copes with playing to these arseholes, screaming to see her tits, grabbing her legs and gobbing at her. I get immense pleasure when she raps one of the wankers with a mike stand or kicks someone on the head who's too amorous . . . " (1999: 107). Siouxsie displays agency within these recorded acts, fighting off members of the audience, but the screaming request to see her breasts shows that though punk rock did not have any standards for its musicians in terms of musical skill or instruments, it was still a male-dominated genre and reflected the patriarchal culture of Britain at the time. In two photographs that Stevenson includes in *Vacant*, Siouxsie wears a shiny rubber bondage outfit, which includes one leg, one arm, fishnet tights, and a bra that exposes both breasts (1999: 43, 45). Her appearance was a performance in itself, as was that of the male punks who wore ripped clothes and safety pins in their jackets, shirts, pants, and flesh. However, Siouxsie Sioux faced a greater risk. Even though she powerfully placed her body in the same public spaces as male punks, such physical exposure for a woman is not only socially unacceptable but dangerous in a typical Western society where many routinely face the threat of violence.

The Slits, an all-women band, and Poly Styrene, of the band X-Ray Spex, also took the stage in the 1970s, placing women in an aggressive site with the power of voice that the microphone brings. In a letter Stevenson copied and included in *Vacant*, Viv Albertine of the Slits refers to that era of Britain's punk rock history as liberating: "We didn't have to pretend to be nice girls. We didn't have to dress, talk, act or write about being nice girls. It was a liberation. And we weren't the freaks, everyone else was" (1999: 96). Within punk rock, nonconformity was the norm, and this included going against women's stereotypical pretty appearances, submissive behaviors, and complimentary conversations. Britain's punk scene came to the US with the Sex Pistols and the Clash. Often wearing a Johnny Rotten pin on stage, Patti Smith became the icon of US women in punk, along with Debbie Harry of Blondie, Maureen Tucker of the Velvet Underground, and Tina Weymouth of the Talking Heads (Stevenson 1999: 99). While only Tucker and Weymouth consistently played instruments on stage, and the music by most of these groups was and is considered more pop than punk, or, in Smith's case, poetry, these were the women that brought the DIY (do it yourself: pick up an instrument or microphone and get on stage) philosophy of punk to the stage at clubs like CBGBs in New York. The courage it took to get up on stage within a male-dominated genre, regardless of the DIY philosophy it spoke to, made them role models for many women in punk in the early to mid-1990s.

The 1980s were an era of rock when women on stage in mainstream public spaces were mostly present as groupies or decorative back-up singers.[4] There was no noticeable movement where women were self-consciously addressing their femininity and gender. Fortunately, there were individual examples, such as Joan Jett and Chrissie Hynde, who were the exception, playing electric guitars on stage and dressing in ways that were often thought to belong only to male rock stars. In the early 1990s, however, Bikini Kill yelled for revolution, girl style now. Tribe 8 shouted out its pro-S/M lesbian desires, and two "loud, abrasive, angry, and obnoxious" bands were pursued by and decided to sign with major labels: Hole went with DGC and L7 went with Slash (Wurtzel 1992: 64).[5] Even though, unlike Bikini Kill and Tribe 8, Hole and L7 signed into the mainstream, these acts still marked a site of resistance to the traditional ways in which women's bodies on stage were consumed as passive objects. Granted, the record industry has, by its capitalist nature, profit and not resistance in mind. Yet, as Rebecca Schneider observes in "After Us the Savage Goddess", resistance lies in revealing the existence of commodification within this oppressive system, defying ways of knowing that are presented as a natural part of the social order: "By showing the show of their commodification and by not completely passing as that which they purport to be, dialectical images . . . can talk or gesture back to the entire social enterprise which secret(e)s them" (Diamond 1996: 158). The key to resisting the image of passive object or commodified subject on stage, then, in combat boots or platform heels, is to talk back, through gesture and word, to the industry selling that image, calling attention to it. Through aggressive, physical rhetoric on stage and discussions of the "girling" of their sound with the press, the bands discussed here can be viewed as revealing the normally hidden presence of patriarchal institutions that Schneider refers to in the quote above as the "social enterprise which secret(e)s them".[6]

In the early to mid-1990s, Hole, L7, Bikini Kill, and Tribe 8 performed interventions in cultural perceptions of women through both radical positionings and postured spectacles. At this time, public displays of anger, aggression, and agency by women were still considered unacceptable in mainstream society, especially through gestures that traditionally belong to desiring subjects (read male) and not objects of desire (read female). What makes such appearances and positionings radical is that they have the potential to change the way audiences view female bodies.

In *She-Bop*, Lucy O'Brien records the practice of aggressive female subjectivity enacted on stage by Courtney Love during a Hole concert: Love "once pulled a breast out on stage [and said]: 'See, I've got my tit out!'" (1995: 163). Love both acknowledges and ridicules any desire to view a sightless and passive object on stage, which the patriarchal gaze of certain audience members may produce. By the mid-1990s, Love, unlike other members of her band, had become infamous for such performances on stage. During the 1995 Lollapalooza tour, Love "referred repeatedly to her yeast infection . . . [and] shoved a doll in her crotch and threw *that* at the audience" (Schoemer 1995: 54). In such a gesture, cultural representations of prettiness expected of femininity, of a female, in the patriarchal mode of viewing, implode. The fissure created is thrown back at the audience on the very doll surface that femininity has traditionally been expected to maintain, particularly in public. In a 1994 interview with Amy Raphael, Love discusses playing with such imagery on stage. Referring to her tour with Nine Inch Nails, Love states: "In Minneapolis, I wore a dress that was so restricting and heels that were five inches high, I could barely stage-dive. Then I got like the best write-ups: for being feminine I guess. I couldn't move well and I was restrained, which equals great review. That's pretty horrid" (1995: 29). Love recognizes the performance on the surface of her body of the passive and bound object that an institution of viewing desires and so praises. Her acknowledgement of this patriarchal way of viewing reveals the damage that such sighting practices cause while they are considered normal by representative voices of mainstream society, as demonstrated here by the reported praise of the media.

Members of L7 have been very vocal about women's bodies on stage and about the media's treatment of those bodies. Like many female performance artists of the 1960s and 1970s, L7, along with Bikini Kill and

Tribe 8, played benefits in support of the equitable treatment of women. At the 1995 Voters for Choice benefit in Washington, D.C., Jennifer Finch spoke to female members of the audience, telling them: "stick your hands down your pants . . . that's yours, and nobody can fucking tell you what to do with it" (Considine 1995: 36). Finch was also, as were many women in all-female or female-dominated bands at that time, frustrated with labels such as "clit-rockers", wanting her band to get the same treatment in the press that other bands, like Nirvana and Cracker, were receiving at the time. In a 1994 *Rolling Stone* article entitled "Ah the Smell of It: L7 Bask in the Sweet Stink of Success", Finch is quoted as saying: "Creating genre out of gender is just horrible to me" (Retna 1994: 26). In an earlier article, band member Donita Sparks speaks from the same perspective, claiming that members of the band are "feminists, but that's not the basis of the band. I think any woman who is in the workplace is lying to herself if she doesn't call herself a feminist" (Joy 1992: 28).

On stage, though, the power belongs to the band and to the non-normative representations of femininity. Discussing the familiar "show us your tits" comment that all-female or female-dominated bands have regularly received from male audience members, members of L7 address the power they have on stage, claiming: "[W]e're the ones with a microphone. To battle us is ridiculous" (Retna 1994: 26). When women on stage are speaking subjects of their own performances, agency may be found in the female-ness that women's bodies as aggressive subjectivities create. In 1992, performing live on the British TV show *The Word*, Donita Sparks dropped her pants and was naked from the waist down. One journalist who had seen the show wrote in an article for *Melody Maker* that " . . . it seemed like an exasperated f*** you gesture. It wasn't the . . . self-worship of Madonna, it wasn't titillating or even disturbing, it was just *there*, an unarguable fact. For me, this kind of sums L7 up . . . for certain wankers – an uncomfortable truth" (Selzer 1992: 26).

That same year at the Reading Festival, Donita Sparks acted with a similarly self-produced subjectivity, through which she charged the space between audience and stage by playing with social constructions of gender and sexuality. Ben Thompson noted the performance for *New Statesman and Society*:

Los Angeles punk-metal quartet L7 took the stage to a mixed reception. A large part of the hostility, and the consequent hail of mud, directed at the band seemed to be based on resentment of the fact that all four of them are women. They replied with a ferocious and impressive performance, but when this didn't put paid to the mud-throwing, a more drastic response was called for. Lead singer Donita Sparks retired to the back of the stage and returned, after a bit of discreet rummaging, swinging a small

but politically charged item over her head. She then released it into the
fractious section of the crowd, to the cheers of the band's supporters, with
a vengeful cry of "eat my used tampon". (1992: 33)

Other than point out Sparks' "drastic response", Thompson fails to
question the anger that a large part of the crowd expressed at women
on stage in the traditionally and predominantly male space of the rock
and roll band. Sparks' act of throwing a tampon, a traditionally hidden
gender signifier, into the face of her audience creates a site for re-
viewing, for an alternate sighting of a woman's body on stage. Such a
gesture illustrates her refusal to be disapproved of for taking the stage
in a manner traditionally associated with male performers in music
culture, playing loud, hard, and moving aggressively with agency on
stage. Instead, Sparks, like Kathleen Hanna of Bikini Kill, demands that
her audience confront her through her body and on her terms.

Hanna was fundamental in creating the Riot Grrrl movement of the
early 1990s, encouraging young women to start their own bands, read
and create their own fanzines, and code their hands with stars and
hearts when they go to shows so that they may recognize and talk with
one other. She would often take the stage topless, mocking male rock
stars of the past. An article in the Spring 1999 issue of Bust features a
1994 picture of Hanna that, according to the author, defined Riot Grrrl
for the mainstream. In this photograph, Hanna is pictured with the
word "slut" scrawled on her stomach and is wearing a halter top with
the words "baby doll" and "cutie pie" printed on it. In response to this
picture, Hanna states:

> I guess insisting these words were in the frame was my way, at the time,
> of having some kind of agency in terms of being photographed. I was also
> trying to take power away from certain words by ridiculously over-using
> them. I sort of anticipated guys thinking, "oh, she's showing skin, there-
> fore she's a slut." So I wrote "slut" on myself as a way to beat them to the
> punch. (Boob 1999: 62)

Hanna goes on to state that she was not aware then as she is now of the
fine line between reclaiming derogatory slang and glamorizing it (Boob
1999: 62). Some critics such as Natasha Stoval viewed the riot grrrl
movement as a "psychological trap", hiding "the potentially much
greater power in being a woman behind a fantasy of childhood
strength" (1996: 69). It is the attempt, though, at physically re-defining
and re-presenting the body on stage that is significant here within the
context of interrogating the possibilities of the creation of aggressive
subjectivities on stage through physical rhetoric. This attempt at re-
inscribing the body, re-naming or re-claiming the power of naming from

the patriarchal institution of viewing, allows for the possibility of re-viewing the created object as creating subject.

Lynn Breedlove of Tribe 8, a San Francisco band made up of five anar-chist, butch, S/M dykes, has also been known to perform topless, mocking not only shirtless male rock stars as Hanna did but also straight women strippers who perform for straight men. With a nipple ring and a drawing of anarcho-venus on her belly, Breedlove is infamous for bringing the first mosh pit to the 20th Michigan's Womyn's Festival, as well as positively portraying S/M culture and performing a mock castration on stage.[7] Also like Hanna and L7, Breedlove encouraged women to join in the traditionally all-male space of the mosh pit. While touring to support their first full-length CD, *First City*, in 1995, Breedlove, wearing a strap-on dildo, told the crowd at CBGB's in New York, "We're not going to play until a guy comes up here and sucks my dick" (McDonnell 1995: 56). By her charged physical rhetoric, Breedlove invades realms of heterosexual freedom and patriarchal privilege. Re-norming practices of viewing, Breedlove offers a reversal of passive images of femininity and subject positionalities of masculinity. Her band's open support of women's active attainment of pleasure as lesbian subjects, as well as straight female subjects, in terms of power and sex also calls into question conservative feminist views on those subjects, especially in terms of S/M culture.

Like the female performance artists of the 1960s and 1970s, bands such as Bikini Kill, Hole, and L7 present images of women on stage as desiring subjects. Tribe 8 clearly shows that women are also subjects on stage to be desired by women, as subjectivity and sight are given overtly not only to straight women but to queer women as well. Women as subjects on stage provide a site through which desires can be imagined and normative representation can be questioned, reconsidered, re-viewed, twisted, and re-presented. As audiences view images of women on stage, their ways of knowing can be changed and exchanged to include lesbian subjects, S/M subjects, and, most importantly, viewing subjects. This interference, produced by the various active representa-tions of images of women's bodies on stage, is important, even vital; for it can, through its destabilizing potential, simultaneously be an inter-ference in ways of viewing women off stage as well.

Notes

1   Carolee Schneemann performed her groundbreaking performance art piece *EyeBody* in her loft in 1963.

2   Note, of course, Jill Dolan's *Presence and Desire: Essays on Gender, Sexuality, Performance.*

3 A significant number of Fluxus artists were performance artists. Architect and graphic designer George Maciunas named the group in 1962.
4 Two exceptions are The Go-Gos and The Bangles, who were, unfortunately, pleasantly passive.
5 Hole has one male member, and there are no men in L7.
6 I use "girling" here to refer to the mainstream media's habit of placing all-women or women-dominated bands in a separate category from other bands. This term can also be used to discuss sexist fan responses that, more than likely, are inspired by the media's condescending categorizations, such as, "You play pretty well for a girl".
7 A mosh pit consists of a group of audience members, usually near the stage, who dance at punk rock shows by physically jumping and pushing themselves against one another.

References

Boob, Betty. 1999: Rebel Girl, Interview with Kathleen Hanna. *Bust,* Spring, 60–2.

Bataille, George. [1928] 1967: *Story of the Eye.* Joachim Neugroschel (trans.), San Francisco: City Lights Books.

Considine, J. D. 1995: Voters for Choice Benefit: Pearl Jam, Neil Young, L7, Lisa Germano. *Rolling Stone,* 9 March, 36.

Duncan, Michael. 1999: Tracing Mendieta. *Art in America* 87, 110–19.

Forte, Jeanie. 1988: Women's Performance Art: Feminism and Postmodernism. *Theatre Journal* 40, 217–35.

Grosz, Elizabeth. 1994: *Volatile Bodies: Toward a Corporeal Feminism.* Bloomington: Indiana University Press.

Harris, Hilary. 1993: Toward a Lesbian Theory of Performance. In Tony Bennett, Simon Frith, Lawrence Grossberg, John Shepherd, and Graeme Turner (eds), *Rock and Popular Music: Politics, Policies, and Institutions.* London: Routledge.

Joy, Sally Margaret. 1992: L7: Maiden LA. *Melody Maker,* 16 May, 28–9.

Koebel, Caroline. 1998: From Danger to Ascendancy: Notes Toward Carolee Schneemann. *Wide Angle* 20, 50–7.

McDonnell, Evelyn. 1995: Beyond the Tracks: Rock's Midsummer Madness. *Interview,* August, 56. *Infotrac 2000* (7 June 1999).

O'Brien, Lucy. 1995: *She-Bop: The Definitive History of Women in Rock, Pop + Soul.* New York: Penguin Books.

O'Dell, Kathy. 1997: Fluxus Feminus, *TDR* 41, 43–60.

Raphael, Amy. 1995: Interview with Courtney Love. In Amy Raphael (ed.), *Grrrls: Viva Rock Diva.* New York: St. Martin's Griffin.

Retna, Honey Salvadori. 1994: Ah, the Smell of It: L7 Bask in the Sweet Stink of Success. *Rolling Stone,* 11 August, 25–6.

Roth, Moira. 1983: The Amazing Decade: Women and Performance Art in America. In Moira Roth (ed.), *The Amazing Decade: Women and Performance Art in America.* Los Angeles: Astro Artz.

Schneider, Rebecca. 1996: After Us the Savage Goddess: Feminist Performance Art of the Explicit Body Staged, Uneasily, across Modernist Dreamscapes. In Elin Diamond (ed.), *Performance and Cultural Politics.* New York: Routledge.

Schoemer, Karen. 1995: On Love's Rocky Road: Hogging the Show at Lollapalooza. *Newsweek,* 24 July, 54.

Selzer, Jon. 1992: Shock Tactics: Faith No More/L7. *Melody Maker,* 28 November, 26.

Stevenson, Nils. 1999: *Vacant: A Diary of the Punk Years, 1976–1977.* New York: Thanks and Hudson.

Stoval, Natasha. 1996: Adult Crash, Rev. of *Reject All American* by Bikini Kill. *Village Voice,* 30 April, 69+.

Thompson, Ben. 1992: Blood on the Tracks: What Happens When Heavy Metal Goes Feminist? *New Statesman and Society* 5, 33.

Wurtzel, Elizabeth. 1992: Popular Music: Girl Trouble. *The New Yorker,* 29 June, 63–70.

Chapter 7

Leaving Las Vegas: *Reading the Prostitute as a Voice of Abjection*

Doreen Piano

It is articulation which must be stressed, not simply representation.
Maggie Humm (1997:57)

FOR AN IDEA of how ubiquitous the celluloid figure of the female prostitute is in Hollywood, one need only read a March 1999 article in *Premiere* magazine entitled "That's Why the Lady Plays a Tramp!" That prostitution is primarily viewed as women's work is left unquestioned not only by the title of the article, but also the special issue called "Women in Hollywood". In the article, Anne Thompson collects an assortment of comments from Hollywood actresses who have played prostitutes. Observations range from Bebe Neuwirth's prostitute-as-victim comment that "The prostitute is the only woman that men are not intimidated by . . . because they can fuck her" to Mira Sorvino's cautiously sex-positive one that "There's something feminist about [prostitution] in a weird, weird way" (Thompson 1999: 79, 96). While many of the actresses interviewed perceived prostitute roles as challenging, quite a few find them depressing and difficult. As Teresa Russell, who starred in Ken Russell's *Whore* (1991), says, "I don't want to go there again . . . Every morning you had to wake up and feel really bad about yourself" (Thompson 1999: 96).

Taken as a whole, these comments construct the prostitute as an ambiguous and compelling figure who has become a site of powerful discourses, both hegemonic (patriarchal control over women's bodies) and counter-hegemonic, (radical and socialist feminists' view of "prostitution . . . as the ultimate objectification of women and the ultimate alienation of labor" (Pheterson 1993: 57). In fact, these discourses have served to smother any that prostitutes themselves can produce (Bell 1994: 73). However, despite or because of this "othering" by anti-sex feminists and patriarchal culture alike, sex workers and pro-sex feminists have begun theorizing a space that contests these discourses through the production of a prostitute political/sexual identity (Bell 1994: 95).

While pro-sex feminists and sex worker activists agree that prostitution, as it is situated within patriarchal culture, contributes to the victimization and exploitation of women, they also claim that eliminating prostitution will not alleviate discrimination or acts of violence against women. Rather, they argue, prostitutes need a legitimate political identity. Thus, prostitutes' rights groups in North America such as COYOTE (Call Off Your Old Tired Ethics) and PONY (Prostitutes of New York) have formed to decriminalize prostitution and to address nineteenth-century medical and social discourses that construct sex workers " as an 'other' against which varieties of white female sexual identity have constructed themselves" (Pendleton 1997: 73).[1] As Shannon Bell claims, in *Reading, Writing, and Rewriting the Prostitute Body*, the nineteenth-century bourgeois subject excluded from its social realm what was perceived as "low"; in other words, anything relating to the body was seen as dirty and contaminating. The prostitute, because of her classification as a sexualized identity, thus became a "negative identity of the bourgeois subject" (Bell 1994: 43). In the twentieth century this dichotomy manifests itself in the establishment of white, middle-class, heterosexual feminism as the norm to which all other categories of "woman" must either conform or be excluded. Thus, excluded feminist identities such as US Third World (or women of color), queer, and pro-sex become "marked with an essence, imprisoned in a given set of possibilities" (Young 1990: 170), representing the devalued term in dichotomies such as feminist/whore, heterosexual/homosexual, and respectable/unrespectable.

Attempting to recover the prostitute body as a legitimate identity, Bell rewrites negative classifications of prostitutes as "disease-producers", "degenerates", "victims" and "commercial objects" by inverting and replacing these terms with "healer", "educator", "sex expert", and "business woman" (Bell 1994: 100). She argues that through acts of counter-identification and dis-identification prostitutes can produce positive sexual identities that "speak back" to dominant vilified images. Whereas the strategy of counter-identification entails resisting dominant representations of prostitutes, dis-identification provides a space for transgressive possibilities, "moving the discourse to a different terrain of meaning" (Bell 1994: 14).[2] Bell reads North American performance artists Annie Sprinkle and Candida Royalle as enacting both counter- and dis-identification through a "prostitute discourse", one that takes on the multiple and contrary meanings – feminist *and* whore, empowered *and* oppressed, respectable *and* unrespectable – that the term "woman" can embody. In this way, Bell argues, the prostitute body can be reclaimed as a site of sexual healing and education by becoming a carrier of its own dichotomous representations. However, because prostitute performance art remains mostly an art house phenomenon, its power as an antidote to prostitute stigmatization is limited to a small audience.

For this reason, the prostitute's persistent presence in mainstream Hollywood films, from comedies and action movies to Mafia flicks and teary-eyed melodramas, calls for an investigation into whether Bell's analysis of "prostitute discourse" found in performance art can be traced in film. A superficial survey, however, reveals that, for the most part, nineteenth-century views of prostitution still persist. For example, *Pretty Woman* (1990) and *Hustling* (1975), while attempting to humanize prostitutes, reproduce stereotypes about unhappy women who can only gain happiness and respect by giving up their jobs and involving themselves in heterosexual relationships. Even worse, most prostitutes in film are punished for their sexual and economic autonomy, as in *Klute* (1971) and *Whore* (1991), before being recuperated into mainstream society while others are tortured and die as in *Strange Days* (1995). Because of these narrowly conceived and often misogynistic story lines, analyzing films about prostitutes through a narrative lens occludes reading any potential challenge or resistance that the prostitute figure poses.[3]

For this reason, a feminist reading strategy entails moving beyond visual and narrative readings to, what Maggie Humm suggests in *Feminism and Film*, "a more complex approach to understand the meaning and diversity of differing sexual representations" (1997: 47). In other words, Humm proposes a feminist strategy that analyzes both visual and verbal discourse, examining how these different elements contain or suppress women's voices as in her reading of *Klute* or, conversely, how they subvert dominant representations of women through visual and linguistic defiance of these codes as in Bette Gordon's *Variety* (1983). I would like to build on Humm's method by proposing to read the prostitute in film as speaking against the cinematic apparatus that attempts to contain and silence her by analyzing her as speaking from a particular location, that of abjection.

As explored in Julia Kristeva's book *Powers of Horror*, abjection is that which must be excluded in order for a subject to take its place within the Symbolic – the social realm in which signification takes place. The Symbolic is where meaning is made, where, for example, identities are attributed, as in gender roles. Thus, in order for signification to occur, the subject must take its place in the Symbolic by rejecting the maternal body – that which is ambiguous, inassimilable, and beyond significa- tion. The separation from the maternal body is a psychical process that occurs at birth and that creates a lack or need in the subject because it is prevented from returning to the maternal body. Thus, because of its exclusion, the abject threatens to return, or as Kristeva states "from its place of banishment, the abject does not cease challenging its master"(2). The abject's proximity, Kristeva claims, is what accounts for cultural taboos such as incest and food prohibitions as well as psychological and physiological processes such as phobias, feelings of repulsion, aversion, and self-loathing.[4]

In *Reading Kristeva*, Kelly Oliver explains that "The abject threat comes from what has been prohibited by the Symbolic order . . . " (1993: 56), anything that "disturbs identity, system, order" (Kristeva 1982: 4). Thus, Kristeva's theory provides possibilities to read minority feminist iden- tities such as the prostitute as enacting a "border crisis", one that disrupts the hegemonic concept of "woman" by calling into question what that term excludes. Similar to Bell's concept of prostitute discourse which relies on dis-identification and counter-identification, the theory of abjection provides a method for reading the prostitute as being capable of disrupting the heterosexual, patriarchal social order that attempts to deny her subjecthood, or more specifically, her right to discourse. Reading films in this way requires digging deeply into the structures embedded in the cinematic apparatus, uncovering the bina- ries that muffle "voices of abjection".

To illustrate this reading method, I would like to analyze *Leaving Las Vegas* (1996) for the disruptions that may occur when the prostitute is perceived through a Kristevan lens of abjection. I analyze this particular film not because of its visual aesthetics or progressive politics (of which it has neither), but rather for its attempt to move outside the conven- tions of Hollywood film in its bleak depiction of a romance between a drunk, Ben (Nicholas Cage), and a prostitute, Sera (Elisabeth Shue), thus providing gaps and interstices for the voice of abjection to surface. In reading Sera as articulating a voice of the abject, I want to argue that despite the camera's male gaze that contains and underscores her sexu- ality, Sera's presence, especially her transgressive body, threatens to disrupt the borders that separate the Symbolic from the abject. Sera's transgressions disrupt a number of binaries in the film that attempt to separate suburban from urban space, legitimate from illegitimate economies, hard from soft bodies, and acceptable from unacceptable forms of female sexuality.

Ultimately, I want to argue that Sera's ambiguity as a prostitute allows her to traverse these binaries, providing her with a voice of abjection that questions the binaries the film itself attempts to maintain. By conveying both sexual and economic autonomy and by passing as a "woman", Sera calls into question women's traditional positioning within the Symbolic as being financially dependent and sexually monogamous. Her ambiguity – that she can play both sides – positions her outside the Symbolic despite her ability to demonstrate the "respectable" qualities of someone within. For many prostitutes, however, autonomy is linked to class and racial privilege. For example, according to Prostitutes Education Network, women prostitutes of color who work the streets are more vulnerable to arrest than whites, with a larger majority of black women going to jail. This is despite a lower percentage of women of color in the "biz" (Zolbrod 1999: 13). Thus, "passing" as a certain kind of "woman" and enacting a "border crisis" are contingent on racial and class factors that determine how effective prostitutes can be in challenging dominant culture.

For example, Sera's ability to disrupt is predicated on her "unmarked" status as a Western white woman. This positionality provides her with certain privileges that sex workers of color and of Third World nationalities often do not possess. Even in global regions where sex workers are primarily women of color or where women of color are heavily desired such as African women in Italy, "white sexual labor is most valued within the global sex industry" (Doezema and Kempadoo 1999: 11). This valuing of whiteness extends to benefits such as cleaner and safer working and living conditions. Thus, for example, in the film Sera lives in a gated community, away from the streets where sex workers are most vulnerable to attack and from police harassment. She is also able to solicit "johns" in hotel lobbies because, although provocatively dressed, she looks like a middle-class white tourist in Las Vegas. It is when she transgresses the societal expectations of her "unmarked" status – making an overt sexual offer to a tourist – that Sera evokes confusion, aversion, and consternation from others. Her transgression becomes threatening because she is disrupting boundaries that distinguish unacceptable from acceptable ways of being white, heterosexual, and female.

In addition, Sera's positionality as a prostitute is often elided by the heterosexual romance between her and Ben that dominates the narrative and labels Sera an "acceptable" woman, one with whom white, middle-class women can identify. Contrasting this feminine ideal is a Latina prostitute who, early in the movie, seduces Ben at a traffic light and later, while simulating oral sex on his finger, steals his wedding ring. That she is Latina conveys a particular type of body, one that transgresses the norms of conventional womanhood. "The brown or black woman is regarded as a desirable, tantalizing, erotic subject suitable for temporary ... sexual intercourse ... and rarely seen as a candidate for a long-term commitment" (Doezema and Kempadoo 1999: 10). Thus, Sera's work, and sometimes her dress, defines her as a prostitute, and not her body, which, when compared to women of color whose bodies are accorded specific sexual associations based on racial stereotyping, affords her a certain anonymity.

Conversely, in *Mona Lisa* (1986), Simone, played by Cathy Tyson, is also able to pass in terms of gaining access to high-income clients in London's high end hotels though this is most likely due to the presence of her white male companion as well as her light complexion and super-model beauty. Historically, as Sander Gilman notes, Western society has associated the black body, male or female, with "deviant" sexuality (quoted in hooks 1997: 114), and, thus, it is no surprise that by the end of the film, Simone's blackness becomes a trope for hidden and forbidden aspects of her life such as her lesbianism that surfaces at the end of the film. In fact the disclosure of her sexuality engenders violence as Simone kills the men who attempt to hurt the young white woman whom she loves. bell hooks' comment about how this moment casts Simone in the stereotypical role of a "mammy" who abdicates any possibility for sexual agency and self-representation by serving the needs of a white woman (1992: 74) reveals the need to consider racial as well as First World/Third World differences in prostitute positionalities when analyzing representations of sex workers. As Kempadoo and Doezema claim, the contrary and diverse experiences of sex workers globally demand feminist analyses that are historically and geo-politically specific (1999: 130).

Thus, in reading Sera as a "voice of abjection", I am positioning her on the margins due to her sex worker status, at the same time I argue that her whiteness affords her "passing" privileges. In other words, Sera has more access to better working and living conditions than many sex workers of color, yet her work ultimately condemns her to the margins. Deemed a "respectable" body because of her whiteness and complementary middle-class markers (articulate, well-groomed, and confident), Sera's proximity to those who have a similar appearance enacts a "border crisis". Thus, the businessman Sera attempts to solicit at the bar, Ben, a formerly married Hollywood executive, and Sera's landlady, all comfortably situated in the white middle-class, experience "border anxiety" when her sexualized identity as a prostitute is revealed.

The threat to these boundaries can be seen in the movement Sera makes between her townhouse apartment and the Las Vegas "Strip" where she works. In the film, safe and unsafe spaces are not defined by typical geographical markers such as urban and suburban, but rather "safe" or "uncontaminated" spaces are found in pockets of the city that are safeguarded from the "Strip's" influence. The Strip, traditionally seen as the seamy side of Vegas, discloses its presence elliptically in the film through the mise-en-scène of privacy. Thus, high walls, keys, security guards, and gates signify an attempt to draw boundaries between public and private spaces. As Iain Chambers notes, in the postmodern world, "referents that once firmly separated the city from the countryside, the artificial from the 'natural', are now indiscriminately reproduced as potential signs and horizons within a common topography" (1990: 54). The Strip is distinguished by its constant movement of being in flux – flashing signs, people, moving cars – whereas the townhouse where Sera lives appears staid and tranquil, an oasis in a desert city. However, that these boundaries are porous is witnessed in Sera's fluid movement between them, occupying both the townhouse with all of its middle-class American trappings – a swimming pool, numerous rooms, electronic devices, privacy – and the glittery, neon-lit, crowded streets where she works.

That Sera's body provides her with a lifestyle more suited to middle-class amenities – a nice townhouse outside of town, material comfort, flexible working hours – is a source of discomfort and fascination to her neighbors, especially the landlady's husband who watches her sally forth in her "evening wear" only to return weary-eyed in the morning. This fluidity between locations is accessible to Sera because she has a certain invisibility due to her ability to pay rent and maintain an appearance that is grounded in middle-class ideals of beauty and success. However, later in the movie after Sera has been brutally raped and beaten, her bruised and "marked" body is a source of horror as her landlady realizes that the border between her townhouse enclave and that of the Strip is not as tightly drawn as she thinks. This realization results in Sera's eviction from the townhouse and her subsequent homelessness, a space that Kristeva would define as the abject's cultural location (1982: 8).

In "The City of Desire: Its Anatomy and Destiny", Pat Califia observes how sexual minorities have been contained and controlled traditionally through the allocation of space in the urban landscape. It is through this parceling out of space that sexual minorities may be barely tolerated and only because "a sex zone must acquire at least a token invisibility to avoid threatening its customers as well as the authorities" (1994: 206). Because Las Vegas is a city that supplies its tourists with a variety of pleasures, prostitutes are part of the public space of the metropolitan. In some ways, it is fitting that Leaving Las Vegas takes place in a city where, to a certain extent, abjection rules. Vice is at the pulse of the city's functioning. Yet, despite vice, both sexual and economic, being a vital energetic force in Las Vegas, it is also imperiously defined by a system that allows state-sanctioned vice to operate at a profit to the exclusion of individual entrepreneurs. For example, although prostitution in Nevada is legal, prostitutes must work in state-run brothels such as Mustang Ranch in order to avoid legal harassment and thereby abdicate any right to define their own working conditions.[5] How long prostitutes can be seen in public before being exposed to regulation and expulsion is dependent on what exactly their presence threatens. If sex workers become a "visible" presence to either the tourist trade or the city's inhabitants, then a tightening of boundaries will occur. Thus, whereas gambling is sanctioned, individual prostitution, part of the city's invisible economy, is not.

Recent conflicts over urban planning and expansion between Las Vegas residents and "the Industry" has resulted not in limiting the growth of hotel and gambling facilities but instead in decreasing the visibility of prostitutes. A combined effort between city planning and civic organizations and gambling establishments has attempted to rid prostitutes' presence on the streets and in the casinos (Littlejohn 1999: 25). Thus, as the legitimate economy of gambling continues to negatively affect the city's residents in terms of available natural resources and the rise of crime and traffic, the illegitimate economy of prostitution, what drives the city's 'othered' pleasures, becomes the abject source that must be expelled.

This privileging of one economy over another is witnessed in a scene at a hotel bar where Sera is trying to turn a trick. Her interaction with an out-of-town businessman reveals how her abject position as a prostitute threatens the economic and social order that determines what is legitimate "business" and who has access to it. As Sera and the businessman begin chatting, he is obviously taken by her assertive manner as well as her beauty. Yet when she asks him if he wants a "date", he recoils from her. "A date? What are you a whore?" he shouts. "I have a wife waiting at home for me."

Repulsion, aversion, fascination, and disgust, Kristeva tells us, are all reactions to the abject which "threatens to dissolve the subject by dissolving the border" (Young 1990: 144). The businessman's disgust stems from his initial recognition of Sera as a woman whom he can seduce and overpower, yet her aggressive sexual advance suggests that she is more of a "professional" like himself. Because this paradox cannot be assimilated, Sera becomes a figure of horror to him, and a threat to the Symbolic, which demands a distinction be made between what respectable and unrespectable bodies can and cannot do. Respectable bodies are unmarked while unrespectable ones are gendered, racialized, disabled, Other. As Marion Young claims "In being chained to their bodily being they cannot be fully and unselfconsciously respectable and professional" (1990: 141). Because of their marked qualities, they are limited economically and socially. In other words, a prostitute, though part of a capitalist economy that sanctions the selling of goods, is denied the ability to sell her body and make a living legitimately. This clampdown is seen in the bartender's sanctioning of the businessman's reaction by telling Sera that she must leave.

Sera's expulsion from the bar, her humiliation, and subsequent loss of a possible trick are her punishment for attempting to occupy a legitimate space through her appearance of being an "acceptable" body. As Califia explains, it is okay for "johns" to visit the forbidden zones of the city yet when these erotic zones encroach on legitimate terrain, their presence becomes "hotly contested" (1994: 206). Thus, a hotel bar as a space where trade and pleasure mingle is only available to "like-minded" folks; when that space is invaded by an excluded "other" such as Sera, its legitimate practices are called into question by the corruption that her trade suggests.

By enacting a business transaction, Sera inadvertently challenges "the economy of heterosexual sex in which men feel entitled to unlimited access to women's bodies" (Pendleton 1997: 79). Hence, the businessman's claim that he has a wife waiting at home for him reveals the assumption that heterosexual sex is free, something for which a man should not have to pay. Using femininity as a disguise, Sera challenges the economies of the hotel bar by acting direct and business-like. It is this which the businessman finds affronting as well as disconcerting. As Eve Pendleton claims "femininity as an economic tool is a means of exposing its constructedness and reconfiguring its meanings" (1997: 79). In this way, the female prostitute body, typically seen as one of unbridled sexuality, exhibits a traditionally "masculine" behavior that dismantles gender distinctions.

Moreover, Sera's buff body can also be seen as challenging normative ideals of femininity and masculinity that assume male bodies are hard while women's are soft. As Lynda Johnston notes in her essay about women bodybuilders: "In order to establish the solid male body, there must be a contrast with the non-solid or liquid female body" (1998: 254). However, Sera's body challenges this binary by being both erotic *and* extremely muscular. While working, Sera wears a leather miniskirt and halter top that makes her appear intimidating, not vulnerable. Like women bodybuilders, she is a producer of her own appearance. Her body is a product of hard work as well as a producer of pleasure. In this way, Sera can be seen as, what Rosi Braidotti calls, the "monstrous-feminine", one that "trespasses and transgresses the barriers between recognizable norms and definitions" (1997: 65). On the one hand, she calls attention to herself on the street as "someone to be looked at" by utilizing feminine markers such as a mini-skirt and high heels, yet the invitation to look is undermined by her leather skirt and hard body, which are more suited for an action film than a melodrama. In this way, her presence on the street is unnerving; her unrespectable body unmasks her middle-class appearance. "The role of prostitute/'street-walker' allows female characters not only to inhabit urban space but to flaunt it . . . and, perhaps, to exhibit the 'toughness' through which working-class masculinities are regularly symbolised . . . " (Tasker 1998: 5). Through her posturing and clothing, Sera deflects the camera's gaze that continually attempts to frame her as being part of the flashiness and allure that constitute the topography of Las Vegas.

However, even though Sera's body is sharply defined and bound in leather, the camera undermines her self-possession and controlled sexuality by focusing on her breasts. This can be seen as a way to contain her transgressive sexuality "through stripping 'woman' of all defenses and portraying her in a naked form" (Ussher 1997: 92). It is through exposure of the female body that male anxiety over female desire can be suspended. Because of the camera's gaze, Sera's breasts become aesthetic rather than dangerous, fetishisized rather than horrific. Yet their constant appearance acts as a trope for the maternal body, and, in this way, signifies a threat by the abject. "Because the maternal body is our first site of desire and of prohibition, mothers represent the in-between, the realm of the abject which must be struggled against to enter the symbolic . . . "(Humm 1997: 74). Sera's sexuality is transgressive, erotic yet prohibited. It makes Ben feel uneasy and threatened as witnessed in his volatile behavior toward her, particularly when he watches her transform from a middle-class subject to a sexualized other.

Stripped of everything that defines him as being within the Symbolic – his job, his family, friends – Ben's own state of abjection is signaled by his state of crisis that manifests itself in excessive drinking, prurient albeit ineffective attempts to master his sexuality, and self-imposed exile from everything that is familiar. As Kristeva notes, the abject is "experienced at the peak of its strength when that subject, weary of fruitless attempts to identify with something on the outside, finds the impossible within" (1982: 5). Ben has rid himself of the *accoutrements* that sustain a life within the Symbolic. His alcoholism and his literal death drive to Las Vegas push him closer to the space where abjection lies, "the one by whom the abject exists is thus a *deject* who places . . . separates . . . situates . . . , and therefore *strays* instead of getting his bearings, desiring, belonging . . . " (Kristeva 1982: 8). As Kristeva notes, the straying that marks abjection is where "he draws his jouissance . . . *a land of oblivion*" (1982: 8). Thus, Ben welcomes being in Las Vegas, a Land-of-the-Lotus-Eaters city, where time and space are reduced to the endless repetition of gambling and drinking. His inebriated state effaces all previous memories, ambitions, and drives. This *jouissance,* what Kristeva defines as a pre-sexual, pre-Symbolic state characterized by bliss, can be seen by his smile when he reads the motel name where he's staying as "The Hole You're In" rather than its actual name: "The Whole Year Inn."

Thus, it makes sense that he and Sera are drawn to each other; both recognize in the other a state of abjection. Yet Ben's abjection seems to stem from a battle within, a dissembling of the self, while Sera's is imposed by the Symbolic order, which maintains narrow definitions of female sexuality and expels those that fall outside of that definition. Her marginalized status is more vulnerable and subject to violence and surveillance. Also, in contrast to Ben, who is emotionally and physically dissipated, Sera conveys a sense of control over her life. Although abject, she represents everything that he has lost – economic stability, sexual power, material gain – even though she cannot gain legitimate status unless she gives up her job. This ability to be both powerful and desirable repels yet fascinates Ben.

Sera contains the multiple discourses about women that the Symbolic attempts to classify, most prominently the distinction between madonna and whore. As Rosi Braidotti claims, "The mother's body as the threshold of experience is both sacred and soiled, holy and hellish; it is attractive and repulsive, all-powerful and therefore impossible to live with" (1997: 65). Throughout the movie, Ben's oscillation between calling Sera a whore and an angel reveals his inability to accept her ambiguity "as is". Instead, he acts in concert with the Symbolic to classify her body as either/or rather than both/and as witnessed by his derisive comments when she transmogrifies from the gal next door to a luscious lady of the night.

Part of Ben's horror may stem from the border anxiety he experiences having his shortcomings as a "man" thrown into relief by Sera's autonomy. Ben's inability to control himself and his excessive irrational behavior compared to Sera's evenhandedness, her self-possession and financial autonomy, disrupt traditional notions of gender roles. His overdetermined need to exert his masculinity by getting into bar brawls and thrown out of casinos reveals a feeble attempt to re-constitute his masculinity at the same time that his sexual impotence and 'soft' body call it into question. As Jane Ussher claims, "The 'unthinkable' is that 'man' takes up the position of 'woman,' that he becomes the 'second sex'" (1997: 91). Ben's attempts to draw distinct boundaries between them are most visible in his need to constantly remind her that she is a "slut" by finding multiple ways to objectify and sexualize her identity.

In this way, *Leaving Las Vegas* becomes a site of confusion about what constitutes legitimate gender identities, and it is the camera's patriarchal gaze that attempts to resolve this confusion by fetishizing Sera's sexuality and expelling her violently from the Symbolic through the mauling and marking of her body in a gang rape scene. Her unrespectable, yet powerful, sexuality becomes a site of dis-ease and violence not only on an interpersonal level between Sera and Ben, but also on a social level when, after Sera is gang-raped, she is mistreated and scorned by everyone she encounters – from a taxicab driver's snide remarks about her being sodomized to the landlady who evicts Sera when she returns to her townhouse. It is striking that only a black cabdriver sympathizes with her "marked" state, and, yet, she forecloses his gesture of solidarity by ignoring his comments. Unable to walk, never mind pass as a "woman", Sera is no longer a threat. Her soiled appearance is easily spotted and shunned, or, in the case of the cabdriver, is acknowledged as speaking from a similar location of abjection. However, whereas Sera's marked appearance will eventually disappear as she heals, the cabdriver's blackness is subject to permanent marking.

Even though her marked appearance defines her as a body open to derision, its visibility challenges the Symbolic in a way that her "passing" strategies could not. Her bruises mar her beauty by calling attention to the existence of misogyny, a strategy of control by the Symbolic that often goes unmarked in public, as seen in Sera's scars on her thighs from her pimp, Yuri. Thus, Sera's body becomes a form of "body art", what Jane Ussher sees as an ability "to subvert the masculine gaze, allowing women to become speaking subjects as opposed to mere objects of the gaze" (1997: 118). Although she obviously has not chosen to be raped and beaten, she does not stay hidden from sight and unmasks herself as a disruptive presence among the glassy-eyed tourists in Las Vegas. For example, in one of the ending scenes, Sera, her face still bruised, walks into a casino, and pointedly ignores a European tourist who mocks her by putting two casino chips up to her breasts. Her rude reaction to this gesture results in her getting kicked out by a casino bouncer. But Sera does not leave so easily. Instead, she turns around and walks back to the bouncer confidently staring him down and spits in his face. This confrontation provides a space for Sera to speak from "a voice of abjection" that openly rather than slyly defies the Symbolic.

This scene sets up the final one between Sera and Ben, where in the throes of death, Ben finally appears to accept Sera's many positionalities, not just the middle-class white one that is most socially acceptable.

The physical consummation of their relationship signifies both an embracing of Sera's abjection and an enacting of a traditional Hollywood ending: the recuperation of the autonomous woman into the social sphere via a heterosexual relationship. This return is magnified by her utter loneliness at the end of the film where the importance of heterosexual romance as the ultimate mode of companionship is underscored.

What is most disturbing about the film is Sera's alienation and isolation from other sex workers. In no way does the film allude to a network of sex workers who can band together to achieve better and safer working conditions as well as attain a sense of solidarity among themselves.[6] Instead, the comfort of heterosexual romance is Sera's only salvation from her work. In fact, Sera's desirability and autonomy appear to be based on her difference from other prostitutes. For example, the other sex workers in the film, a Latina prostitute, a stripper at a bar, and a prostitute who has sex with Ben are all in some way used to evoke sympathy and respect toward Sera who contrasts sharply with their slatternly representations. Sera's only other friend besides Ben is the camera that she addresses and that is positioned as her "therapist". Thus, while *Leaving Las Vegas* provides alternative reading possibilities for exploring the prostitute in film as a powerfully ambiguous presence, its prostitute discourse is diminished by a conventional Hollywood ending that represents Sera not as a successful sex worker but as a grieving, broken-hearted woman.

Acknowledgments

The author is immensely grateful to Hosam Aboul-Ela, Mary Brewer, Jeff Brown, and especially Ellen Berry, for their helpful suggestions and feedback on various drafts of this chapter.

Notes

1   COYOTE and PONY are two of many international sex workers' rights organizations fighting for better working conditions and political representation. For more information on global sex workers' movements, see Commercial Sex Information Service (CSIS) at http://www.walnut.org/csis and Prostitutes Education Network at http://www.bayswan.org.
2   See Bell, chapter 5 for an elaboration of the terms counter- and dis-identification.
3   For analyses of Hollywood films about prostitutes that read "against the grain" of stereotypes, see Veronica Monet's article "The Balcony is Closed-Minded: At the Movies with Prostitutes".
4   See Oliver *Rereading Kristeva* 55–60 and Young *Justice and the Politics of Difference* 141–5, for excellent discussions of abjection in terms of feminist

theory (Oliver) and political theory (Young).

5   Read Laura Anderson's critique of working in a state-run brothel at http://www.bayswan.org/Laura.html.

6   For films that show solidarity among sex workers, see non-Hollywood films such as Lizzie Borden's *Working Girls* (1986), Frederico Fellini's *Nights of Cabiria* (1957), Bette Gordon's *Variety* (1983), and most recently, Vicky Funari and Julie Query's documentary, *Live Nude Girls Unite!* (2000).

References

Bell, Shannon. 1994: *Reading, Writing & Rewriting the Prostitute Body.* Bloomington: Indiana University Press.

Braidotti, Rosi. 1997: "Mothers, Monsters, and Machines". *Writing on the Body: Female Embodiment and Feminist Theory.* Eds. Katie Conboy, Nadia Medina, and Sarah Stanbury. New York: Columbia University Press, 59–79.

Califia, Pat. 1994: "The City of Desire: Its Anatomy and Destiny". *Public Sex: The Culture of Radical Sex.* Pittsburgh, Pennsylvania: Cleis Press, 205–13.

Chambers, Iain. 1990: *Border Dialogues: Journeys in Postmodernity.* New York: Routledge.

Doezema, Jo and Kamala Kempadoo. 1999: *Global Sex Workers: Rights, Resistance, and Redefinition.* New York: Routledge.

hooks, bell. 1996: Reel to Real: Race, Sex and Class at the Movies. New York: Routledge.

——. 1997: "Selling Hot Pussy: Representations of Black Female Sexuality in the Cultural Marketplace." *Writing on the Body: Female Embodiment and Feminist Theory.* Eds. Katie Conboy, Nadia Medina, and Sarah Stanbury. New York: Columbia University Press, 113–28.

Humm, Maggie. 1997: *Feminism and Film.* Bloomington: Indiana University Press.

Johnston, L. 1998: Reading the Sexed Bodies and Spaces of Gyms. In H. Nast and Pile, S. (eds). *Places through the Body.* London: Routledge, 244–62.

Kristeva, Julia. 1982: *Powers of Horror: An Essay on Abjection.* New York: Columbia University Press.

Littlejohn, David. 1999: "Introduction." *The Real Las Vegas: Life Beyond the Strip.* Ed. David Littlejohn. New York: Oxford University Press, 1–31.

Monet, Veronica. 1999 (Fall): The Balcony is Closed-Minded: At the Movies with Prostitutes. *Bitch: Feminist Response to Pop Culture* 11, 42–7.

Oliver, Kelly. 1993: *Reading Kristeva: Unraveling the Double-Bind.* Bloomington, Indiana: Indiana University Press.

Pendleton, Eve. 1997: "Love for Sale: Queering Heterosexuality." *Whores and Other Feminists.* Ed. Jill Nagle. New York: Routledge, 73–82.

Pheterson, Gayle. 1993 (Winter): "The Whore Stigma: Female Dishonor and Male Unworthiness". Ed. Anne McClintock. *Social Text* 37, 39–64.

Russo, Mary. 1997: "Female Grotesques: Carnival and Theory." *Writing on the Body: Female Embodiment and Feminist Theory.* Eds. Katie Conboy, Nadia Medina, and Sarah Stanbury. New York: Columbia University Press, 318–36.

Tasker, Y. 1998: *Working Girls: Gender and Sexuality in Popular Cinema*. New Brunswick: Rutgers University Press.

Thompson, Anne. 1999 (March): That's Why the Lady Plays a Tramp! *Premier Magazine*, 79–81, 96–7.

Ussher, J. 1997: *Fantasies of Femininity: Reframing the Boundaries of Sex*. London: Routledge.

Young, Marion Iris. 1990: *Justice and the Politics of Difference*. Princeton: Princeton University Press.

Zolbrod, Zoe. 1999: "Dollars, Sex, Sense, Rights". *Maxine* 4, 12–15.

Part III

Challenging Universalism in Feminist Theory and Practice

A LYSSA O'BRIEN's *Theorizing Feminisms: Breast Cancer Narratives and Reconstructed "Women"* foregrounds the way in which women with breast cancer are subjected to the discursive and physical control of medical institutions as well as alternative health philosophies and practices. The essay addresses the proliferation of articles, interviews, public speeches and videos made by women from a range of social classes, races, ages and sexual orientation that aim to assist women in maintaining control over their bodies while fighting breast cancer. O'Brien identifies as a crucial part of Breast Cancer Activism the narration women use to forge self-consciously mediated representations of their material experiences and interactions with agents of institutional power. She demonstrates how women's breast cancer narratives can stand as a model for a contemporary feminist praxis by providing a new ground for feminist political action, and she argues that these stories are as important as the more overtly political actions taken by activists insofar as they contribute to the re-construction of women as an epistemological category.

Having grown up on the Listuguj First Nation in Quebec, the child of a white mother and an aboriginal father, Angela Slaughter is uniquely placed to speak about the cultural barriers that have made it difficult for aboriginal women to participate as equals in the Canadian Women's Movement. *Aboriginal Women and the Canadian Women's Movement* draws further on the author's recent experience as a graduate student at a predominantly white university, where her encounter with mainstream feminism on a Women's Studies course leads her to conclude that aboriginal women must devote their energy and resources firstly to establishing a women's movement independent from the mainstream. Only then, Slaughter suggests, can aboriginal women consider forming strategic alliances with mainstream groups. This paper makes the case that in order to resist the exclusionary and sometimes racist practices of mainstream Canadian feminism Aboriginal women must be able to deal from a position of strength, a position unlikely to be achieved outside of their own culturally-based movement.

Where Metaphor Meets Materiality: The Spatialized Subject and the Limits of Locational Feminism, by Rebecca Walsh, considers feminism's adoption of spatial models as a way to account for the multiple and shifting aspects of female identity. Walsh examines the difficulties inherent in trying to make identity "thematic" through the use of a geographical epistemology and the metaphors and tools that accompany it. For somewhere in the attempt to wed geography and identity, she argues, locational feminism risks "endorsing" only those aspects of identity that are most easily seen. The essay focuses on the complicated nature of the lesbian's relationship to metaphorical and material space as a way of indicating how locational feminism might consider in a more substantial way the difference it makes that some differences are more visible than others. Walsh concludes that locational feminism must consider more carefully the implications of what it is trying to chart, especially how its project feeds into existing debates within the gay and lesbian community about issues of visibility, categorization, and subversion.

Chapter 8

Theorizing Feminisms: Breast Cancer Narratives and Reconstructed "Women"

Alyssa O'Brien

And of course cancer is political.
Audre Lorde (1988: 98–9)

EMINISTS PAULA TREICHLER and Lisa Cartwright have noted "a new wave of activism toward institutionalized science and medicine" in response to health-related crises in the past ten years (1992: 5). Eve Kosofsky Sedgwick has termed this phenomenon "the recent crystallization of a politics explicitly oriented around grave illness" (1993: 13). One such political arena is the battle concerning what has been termed the "epidemic" of breast cancer. As Treichler and Cartwright explain, "modeling their strategies in part on those of AIDS activist groups like ACT UP, feminists are scrutinizing all dimensions of standard breast cancer care – routine mammograms, treatment options, choices in reconstruction and prosthesis, theories of etiology, insurance coverage policies, federal funding, and basic partner education – and finding them wanting" (1992: 14). *Ms.* writer Susan Rennie also remarks on the politicization of what has historically been rendered a personal and private trauma: "Women, taking their cue from AIDS activists, have also begun to 'act up,' by organizing, demonstrating, agitating, lobbying" (1993: 38). The new visibility of women is incurring significant social change – not only in terms of breast cancer care, but also in the development of a coalitional feminist praxis that insists on attending to differences between women. Breast cancer activists from varied social positions have begun to challenge the epistemological construction of the breast cancer patient by both the medical establishment and "alternative" medical programs and philosophies. A crucial part of this challenge is located in the narration women use to forge self-consciously mediated representations of their experiential materiality and interactions with agents of institutional power.

Through a proliferation of articles, interviews, public speeches, and videos, women from a range of social classes, races, ages and sexual orientations are mounting a collective response. In these diverse and multi-positioned texts, women fulfill Audre Lorde's injunction not to be silent. "For silence and invisibility go hand in hand with powerlessness," Lorde wrote in *The Cancer Journals* (1980: 61). Breast cancer activists now emulate Lorde's courageous act of speaking out about her disease from her position as a self-identified black lesbian poet in order to claim power over their own lives and the narratives used to construct meaning about their material experiences as female bodies combating cancer. In their work, the deliberate use of personal narrative stands as a model for a contemporary feminist praxis by providing a new ground for political action.

An examination of a number of local discourses, or narratives by women who have experienced breast cancer, demonstrates how feminist political action takes place in personal narration through the contestation of disempowering tactics and discourses used by social institutions that reduce the ill body to abjection. These stories are as important as the more overtly political actions taken by activist groups for they contribute to the re-construction of "women" as an epistemological category. Specifically, the narratives provide an alternative epistemology to that circulated by the medical establishment through which to comprehend the patient's body; they allow for a disruption of the homogenization common in medical discourses by foregrounding the radical positionality of the speaker in her particular social location. As Roseanne Lucia Quinn explains in her discussion of women's responses to what she terms misogynistic representations of women with breast cancer, "what has been most important in these women's words is their exposing of the particularity of their exploitation as women burdened with breast cancer in a sexist, racist, classist, ageist, homophobic society" (1995: 267–8). By grounding their discourses in what Rey Chow theorizes as "the local" (1992: 114), women are demanding that the strategic narratives of their material experiences contribute to a re-theorization of the subject in health and medical contexts and that their socially specific needs be addressed. These are not women "simply giving voice to suffering" as Judith Butler fears (1993b: 12), but rather women articulating a discourse of patient demand and epistemological renegotiation.

Studying the varied localized discourses of women with breast cancer, I have found that the upsurge in personal narrative used as a strategic intervention to social and medical constructions of "woman" and "patient" provides a means for such women to insist on the relevance of social categories such as race, class, sexuality, and age. Their strategic stories take advantage of what Joan Scott theorizes as the inevitable mediation of experience through narrative (1992: 22). Consequently, their stories emphasize the power of discourse as a new ground for a progressive and socially transformative feminist praxis. This work fills a crucial void in current feminist attempts to merge theory with societal change.

The Need for Contemporary Feminist Praxis

Cancer is not the end. It is a new way of living.
Joan M. O'Brien (1996a: 7)

Like other breast cancer activists and feminists, I do not have breast cancer, but I was brought to political consciousness of the disease as a result of my mother's battle with it over the past several years. Observing my mother's material struggles with a body under siege, her attempts to articulate agency concerning her treatment, and her struggle to comprehend a disease that has not been – until recently – publicly discussed, I realized that the postmodern theoretical paradigm which eradicates "woman" as a subject is inadequate to meet the needs of women from diverse subject positions who share a crisis of health of staggering severity. My mother's cancer raised the stakes for me as a feminist critic and fueled my interest in articulating a political response to the epistemological de-construction of "women" as a tenable category for feminist praxis. I could no longer consider the category of gender solely in terms of philosophical or academic formulations but was forced to assess the political and social consequences of our ways of talking about female bodies, experience, power, and discourse. I realized that contemporary feminism lacked the means to theorize the everyday battles of women from diverse social positions, particularly in the face of the medical establishment's transformation of women with breast cancer into abject bodies and alternative medicine's imposition of blame upon women who struggle to find ways to survive and combat the biological processes ravaging their bodies.

My mother's increasingly vocal and public response to her experience – through a number of community lectures – inspired me to theorize a new ground for contemporary feminist praxis. As she worked through

151

her treatments, my mother moved from personal healing to public activism, and thus encouraged me to begin the work that daughters, friends, and lovers of women with breast cancer can do as comrades in the fight against the disease and the social institutions that control breast cancer discourses. Her strategic narratives showed me how we might bridge the gap between what Teresa Ebert calls ludic feminism and materialist feminism such that a contemporary feminist praxis can emerge: one which takes the insights of discourse theory and uses it for real concrete change. In other words, the mediation I propose here is not the use of discourse as *play* or what Teresa Ebert terms the language-effects of ludic feminist theorists (1996), but rather the strategic use of language articulated from a particular social position as an intervention to the operation of social power.[1]

From my mother's numerous talks, I recognized that the strategic narrations that women perform as self-consciously mediated representations of their experience constitute political work. These stories critically challenge their interactions with the medical establishment – interactions which may be necessary but that need to be radically improved – and insist upon attention to the different needs of various female subjects as unique patients. Through personal testimonies from a local position, what Adrienne Rich calls "a politics of location" (1986), Rey Chow calls, "radical materiality" (1992: 114), and Gayatri Spivak calls "the strategic use of essentialism" (1993: 3–5), the subject is re-constructed to demand important changes.[2]

These narratives are as significant as the lobbying, fundraising and other more "active" activism, for the stories challenge the epistemology of the gendered patient's body circulated by the medical establishment and its supporting networks. As Stacey Young argues in her discussion on the importance of "discursive politics" for contemporary feminism, "Structural, fundamental material changes come about when ideologies, expectations, and norms – the grammar through which we make sense of our world – are transformed" (1997: 208). Similarly, Sandra Harding argues that "women speaking women's experiences is a crucial act, and an epistemological one, too" (1994: 12).[3] Although she does not discuss breast cancer politics, a striking aspect of Harding's work is that she foregrounds the importance of "speaking" as resistance to the scientific community, those experts who occupy a privileged social position such that "most people who count as scientists will tend to hold sexist, racist, and class exploitative assumptions" (1994: 29). As a practice of resistance, subversion, and re-construction of subjectivity, such strategic narratives of personal, located experience signify not an unexamined return to the body as an ahistorical object unshaped by cultural formations – or what Sara Suleri terms "biological fallacy" and "low-grade romanticism" (1994: 248) – but rather the narratives signify a process of rewriting the cultural view of the body and the subject who claims it. To use Butler's words, strategic discourses "might force a radical rearticulation of what qualifies as bodies that matter, ways of living that count as 'life'" (1993a: 16). What critics such as Suleri ignore is that the strategic use of personal narration relies on material experience but foregrounds the act of framing, articulating, and disseminating; it is a feminist political action based not on experience alone, but on the practice of making sense of it (mediation) and making it known (dissemination) through language and in context.

The strategic use of narrative as epistemological renegotiation is an important form of political activism for women: it suggests a coalition of individuals from different social locations who are collectively resisting control over their bodies. A crucial aspect of this political feminism is the emphasis on the particularity of each woman's experience: her changing social position and consequent needs, her financial and social resources, her specific decisions about treatment and recovery, and the ways in which such decisions are mediated by the information and options available to her. A material analysis of such powerful discourses shows that the strategic use of narratives which re-construct the category of "woman" can serve, individually and collectively, as a meaningful and transformative feminist practice. These stories impel the legislative lobbying, the charity fund-raisers, the appeals to the scientific community and funding institutions. They force a reconsideration of the very terms used to construct the battle over breast cancer: "woman" and "patient".

Discursive Politics: Speaking Out as Feminist Work

Your silence will not protect you
Audre Lorde (1980: 20)

Alicia Ostriker's poems in *Ms.* and *The American Poetry Review*, and Leatrice Lifshitz's collection of poems by various women entitled *Her Soul Beneath the Bone: Women's Poetry on Breast Cancer*, bring breast cancer histories out of the silent darkness which formerly surrounded them and challenge Susan Sontag's declaration that "cancer is a rare and still scandalous subject for poetry" (1977: 20). In Midge Stocker's volume, *Cancer as a Women's Issue: Scratching the Surface*, nearly twenty women of diverse social locations speak against the medical control of their bodies and the medical establishment's epistemological construction of their bodies as gendered subjects. Their writings ground themselves in particular social locations to refute a homogenized representation of women with breast cancer as uniformly abject bodies. Similarly, the collection *1 in 3: Women with Cancer Confront an Epidemic* presents forty-eight different voices which articulate a new feminist political practice, that of "Challenging the Establishment", to use a title of one of the essays (Brady 1991). In such texts, women with breast cancer use strategic narratives to produce a new epistemology of the patient. They demonstrate what Linda Singer calls the increasing rejection "of the posture of placing faith in doctors" as well as the rejection of "'being a good patient' or pious recipient who accepts whatever is offered gratefully and without question" (1993: 106).

Collectively, the stories of these women form a feminist praxis in which difference becomes an empowering starting point. As Kay Cook, a graduate student and breast cancer survivor who wrote of her experience, explains: "A collective voice is *not* an essentialist voice. It does not derive from our inherent human natures or the size of our brains. Rather, it is a choral refutation of the discursive complexity and cold objectivity with which our essential parts (ovaries, uterus, breasts – yes, I *know* that even these words are linguistic constructs, signifiers) are discussed, treated, depicted, valued, and, above all, removed, amputated" (1991: 93). Strategic narratives from localized positions demand political, medical and communal attention to breast cancer; they mobilize the AIDS activist cry, SILENCE=DEATH, through voicing a resistance to the practice by which, to cite activist Susan Shapiro, "women with cancer may be not only silenced but blamed" (1989: 18). By learning from AIDS activists and using articulation as political resistance, women are now conducting a feminist political practice which is, in Audre Lorde's words, "the transformation of silence into language and action" (1980: 22).

Gracia Buffleben's story in *Ms*. Magazine, for example, articulates how she became politically involved as a result of frustration with the medical establishment's lack of progress: "At about that time [when the breast cancer recurred after three years], I became interested in Breast Cancer Action. Its model is ACT UP. No, I was never an activist, never in my life. I joined because nothing was happening. The treatments are the same as 20 years ago, and the mortality rate hasn't changed much" (1993: 41). Buffleben's story not only demonstrates how women with breast cancer are using the politically progressive work of AIDS activists to demand changes in the funding and treatment of breast cancer, it also challenges the silence that shrouds the disease. Buffleben does this by speaking from her body: "Now, I'm bald", she says. "I wear a hat occasionally. I don't wear a wig because I feel that over 46,000 women a year are dying of breast cancer, and what are we hiding? What are we afraid of?" (1993: 41). Buffleben's articulation of her refusal to mask the ravages of chemotherapy inflicted upon her body forces recognition of the destruction done to patients in the name of "treatment". Her narrative produces a new epistemology of the patient which is, to use Linda Singer's terms, "cast in the language of *the demand*" (1993: 106).

The prevailing epistemology of gendered subjects as patients in the medical establishment against which women are speaking, theorizing, and mobilizing can be best described by Linda Singer: "To be a patient, one must also be patient" (1993: 102). Women telling stories about breast cancer challenge this epistemological representation of the female patient as a passive and non-autonomous vessel to be manipulated by a group of medical "experts". They demand a multiplicity of treatment options, a renegotiation of the relationship between physician and patient, and an overt social recognition of the consequences of prescribed medical treatment – what Dr. Susan Love describes as "slash, poison, and burn" (1990). Susan Rennie argues that the medical establishment prefers to control women's bodies through invasive alterations rather than grant women confirmation of what their bodily experience suggests: that environmental pollutants are a significant cause for breast cancer. She points to the cancellation of the Women's Health Trial, a study designed to investigate the link between consumed fat content in food and incidence of breast cancer, in favor of "chemoprevention", a study of the potent anti-estrogen chemical Tamoxifen (1993: 46). Similarly, Liane Clorfene-Casten asserts that "as a result of the continuing ascendancy of treatment over prevention, the push has been largely for expensive, often highly toxic drugs to be used in the treatment of cancer", the effects of which women are often asked to conceal (1993b: 57).[4] Such preferences for prescription treatments over prevention necessarily elide the concerns of lower-class women whose access to health care and preventative education is limited, while their diets often reflect the precise factors thought to contribute to the incidence of breast cancer. The epistemological model of the subject in medical circles, however, often overlooks the material circumstances of socially disadvantaged women.

In contrast, strategic stories by women from various social positions point to the significance of environmental factors such as nuclear power plants, radiation exposure, pesticides, hormones and anti-bodies given to farm animals, and polluted air and water. In their testimonies, women also point to the fact that the chemical toxins, hormones, anti-bodies and pesticides found in fatty foods have been linked to cancer. Susan Shapiro, in her article, "Cancer as a Feminist Issue", delineates a range of social, environmental and structural factors implicated in cancer to debunk the notion of cancer as a mysterious family disease or a spiritual message that a woman has been working too hard at her job or neglecting her family. Shapiro begins by depicting her initial compliance with the hegemonic representation of cancer patient: "Like most people, I had learned that cancer was a personal tragedy, a family tragedy; it was not a community issue, certainly not within the realm of feminist causes", she writes (1989: 18). Shapiro then links her experience to that of others: "Most of the women I interviewed expressed some feeling of being 'left out' or 'incredibly alone,' even those who had support from friends and family. I think that what was missing was the sense of being part of a community that cared" (1989: 19). In reaction against this situation, Shapiro developed a support group and publicly shared her narrative as a means to combat the isolation which previously shaped the social interpretation of breast cancer. Her example demonstrates the way in which self-consciously mediated discourses of material experiences can be disseminated to incur significant change at both local and structural levels. By strategically narrating their experiences, women such as Shapiro, Buffleben, and the many women poets and writers in recent collections, engage in a war against a medical establishment which constructs them as silent, solitary and passive victims in the hands of cancer "experts". Through a politics of articulation they include themselves as experts in their own care. In this way, women from varied classes and races are working together as committed political activists refusing to be silent.

Significantly, women engaged in a contemporary feminist praxis of strategic narration criticize not only the medical establishment; they also expose "new age" alternatives and the accompanying epistemological construction of the female subject which uncannily recalls the homogenized gendered body constructed by the operations within the medical establishment. As Sue Wilkinson and Celia Kitzinger explain, the allure of alternative therapies is that they provide an epistemology of the patient which ostensibly grants women power and agency to confront their illness. Yet too often such alternative medical practices blame women's psychological or emotional processes for the onset of the disease. The promise of agency becomes accusation, and empowerment becomes faultfinding. In their review of self-help guides, Wilkinson and Kitzinger assert that "these books and tapes say we are responsible for giving ourselves cancer; that we can cure ourselves of it; that we choose whether to get well or not; that it is our fault if we die. Individual, personal responsibility at every step is the overwhelming message of the 'self-help' literature" (1993: 233). As a polar reaction to conventional medical practices, alternative therapies place all responsibility upon women's bodies and minds with the consequence that larger structural and societal causes are again ignored.

Louise Hay's tape, *Cancer: Discovering Your Healing Power*, exposes how the operational logic of self-help guides to breast cancer make healing a performance of "mind over matter". Hay asserts that "we are each 100% responsible for every experience in our lives – the best and the worst. We each create our experiences by the thoughts we think and the words we speak . . . resentment, long held, eats away at the body and becomes the dis-ease we call cancer" (quoted in Wilkinson and Kitzinger 1993: 233). This message renders women solely accountable for the cancer and ignores the growing evidence of environmental pollutants and even recent work in genetic research. Similarly, Joy Hopkins-Hausman's video, *Cancer: Just a Word . . . Not a Sentence*, demonstrates the way in which alternative medical practices control women as subjected "patients". In one scene, Joy films an office visit with Dr. Bernie Siegel, author of *Love, Medicine and Miracles* as well as psychological and spiritual guide for many breast cancer patients. Hopkins-Hausman tells Siegel that her recent reconstructive surgery did not work: "I had some reconstructive surgery done . . . a few months ago. It didn't work. I have to have it redone." Siegel responds, "Well, it's a foreign body in your body and so you react to it. If you do it [the surgery] again, tell your body not to react, you want it there, and also you can start immediately manipulating, pressing, squeezing." At this point Hopkins-Hausman interrupts him, asserting, "I did all that – I tried that." Siegel replies, "Maybe you have to do it harder . . . Remember it's always back to you" (Hopkins-Hausman 1989). There is no mention in Siegel's discourse of the surgeon's contribution to the failed reconstruction; Hopkins-Hausman's video reveals the startling way in which alternative medical practices, while attempting to wrestle control from the medical establishment's dominance over breast cancer treatments through surgical and pharmaceutical "solutions", actually signify an equally undesirable extreme. Self-help and "new age" solutions place all blame squarely on the bodies and psyches of particular women. These alternative medicines, moreover, are often aimed at a particular social stratum of women who have the means to avail themselves of their therapies, texts, workshops, and "cures".

Strategic stories by women with breast cancer thus expose how alternative medicine's supposedly preferable epistemology of the patient persists in imposing a paradigm of domination upon the subject and is complicit with medical practices in transforming her into an abject body. The political work of women's theorized narratives is clear: using discourse to produce concrete changes in material conditions for themselves and those in their particular communities, women with breast cancer are beginning to challenge opposing constructions of the patient as either completely powerless or solely accountable. Rather than have to choose between the binary oppositions of standard medical practices and their alternatives, perhaps we might follow their example and mobilize discourse to articulate criticisms of social structures on a broader scale. We might then concede with Wilkinson and Kitzinger that "a feminist analysis of health and illness begins by acknowledging that we ARE victims – victims of a patriarchal world and a heterosexist health system, which, as feminists, we struggle against". The feminist approach to breast cancer espoused by Wilkinson and Kitzinger "continues with campaigns and community action: to change current medical, social, and political approaches to cancer, and to provide information and support for all who need it" (1993: 237–8). Crucial in this campaign is the articulation by "those in need" of their situation-specific demands and struggles in the battle for survival and quality of life.

Coalition Emerging through Difference

It's probably not surprising that gender is so strongly, so multiply valenced in the experience of breast cancer today. Received wisdom has it that being a breast cancer patient, even while it is supposed to pose unique challenges to one's sense of "femininity", nonetheless plunges one into an experience of almost archetypal Femaleness. (Eve Sedgwick 1993: 13)

By grounding their discourse in "the local", women are demanding that the strategic narratives of their material experiences contribute to a re-theorization of the subject in health and medical contexts and that their socially specific needs be addressed. As Audre Lorde explains, "Our battle is to define survival in ways that are acceptable and nourishing to us, meaning with substance and style. Substance. Our work. Style. True to ourselves" (1988: 98–9). Following Lorde, women are articulating a discourse of specific materiality to disrupt the homogeneous representation of women as gendered subjects in medical and political discourses. Roseanne Lucia Quinn describes the problem well: "medical literature by and large represents 'women with breast cancer' in mono-lithic terms, with no allowance for differences of culture, class, age, race, sexuality, or even biology" (1995: 271). The result of such homogeniza-tion is that socially disadvantaged women are not represented in statistical information disseminated by the medical establishment as "educational" material. In addition, the specific needs of particular women are too often not acknowledged. The strategic narrations by women who do not conform to the homogenized medical construction of white, middle-class, heterosexual women in their forties and fifties necessarily challenge a monolithic construction of "woman" and demand that attention be paid to the specific and diverse social situations of those affected by breast cancer.

As P. J. Viviansayles explains in an interview with *Ms.* Magazine: "My issues [with breast cancer] are different from the issues in the white community. My experience is, right now, all my bills are due" (1993: 55). Viviansayles' narrative of her social location mobilizes the materiality of her experience to articulate a political protest against the invisibility of black women in the social category "woman". In this, she follows a history of black feminist protest against homogenizing "women" to signify only white subjects. Viviansayles' means to protest is through her personal narrative: "The thing that most devastated me about breast cancer was finding this major hole in the black community, this land of the lost. Every woman who gets cancer in the black community gets sucked into it" (1993: 55). Moving from the specifically located to the collective by aligning her plight with "every [black] woman" begins the process of political action. Viviansayles has founded the Women of Color Breast Cancer Survivors' Support Group which now has four locations in Los Angeles. Crucial to her project is the use of strategic narration: "I make presentations about prevention. In the underserved community, you have women whose health gets pushed to the side. I enlighten them. It's about care of one's body. They don't even know they're at risk" (1993: 55). By narrating her experience and bringing together other women structurally disadvantaged by race and class, Viviansayles disrupts the medical and white feminist practice of rendering black women invisible in breast cancer discourses.

In *Cancer as a Women's Issue,* Jackie Winnow articulates the particular problems faced by lesbians with breast cancer: "If you have cancer, you wait endlessly for a support group, which if you are lesbian, a woman of color, working class, or believe in alternative [medicine], you don't fit into anyway" (1991: 27). Winnow uses her personal experience to launch a political criticism against the lack of structural support for lesbians with breast cancer. In this way, she highlights the diversity of women experiencing serious illness. In response to this problem, she, like Viviansayles, formed a support and action collective called the Women's Cancer Resource Center which now thrives despite the homophobia which makes funding scarce. Winnow explains: "we have support groups; we do forums and educationals, and information and referral and counseling and *speak out* about the politics of cancer" (1991: 28). Her narrative ends with a call for women to articulate, loudly and strategically, their material experiences and political agendas: "We need to be *screaming* in the streets that we will not be killed by the dissolution of the earth and make the government accountable to the people" (1991:

Alyssa O'Brien

34–5). Winnow's strategic story transforms her personal experience into a political call to action; it signifies contemporary feminist work.

Like Winnow, self-identified lesbian writers Eve Sedgwick and Audre Lorde narrate political protests against the homogeneous construction of the gendered subject as heterosexual and narrowly feminine. Their anger forms a productive critical response to the hospital social worker or Reach for Recovery volunteer who offers cosmetic advise on disguising the lack so that "no one will ever know" the difference. "I knew sure as hell *I'd* know the difference", Lorde writes. She then expresses a question specific to her subject-position as a lesbian: "What is it like to be making love to a woman and have only one breast brushing against her?" (1988: 42–3). Lorde's insistence on the particularity of her needs and material concerns as a black, lesbian woman provides a crucial disruption to the universalism in standard and alternative health practices. Her narrative is compelling evidence that a politics of articulation can work through discourse to transform the epistemological constructs of "woman" and "patient".

The importance of this work to contemporary feminism is that from such deliberate and crucial emphasis of localized difference, shared needs and agendas arise. Audre Lorde's resistance to the Reach for Recovery volunteer, for example, signifies a common theme in breast cancer narratives. Heterosexual women also create stories that strategically protest the cancer establishment's Reach for Recovery and "Look Good-Feel Better" programs that attempt to cover up breast cancer with cosmetics. In "Beauty Tips for the Dead", Judith Hooper uses sarcasm to narrate her particular response to the beauty campaign: "While this information is useful (I myself have found that long, dangly earrings can do a lot to compensate for the lack of a hairdo), it doesn't help with the real problem . . . Does the American Cancer Society imagine that a woman with a deadly disease will really feel a whole lot better once she gets some expert cosmetological advice?" (1994: 110–11). Speaking from her specific position as a heterosexual mother and author, Hooper contributes her discourse to a growing amalgamation of strategic narratives which collectively can challenge the monolithic construction of the gendered patient.

The fact that Hooper's complaint, located in her specific experience as a heterosexual white woman, coincides with Lorde's suggests that coalitional politics might derive from an exchange of particularized narratives. In other words, the dissemination of strategic stories from a local position works paradoxically to reunite women through insistence on their situated subjectivities. Both Lorde and Hooper speak against the social concern with "normalizing" women "back" into a narrowly defined heterosexual femininity through means that often entail surgically and cosmetically altering women's bodies to maintain adherence to the male-established gender norm. Their shared resistance to proscribed notions of gendered subjectivity and regulatory norms shaping women's bodies connects them in a shared moment of coalition. Viviansayles, Winnow, and Shapiro all articulate the lack of community for them in their particular subject positions. Their common lack speaks to a dearth of social resources for women with illness across a range of races, classes, and sexualities. The parallel stories speak to a need for larger structural change to benefit women from a variety of social locations. In other words, it is through the enunciation of diverse localized needs and social positions that the realization of a shared front becomes possible.

The dissemination of strategic stories thus works to offer feminists a way to connect across what are seen by many as impassible differences in social and economic situations. By talking back and educating others, women from every social strata are resisting what Eve Sedgwick, another breast cancer survivor, calls "the formal and folk ideologies around breast cancer [which] not only construct it as a secret, but construct it as the secret whose sharing defines women as such" (1993: 262). Through emphasizing their differences, women are coming together like AIDS activists to demand changes in the ways that social discourses and material practices treat them on an individual level.

Registering Changes, Looking Ahead

I think of what this means to other Black women living with cancer, to all women in general. Most of all I think of how important it is for us to share with each other the powers buried within the breaking of silence about our bodies and our health, even though we have been schooled to be secret and stoical about pain and disease. But that stoicism and silence does not serve us nor our communities, only the forces of things as they are. (Audre Lorde 1988: 118–19)

Lorde writes that "for Black women, learning to consciously extend ourselves to each other and to call upon each other's strengths is a life-saving strategy" (1988: 123). My argument here is that strategically speaking across and about differences actually produces a coalition of multiply situated activist voices which collectively challenge the control assumed by the medical establishment and its binary alternative, "new age" remedies. These two opposing medical practices reduce the epistemological construction of the female patient to abjection and foreclose the articulation of narratives that theorize experiential materiality as a form of political work. However, women like Gracia Buffleben, Susan

Shapiro, P. J. Viviansayles, and Jackie Winnow are now speaking out as a feminist response to the status quo; their words present a feminist challenge to the current state of discursive and physical norms in breast cancer politics. In this way, women of diverse races, classes, ages and sexual orientations are articulating a political message. It is time to listen.

Fortunately, the strategic discourses of localized positions, particular needs, and situation specific critiques are indeed beginning to change the way that breast cancer is viewed, treated, and discussed. Finally adhering to the demands of women with breast cancer, many medical establishments are becoming more open to holistic treatments and philosophies, thereby reducing the tension between formerly competing practices. Moreover, the previously grim irony of having to sign an "informed consent" release when no alternatives seemed available is dissipating. Impelled by complaints by women like Linda Singer, new technologies are changing the meaning of "informed consent" to be less of a misnomer. Ann Barry Flood is working to disseminate knowledge about the development of interactive video programs which "promote shared decision-making" about cancer treatment and transform the meaning of "informed consent" into educated participation in health care. In such new medical tools, even the option of "doing nothing" is rendered an active choice by the patient; it has been renamed "watchful waiting" (Flood 1992: 225–6).[5] Significantly, with these new technologies, patients make a decision after receiving education about aspects of cancer that effect their particular social location and personal history. These videos thereby dismantle the dominant social model of the homogenized medical subject by attending to differences and by using positionality as the ground for decisions and actions concerning health.

A further change is evident in recent publications by medical establishment professionals who interrogate not only the epistemological and homogenized construction of breast cancer patients, but also the means by which medical practitioners approach the disease through treatments which incur serious side effects such that, as Susan Rennie observes, women potentially "trade one disease for another, one type of death for another" (1993: 46). Susan Love's best-selling manual, *Dr. Susan Love's Breast Book*, frequently cites Audre Lorde and encourages women to tailor their treatment and healing strategies to fit their particular social positions. Similarly, Barbara Joseph uses both her material experience with breast cancer and her social position as an obstetrician and gynecologist to produce a new model of illness. Joseph breaks new ground by overtly implicating environmental factors as contributors to breast cancer ("food is political", she writes), and by debunking the discursively constructed expertise of the medical institution: "The male scientific . . . mechanistic model is seriously flawed. In this model, breast cancer needs only to be eradicated" (1996: 7). Joseph's proposed solution is not adherence to medical expertise nor acquiescence to the alternative of self-healing, but rather coalitional progress towards social and global transformation: "My intention is to share my experiences and the knowledge I've gained for the greater cause, so that other women can make their own proactive choices in the pursuit of their own individual health as well as the health of our planet. . . I believe we all face breast cancer together and we must all deal with the issues it poses, both individually and collectively" (1996: 9–10).

As these testimonies reveal, the strategic use of narrative to challenge what Lorde calls "the force of things as they are" is crucial political work at this historical moment. It is contemporary feminist praxis in process and in the trenches where real bodies and lives are at stake. These multiple and varied voices tell us that we must be wary of discourses from holistic medicines which perpetuate a model of illness, health, and healing as restrictive and controlling as standard medical practices. The stories of breast cancer activists reveal how we can move from theory to practice, and use our words, our lives, and our bodies to contest the homogenizing constructs and damaging practices that endanger our survival as much as the disease itself does. Moreover, they show us that it is from the grounds of particular social locations that we can begin to self-consciously reconstruct the "female subject" for concrete social change. Our discourses can contribute to the formation of a coalitional front against the social and political controls over women's bodies. As Jackie Winnow explains: "Although each of us experiences cancer individually, it is through collective support and action that changes take place" (1991: 27). By sharing stories for support and change, such variously positioned women engaged in a contemporary feminist praxis are making a difference – to use my mother's words – "for all cancer survivors" (1996b: 3). In this way, the strategic use of narrative signifies a progressive and socially transformative feminism for the twenty-first century. We might learn a lesson from the discourses of breast cancer activists and begin to implement their politics of articulation in other important areas under social contestation that impact women's bodies and women's lives.

Notes

1   For further discussion of recent developments in feminist theory around language, agency, power, and social change, see the work of Teresa L. Ebert (1996), Eileen Schlee (1993: 70–80), as well as Nancy Fraser and Linda J. Nicholson (1990: 19–38).

2   Adrienne Rich asserts that for many women, "the need to begin with the female body – our own – [is] locating the grounds from which to speak with authority *as* women." This feminist position bridges the gap between theory and practice by locating feminist discourse in the body; it serves "to reconnect our thinking and speaking with the body of this particular living human individual, a woman" (1986: 210–31). Similarly, Rey Chow insists on the necessity of maintaining specific positionality, what she terms "the local": "Pressing the claims of the local therefore does not mean essential-izing one position; instead it means using that position as a parallel for allying with others." Chow foregrounds the need for collective political work while she cautions against naturalizing the grounds from which posi-tions are articulated: a feminist's "own 'locality' as construct, different, and automaton means that pressing its claims is always pressing the claims of a form of existence which is, by origin, coalitional" (1992: 114). The important idea here is self-conscious positionality, or what Gayatri Spivak famously termed strategic essentialism.
    Discussing the misuse of this tactic among academics, she explains, "it's the idea of a *strategy* that has been forgotten"; a self-conscious focus on positionality avoids this danger: "The strategic use of an essence as a mobilizing slogan or masterword like *woman* or *worker* or the name of a nation is, ideally, self-conscious for all mobilized . . . If one is considering strategy, one has to look at where the group – the person, the persons, or the movement – is situated when one makes claims for or against essen-tialism. A strategy suits a situation" (1993: 3–5). Spivak's assertion elsewhere that collective social change can originate from subjects who mobilize their particular social locations for a purpose demonstrates how strategic narration can serve as feminist political action: "one can self-con-sciously use this irreducible moment of essentialism as part of one's strategy" (1990: 109).

3   Harding's standpoint theory, which emphasizes particular social locations of gendered subjects, has been criticized by feminists such as Christina Crosby for using "the personal" as grounds for epistemology (1992: 130–43). Crosby's argument, however, falls subject to the escapist fantasy of many poststructuralist theorists who, in the words of Susan Bordo, "refuse to assume a shape for which they must take responsibility" (1990: 144).

4   Similarly, Dr. Samuel Epstein in *The Politics of Cancer* condemns the medical establishment for "remain[ing] myopically fixated on obsolete 'blame-the-victim' theories of breast cancer causation [by pointing to family history, genetics and lifestyle factors], while ignoring growing evidence of the role of environmental contaminants" (quoted in Clorfene-Casten 1993a: 54).

5   For detailed discussion of such interactive video programs, see Joe Henderson (1992: 232–9).

References

Bordo, Susan. 1990: Feminism, Postmodernism, and Gender-Skepticism. In

Linda. Nicholson (ed.), *Feminism / Postmodernism*. New York: Routledge, 133–56.

Brady, J. 1991: *1 in 3: Women with Cancer Confront an Epidemic*. Pittsburgh: Cleis Press.

Buffleben, Gracia. 1993: Interview. *Ms*. 3 (6), 41.

Butler, Judith. 1993a: *Bodies That Matter: On the Discursive Limits of "Sex"*. New York: Routledge.

——. 1993b: Introduction. In Linda Singer, *Erotic Welfare: Sexual Theory and Politics in the Age of Epidemic*. New York: Routledge, 1–15.

Chow, Rey. 1992: Postmodern Automatons. In Judith Butler and Joan W. Scott (eds), *Feminists Theorize the Political*. New York: Routledge, 101–17.

Clorfene-Casten, Liane. 1993a: The Environmental Link to Breast Cancer. *Ms*. 3 (6), 52–6.

——. 1993b: Inside the Cancer Establishment. *Ms*. 3 (6), 57.

Cook, Kay. 1991: Filling the Dark Spaces: Breast Cancer and Autobiography. *A/b: Auto/Biography Studies* 6 (1), 85–94.

Crosby, Christina. 1992: Dealing with Differences. In J. Butler and Joan W. Scott (eds), *Feminists Theorize the Political*, New York: Routledge, 130–43.

Ebert, Teresa. 1996: *Ludic Feminism and After: Postmodernism, Desire, and Labor in Late Capitalism*. Ann Arbor: University of Michigan.

Flood, A. 1992: Empowering Patients: Using Interactive Video Programs to Help Patients Make Difficult Decisions. *Camera Obscura* 29, 224–31.

Fraser, Nancy and Nicholson, Linda J. 1990: Social Criticism without Philosophy: An Encounter between Feminism and Postmodernism. In Linda J. Nicholson (ed.), *Feminism / Postmodernism*. New York: Routledge, 19–38.

Harding, Sandra. 1994: Starting Thought From Women's Lives: Eight Resources for Maximizing Objectivity. In Philip Goldstein (ed.), *Styles of Cultural Activism: From Theory and Pedagogy to Women, Indians, and Communism*. Newark: University of Delaware Press, 17–31.

Henderson, J., Baumgartner, E., Chesnut, S., Driscoll, B., Henderson, A. and Hurd, L. 1992: Camera Informatica: Producing Interactive Media: Programs for Patients Facing Difficult Choices. *Camera Obscura* 29, 232–9.

Hooper, Judith. 1994: Beauty Tips for the Dead. In Patricia Foster (ed.), *Minding the Body: Women Writers on Body and Soul*. New York: Anchor Books, 107–37.

Hopkins-Hausman, Joy. 1989: *Cancer: Just a Word . . . Not a Sentence*. Video, Producer Tobe Carey. New York: Willow Mixed Media.

Joseph, Barbara. 1996: *My Healing From Breast Cancer: A Physician's Personal Story of Recovery and Transformation*. New Canaan, Connecticut: Keats Publishing.

Lifshitz, Leatrice H. (ed.). 1988: *Her Soul Beneath the Bone: Women's Poetry on Breast Cancer*. Urbana: University of Illinois Press.

Lorde, Audre. 1988: *A Burst of Light: Essays by Audre Lorde*. Ithaca: Firebrand Books.

——. 1980: *The Cancer Journals*. San Francisco: Aunt Lute Books.

Love, Susan. M. 1991: *Dr. Susan Love's Breast Book*. Reading: Addison-Wesley Publishing.

O'Brien, Joan M. 1996a: *People of God*. Lecture, Emmaus Retreat Weekend. Norfolk, Connecticut.

_____. 1996b: *Your Legal Rights on the Job and in Health Care*. Lecture, Stamford Hospital. Stamford, Connecticut.

Quinn, Roseanne Lucia. 1995: Mastectomy, Misogyny, and Media: Toward an Inclusive Politics and Poetics of Breast Cancer. In Deirdre Lashgari (ed.), *Violence, Silence, and Anger: Women's Writing as Transgression*. Charlottesville: University Press of Virginia, 267–81.

Rennie, Susan. 1993: Breast Cancer Prevention: Diet Vs. Drugs. *Ms*. 3 (6), 38–46.

Rich, Adrienne. 1986: *Blood, Bread, and Poetry: Selected Prose 1979–1985*. New York: W.W. Norton.

Schlee, Eileen. 1993 (Fall): The Subject is Dead: Long Live the Female Subject! *Feminist Issues* 70–80.

Scott, Joan W. 1992: Experience, In Judith Butler and Joan Scott (eds), *Feminists Theorize the Political*. New York: Routledge, 22–40.

Sedgwick, Eve Kosofsky. 1993: *Tendencies*. Durham: Duke University Press.

Shapiro, Susan. 1989 (September): Cancer as a Feminist Issue. *Sojourner: The Women's Forum*, 18–19.

Singer, Linda. 1993: *Erotic Welfare: Sexual Theory and Politics in the Age of Epidemic*. New York: Routledge.

Sontag, Susan. 1977: *Illness as Metaphor*. New York: Farrar, Strauss and Giroux.

Spivak, Gayatri. 1993: *Outside in the Teaching Machine*. New York: Routledge.

——. 1990: Practical Politics of the Open End. In S. Harasym (ed.), *The Postcolonial Critic: Interviews, Strategies, Dialogues*. New York: Routledge, 95–112.

Stocker, Midge. (ed.). 1991: *Cancer as a Women's Issue: Scratching the Surface*. Chicago: Third Side Press.

Suleri, Sara. 1994: Woman Skin Deep: Feminism and the Postcolonial Condition. In Patrick Williams and Laura Chrisman (eds), *Colonial Discourse and Post-Colonial Theory*. New York: Columbia University Press, 244–56.

Treichler, Paula. A. and Cartwright, Lisa. 1992: Introduction. *Camera Obscura* 28, 4–18.

Viviansayles, P. J. 1993: Interview. *Ms*. 3 (6), 55.

Wilkinson, Sue and Kitzinger, Celia. 1993: Whose Breast Is It Anyway? A Feminist Consideration of Advice and "Treatment" for Breast Cancer. *Women's Studies International Forum* 16 (3), 229–38.

Winnow, Jackie. 1991: Lesbians Evolving Health Care: Our Lives Depend on It. In M. Stocker (ed.), *Cancer as a Women's Issue: Scratching the Surface*. Chicago: Third Side Press, 23–35.

Young, Stacey. 1997: *Changing the Wor(l)d: Discourse, Politics, and the Feminist Movement*. New York: Routledge.

Chapter 9

Aboriginal Women and the Canadian Women's Movement

ANGELA SLAUGHTER

I RONICALLY, THE THOUGHTS behind this chapter sprouted from an administrative error at Carleton University that resulted in me taking a "Women's Studies" course for the first time in my final year of graduate school. I am an Aboriginal woman of Mi'kmaq heritage and was raised as a member of the Listuguj First Nation in Quebec. The primary focus of my academic research has always been Aboriginal issues. Truthfully, I was not really even sure what "Women's Studies" was about, but I was confident that I would be able to direct my research towards Aboriginal women.

Being the only Aboriginal woman in the class, I was continually amazed at the stereotyping done about Aboriginal issues by the remainder of the predominantly white, middle-class students. Although I was raised in a First Nations community, my mother was raised as a white middle-class American and she, obviously, as all mothers are, has been a critical influence in my life. Growing up in this type of situation, in a First Nations community with an Aboriginal father and a white mother, I have always found it easier than some of my Aboriginal friends and family to live with a foot in each culture. I like to think that I can see the strengths and weaknesses of both cultures through comparison.

What I was not prepared for in this class was the feeling of not belonging. These feelings did not derive from blatant rudeness or racism on the part of my classmates. Most of the women in the class, I believed, were not racist, just misinformed or plainly uninterested in Aboriginal issues. After a few months of classes, it was difficult not to notice the eyes of a couple of classmates glazing over with boredom whenever I would interject on the topic of the day with an Aboriginal perspective. I must confess this did have a silencing effect on me after a while.

The feelings of not belonging, however, were more than this. I realized that I felt like I did not belong because of my own experiences and beliefs, not because of anything that was said or done in class. The problem was in the very word "feminist". It was not a word I had heard in childhood, nor did any of my family or friends identify themselves as being a feminist. I became fascinated with why this was so. I knew first hand that there were many Aboriginal women who were educated, strong, powerful women. I looked at these women as role models, certainly, but never as feminists.

I knew growing up that there were Aboriginal women who were fighting for change. I was a young girl when Bedard and Laval[1] were taking their cases to court to fight for re-instatement of their Indian status, which they were stripped of when they married non-Aboriginal men. I was in high school when Sandra Lovelace also challenged her loss of Indian status and won her case with the United Nations.[2] We talked about these cases in our home. I knew that my white mother had Indian status because she married my father. I also knew that if I married a white man I would lose my status and never be allowed to come home again. I understood that the "smart thing", although never spoken outright, was simply not to get married. Of my father's eight sisters, my aunties, only one was married. She had an Aboriginal partner. The others were either single mothers or living common-law with their white partners. Bill C-31[3] was passed and changed that when I was in the last year of high school in 1985. Throughout all of this, never did I hear the word "feminist".

In this paper, I want to explore a few of the reasons why Aboriginal women generally do not identify themselves as feminists, and why they, as a group, to date have not participated widely in the white women's movement of Canada. More importantly, I would like to review what Aboriginal women have accomplished in their own women's movement.

There are a number of reasons why Aboriginal women have not participated in the feminist movement of Canada in large numbers. The most important of these reasons is cultural differences. Examples will be used to illustrate that Aboriginal women are starting from a culturally different mind set than white women. This does not mean that their outlooks are "better" or "worse" than white women's, just that their outlooks differ given their particular cultural location. Following my discussion of cultural differences, colonialism and the Indian Act will be examined as other reasons why Aboriginal women have become marginalized in both their own communities and Canada at large. This chapter will address these, and other, variables to illustrate why many Aboriginal women find it difficult to belong to any women's movement except their own culturally-based women's movement.

Cultural Differences

One Aboriginal woman wrote: "The overused and flimsy phrase, 'cultural differences', comes nowhere near describing the tidal waves of changes that I, my family, and my ancestors have undergone" (Larocque 1990: 79). For anyone who has lived in an Aboriginal society and has had any exposure to non-Aboriginal culture, the phrase "cultural differences" can certainly be described as "flimsy". Some of these differences are more obvious than others at first glance.

One point that must be remembered is that all Aboriginal peoples have their own histories, traditions, ceremonies and ways of doing things that are not always homogeneous with other Aboriginal groups. On the other hand, it cannot be denied that there are clearly commonly shared Indigenous themes which can be found in all First Nations traditions such as holistic approaches, non-interference, respect for individual autonomy, and different timing expectations to name but a few.[4] With this in mind, this chapter will concentrate on these areas or themes of Aboriginal culture that are generally accepted as being similar between groups. This will allow for a broader comparison than if speaking about one Aboriginal group in particular.

Aboriginal cultures stress a holistic approach that is often linked to the medicine wheel or circle. On an individual level, the "medicine wheel encompasses the total personality and can be expanded to include the emotional, physical, mental, and spiritual aspects of a human being" (Loomis 1991: 38). If any of these parts is not "healthy" or is neglected, the others will also be "hurting".

Holistic approaches are especially favored by a growing number of Aboriginal communities in terms of justice systems. They believe that there is a better way of dealing with offenders in their communities than the current Canadian systems. Differing views on justice delivery are a major consideration when pointing out cultural differences between Aboriginal and mainstream Canadian society. White feminists state that violence against women is an issue for all women in Canada, including Aboriginal women. While this is true, and much research has been done on and by Aboriginal peoples about violence in Aboriginal communities,[5] desired results and recommended solutions to this problem differ greatly between Aboriginal and white women.

For example, white communities, including feminists, tend to favor a penal system for crimes against the person. At the same time, in many Aboriginal communities, there is a continuing interest and growing use of customary laws and traditional practices of Aboriginal peoples in all parts of Canada. Many of the differences between Aboriginal and white peoples in viewing the role of justice systems can be narrowed down to differences in value systems. The focus of Aboriginal justice is on "peacekeeping" measures within the community, while the primary focus of the mainstream Canadian justice system is on "punishment" measures. Another important difference is that Aboriginal communities tend to prefer the use of measures that will allow the offender a way to redress any wrongdoing and remain in the community, while the existing system tends to "lock-up" offenders removing them from the community and their family members. [6]

Returning to the idea of the medicine wheel, Aboriginal women know that the different parts of a person as identified above in regards to the medicine wheel cannot be separated. They argue that it is impossible to punish the *physical* side of a person through incarceration miles from their roots and family ties, while at the same time reason with the *intellect*, heal the *emotional*, and nurture the *spiritual*. All sides of a person must be healed together as they are all connected according to traditional Aboriginal teachings. The pursuit of holistic healing, for both men and women, therefore is an important cultural difference that separates mainstream feminists and Aboriginal women. As pointed out in the findings of the Royal Commission on Aboriginal Peoples (RCAP), "Aboriginal women are profoundly aware of the need for healing, not just of the body, but of the mind, spirit and environment. Overall wellness is the ultimate goal. Aboriginal women spoke about healing as an essential component in all areas of Aboriginal life."[7]

Another significant difference between Aboriginal and white cultures is the role of children in everyday life. Undoubtedly, access to adequate day care *is* a concern for some Aboriginal women, but not as major a concern compared to white women. This is because in typical Aboriginal communities, family networks are often close; so many Aboriginal women find it more convenient, and natural, to leave their children with available family members. These family members often see it as their role to assist in raising the children. Urban Aboriginal women may see access to day care as more of an issue than their on-reserve sisters.

With that being said, it should be pointed out that in urban centers there often exist other child-related issues such as social services that are more important and relevant to the urban Aboriginal woman's agenda. Issues such as racism and cultural misunderstandings within these social structures that have such a direct effect on Aboriginal women and their children tend not to be a major priority for mainstream women's groups.

This is evidenced further in a story told by Roger Spielman, a Native Studies Professor, in his book *You're So Fat*. Spielman and his family, who are white, lived among the Anishnabe for eleven years. Subsequently, Spielman wrote a book about his experiences and his observations of the differences he found between the cultures:

> When we first moved to Pikogan, we observed that the kids on the reserve seemed to run around with no supervision. The parents seemed to take a hands-off approach to child-rearing, at the very least. After a while, though, we realized that the children were being looked after very carefully. All of the adults in the community shared a sense of guardianship for them. In time, we too began to feel more at ease letting our own children run free in the community. We knew that they were being watched by others on the reserve and we began to take on that responsibility, too, when there were youngsters playing in our "space". From a cultural outsider's perspective, it appeared that the children were running around wild (to use an expression we heard more than once). This is no small matter, because there are non-Native people who are in positions of authority with respect to Aboriginal families and communities, and judgments based on ignorance have had (and continue to have) devastating affects on families and communities. (1998: 39)

These problems exist because of culturally different ways of viewing the facts. Feminists have yet to come to terms with this concept.

A holistic approach to children among Aboriginal cultures is advantageous since society members accept children as part of life and do not penalize women for being mothers. In other words, in mainstream society, a woman may be a mother, a daughter, an auntie or a sister with family obligations, but when at work her identity is primarily that of a worker. Aboriginal people and Aboriginal workplaces tend to accept a woman for all her roles in a holistic sense. An Aboriginal woman is not penalized when the roles overlap, except of course when she finds herself working in mainstream society for a non-Aboriginal organization.

In terms of how this way of viewing things matters to the women's movement, Jill Vickers explains: "This difference in philosophy has limited the practical interaction between aboriginal women and most majority feminists. In general, the stance of the majoritarian movements has been to 'integrate' (incorporate) aboriginal women and their projects. Many aboriginal women have resisted this trend, especially in the last decade" (1993: 266).

Angela Slaughter

Colonialism

"Colonialism" is a fact of life for Aboriginal peoples in Canada, who have been under the influence of colonization by European people for over 500 years, depending on geographic locations. The RCAP points out that "The colonial and post-Confederation legislation applied to Aboriginal people finds its conceptual origins in Victorian ideas of race and patriarchy. Its effect increasingly has been to marginalize women in Aboriginal society and to diminish their social and political roles in community life."[8] The long term result of this process of colonization has been the tremendous growth in social problems found within Aboriginal communities. Outsiders (i.e. white feminists) looking into these communities, however, often determine that the problems Aboriginal women face are the results of gender oppression by their male Aboriginal counterparts. Many Aboriginal women do not believe that this is the case. Roger Spielman notes that "In many Aboriginal communities it is common to hear the elders express the following concerns when approached by non-Natives: 'Why do your people keep trying to tell us who we are? Why can't you accept us for who we are?' Non-Aboriginal people do too often write off Aboriginal people as 'assimilated' or 'just like white people'" (1998: 24). I argue that, at times, feminists, and white society in general, seem to look at Aboriginal communities as little brown "white mainstream wanna-be" communities. It appears to be difficult to view Aboriginal communities through anything but their own filtered cultural lens. White people sometimes believe that given a chance Aboriginal peoples will achieve the same results as white society because that is what their desired goal is. They are wrong! It must be understood that:

> Aboriginal society is not ordered around the same values, such as sexuality, equality and especially freedom of speech, as Canadian society. Expecting Aboriginal society to be ordered around the same principles as Canadian society ignores the possibility that differences can exist. It also ignores the fact that Aboriginal societies have survived colonization (and that Canadian society colonized). This is a fundamental difference between the two communities. (Monture-Angus 1995: 176)

This fundamental difference cannot be ignored. White feminists cannot impose their analysis upon Aboriginal communities. There must be an agreement that what makes a white man violent, towards other men, women, children or people of other races, is probably not the same as what makes an Aboriginal man violent. There are important differences between the experiences of the races and colonialism is a significant one.

The Indian Act

The most lasting product of colonialism in Canada has been the Indian Act which remains a strong force in Aboriginal lives even today. Enacted in 1869, the Indian Act was a colonial tool to aid in the assimilation tactics of the Canadian government of the day. It was, and remains today, discriminatory towards Aboriginal women and their children.

When the government implemented the Indian Act in 1869, many Aboriginal men strongly objected to the legal differentiation between men and women in regards to marriage. The clause 12 (1) (b) was the most dramatic in terms of discrimination towards Aboriginal women. Caroline Lachapelle explains:

> The clause specifies that if an Indian woman marries a non-status Indian (a person of Indian heritage who is not legally registered under the *Indian Act*) or a non-Indian man, she no longer has the legal recognition of the status of Indian. In other words, she is no longer an Indian. She cannot live on the reserve, nor can she hold or inherit property on the reserve. The children of her marriage are not considered Indian and have no rights to reserve life. (1982: 258)

Ovide Mercredi states that "What is especially hurtful about the *Indian Act* is that while we did not make it, nor have we ever consented to it, it has served to divide our peoples. We sometimes buy into Indian Act definitions and categories in our own assessment of people and politics. This is part of the legacy of colonialism" (1993: 88–9).

The RCAP notes that:

> Thus, aboriginality has been broken down for purposes of colonial and later federal policy into the categories of Métis, Inuit and Indian, with the latter further broken down into status and non-status Indians. Even within the status category, there are "new status" and "old status" Indians, on-reserve and off-reserve status Indians, subsection 6(1) status Indians and subsection 6(2) status Indians, and on and on. Each new category brings with it different rights and risks. These categories have little to do with culture, upbringing or identity and everything to do with administration, bureaucracy and an apparently continuing federal policy of assimilation that persists to this day.[9]

Although important changes have been made through the efforts of Aboriginal women in Canada, the Act, unfortunately, remains discriminatory on the basis of sex. It is important to realize that the discriminatory nature of the Indian Act united Aboriginal women

173

across Canada with each other and, for a time, with some factions of the mainstream women's movement.

Related to this, it should be noted that while white feminists and the media were instrumental players in assisting Aboriginal women's groups with their struggle to amend the Indian Act, once Bill C-31 was passed, white women considered the job to be complete. The issue was, and is, far from resolved. Most white women did not, and many still do not, realize that the Indian Act provisions regarding Indian status remain discriminatory against Aboriginal women and their children today.[10] Other problems caused by Bill C-31 such as the lack of resources, adequate housing, and federal funding do not appear to be priority items for white feminists in Canada or the mainstream Canadian women's movement.

Racism and the Women's Movement

Racism is a form of discrimination felt by all Aboriginal people to differing degrees. Some Aboriginal women view the white women's movement in general as being racist. It would certainly not be fair to generalize with a blanket statement that all white women who are part of the women's movement are racist. We know that there are certainly many white women who, individually, are not. At the same time, it must be acknowledged that many of the policies and practices of the white women's movement have been largely interpreted by Aboriginal women to be exclusionary at best, racist at worst.

One Aboriginal woman writes: "White women invite us to speak if the issue is racism or Native people. We are there to teach, to sensitize them or to serve them in some way. We are expected to retain our position well below them, as their servants. We are not, as a matter of course, invited as an integral part of "their movement" – the women's movement" (Maracle 1996: 18). At the same time, while Aboriginal women feel excluded from the women's movement because of their race, they do not necessarily want to be part of the women's movement. This same writer states later that "I am not interested in gaining entry to the doors of the 'white women's movement'. I would look just a little ridiculous sitting in their living rooms saying 'we this and we that'" (Maracle 1996: 18).

Some Aboriginal women can sound almost bitter when speaking about the white women's movement. For example, Lee Maracle, the Aboriginal writer quoted above, states: "That the white women of North America are racist and that they define the movement in accordance with their own narrow perspective should not surprise us. White people define everything in terms of their own people, and then very magnan-imously open the door to a select number of others. They let us in the door as we prove ourselves to be civilized" (1996: 137).

Clearly Aboriginal women who share her view cannot imagine being part of the white women's movement. Other Aboriginal women also see the problems that exist within the white feminist movement, but would possibly consider some sort of limited involvement if their concerns were met. As an example, Patricia Monture-Angus, another Aboriginal writer, argues that "The recognition of distinct Aboriginal ways of being is the minimum precondition of my involvement in mainstream relations such as the women's movement. I cannot come to any discus-sion while at the same time always having to explain and defend why I am different and deserve different treatment. This places an oppressive burden on Aboriginal women" (1995: 178). Until these barriers are addressed substantively, meaning less critically on the part of Aboriginal women and less defensively on the part of white women, then it is certain that little will change.

Class Differences

Economics also plays a part in determining Aboriginal women's oppor-tunity to participate in the white women's movement even if they so desire. Caroline Lachapelle points out that "The socioeconomic status of native and white women is a significant factor contributing to the lack of involvement of native women in the women's movement" (1982: 261). The following statistics present the sorry facts. They are derived primarily from two documents. The first was prepared by the Department of Indian and Northern Affairs in 1996 and is entitled "Aboriginal Women: a Demographic, Social and Economic Profile". The second is a more recent document prepared in March 1998 by Madeleine Dion Stout and Gregory D. Kipling for the Status of Women, Canada's Policy Research Fund, and is entitled "Aboriginal Women in Canada: Strategic Research Directions for Policy Development".

Until now, this paper has used the term "white women" when refer-ring to the women's movement and feminism. This section will use the term non-Aboriginal only because that is how the statistics on women have been collected. In other words, there is no breakdown in data between white women and women of color. The only breakdown that is presented is between Aboriginal women and all other women in Canada.

"Aboriginal women are far more concentrated in the youngest age cohorts than is the case among Canadian women at large, with over one third of the total (34.3%) aged 14 years or younger" (Stout and Kipling 1998: 15). With such a large percentage of Aboriginal women in the younger age groups, it is possible that their concerns are less likely to overlap with the views of older non-Aboriginal women who dominate mainstream feminist groups. For one thing, younger women of any culture will be likely to have less income or material wealth when they are younger. At the very least, the differences in ages will lead to a class difference with Aboriginal women being in the lower class.

"Aboriginal women tend to have significantly larger families, with almost 6 percent of them reporting having seven or more children, as contrasted with 2.7 percent for non-Aboriginal Canadian women" (Stout and Kipling 1998: 15). Larger families are another indication of a lower class as defined by Canadian society in terms of material wealth. A larger family may be deemed to be an asset of a different kind in Aboriginal communities, but it certainly does not help in closing the class gap between them and non-Aboriginal people in an economic sense.

When class divides people into different groups it usually means, in simple terms, that some groups of people have access to goods and services and others do not. Class, as a division of people, means more than simply one group being able to obtain better-quality, more expensive material goods. It means that some people will not always have access to the necessities of life such as proper medical care for themselves or their children, adequate living conditions that are not overcrowded or enough food to eat. Aboriginal people are most likely to suffer from the effects of class oppression in Canada. Vivian Ignace, an aid with the Vancouver Indian Centre, answers the question "What is the major barrier between white and native women?" with another aspect of classism: "Many of us have no mobility. Even if we could get around we are demoralized because we can't dress as well as white women" (Roach, Cohen, Bourne, Masters 1993: 248). Clearly Aboriginal women are at a distinct disadvantage economically in comparison to the white middle-class women who are active in the Canadian feminist movement.

Behavioral Differences

Class differences and Aboriginal women's lack of economic resources can lead to and exaggerate behavioral differences between Aboriginal women and mainstream feminists. For example, Vivian Ignace points out that another problem is the way in which white women view Aboriginal women: "The Indian woman is shy in public, soft-spoken.

People think we are backward because we don't speak up, but we are vocal amongst our own friends" (quoted in Roach, Cohen, Bourne, Masters 1993: 248). Some would argue that this idea is perpetuating a stereotype and that there are many Aboriginal women who are incredibly articulate and have no trouble speaking in public. While this may be true, it cannot be ignored that behavioral differences do exist between Aboriginal women and white women in the Canadian feminist movement.

In the *Canadian Journal of Psychiatry*, Clare Brant "lists a number of behavioral differences between Native people and non-Natives which, when not properly understood, he believes leads to much confusion, tension, and stereotyping among non-Native people" (quoted in Spielman 1998: 36). One of these values is that of "non-interference". It is appropriate to present another story by Roger Spielman at this point to illustrate this value:

I think the term has taken on a life of its own, one which tends to distort what is really going on in relationships between Aboriginal people. In the community of Pikogan, for example, I noticed quite early on that people don't force their thinking on you. In my non-Native tradition it seems common to hear people telling others what they should or ought to do. I remember being in the bush with one of the men from the reserve. His family had a small cabin on their traditional hunting and trapping grounds, far from the beaten path, and situated on a beautiful lake. At one point I decided to go fishing from the shore of the lake with a borrowed fishing rod. He watched me as I became more and more frustrated: I wasn't even getting a nibble. After a while he said to me, "One time my uncle tried fishing there. He didn't catch anything. Then he moved over to where the rocks are. He caught lots of fish there." I thought about that and finally decided to go over and fish by the rocks. But it got me thinking. In my experience, the common thing to say would be something like: "Hey, man, you aren't gonna catch any fish there! It's too shallow. You should go over where those rocks are to fish." In other words, "Don't be stupid. Do what I tell you to do and you'll catch fish." But the way my Native friend got the message across was by telling me a story about his uncle. Whether I got up and moved to another spot was my decision, and he respected that. (1998: 37).

Observations such as this do not reflect classism or racism in itself. However, the cultural tendency for Aboriginal peoples, including women, to be more subdued or subtle in their actions and mannerisms can be, and sometimes is, interpreted by white people as their being less intelligent about a subject or less passionate about a cause.

Another blatant example of this misinterpretation of the Aboriginal way of doing things can be found in yet another experience by Roger Spielman:

> I remember hearing Ovide Mercredi, the former national chief of the Assembly of First Nations, when he spoke at Laurentian University. The audience was a mixture of Native people and non-Natives and when he finished his presentation he invited people to ask questions. After two or three questions a non-Native woman stood up and said, "Look, I've noticed that the first few questions have been asked by non-Natives. I think we need to give the Indians a chance to ask questions, too!" After a bit of a pause Chief Mercredi said very diplomatically to her, "You don't need to worry about the Native people here. Just because they're not talking doesn't mean they're not thinking about what is being said. When any of the Native people here are ready to ask a question, they will. You don't have to worry about us or feel that you have to stand up for us. We're perfectly capable of doing that for ourselves." Eventually, when the time was right, a number of Native people began to ask questions. To me, it goes back to different ways of doing things, different timing expectations, and a different perspective on what it means to interact with people in a Native kind of way. (1998: 41)

This story also illustrates how white people, including mainstream feminists, can sometimes act in a paternalistic manner out of good intentions. No doubt the woman in the story above believed that she was doing the right thing, when obviously she merely didn't understand the cultural differences that existed between the groups.

Beyond this, Aboriginal women, because of their class, often have "more important" problems in their daily lives. As pointed out by Caroline Lachapelle: "Native women must concentrate on sheer survival, they do not have the time and resources to become involved in the women's movement, particularly to attend meetings or rallies" (1982: 261–2). Class, classism, and behavioral differences, therefore, have a major influence on whether or not Aboriginal women want to, or are able to, become involved in the Canadian women's movement.

Conclusion

This chapter has illustrated a number of reasons why Aboriginal women find it difficult to belong to any women's movement except their own culturally relevant one. This is not because Aboriginal women have no "feminist" issues that they need to resolve. For decades, Aboriginal women have organized themselves around issues that are important to them and established organizations to represent their views. This chapter provides an understanding of why Aboriginal women have repeatedly chosen to fight for their issues such as changes to the Indian Act, family violence, colonialism, treaty rights, and employment equity, to name a few, separately from white feminist organizations. Aboriginal women know what they want for themselves, for their families and for their communities. They do not need to be judged or counseled by white women of the feminist movement on how to better their lives or given goals that are not their own. Aboriginal women are capable of setting their own goals. White women have set goals for themselves in terms of the feminist movement. If at any time Aboriginal women see an inter-mixing of these goals that women of both groups have set, there can be talk of a coalition. Until that time, Aboriginal women must be given the freedom to walk their own path on their own terms. For this reason, I do not view Aboriginal women as being "left out" of the white feminist movement. To hold this view belittles Aboriginal women and every-thing they have accomplished to date. Rather I view the Aboriginal women's movement as a strong force in Canada separate from the white women's movement.

Notes

1   Jeannette Corbiere and Yvonne Bedard were the first women who legally challenged their loss of Indian Status under the Indian Act because of their marriages to white men.

2   Sandra Lovelace, a Malicite woman, also challenged her loss of Indian status under the Indian Act because of her marriage to a white man. She chose to take her challenge outside Canada to the United Nations as a question of human rights.

3   Bill C-31 refers to legislation passed in 1985 that amended the Indian Act, granting women the right to retain their status upon marrying non-status or non-Aboriginal men. Women who had previously lost status could also have it re-instated. As discussed by Olive Dickason in *Canada's First Nations: A History of Founding Peoples from Earliest Times*, it had been esti-mated that approximately 50,000 people (primarily women and their children) would be eligible to apply for reinstatement but that fewer than 20% would apply. By 1991, 69,593 individuals had been reinstated.

4   For a full discussion of this see Spielman 1998.

5   Canadian Council on Social Development and Native Women's Association of Canada, *Voices of Aboriginal Women: Aboriginal Women Speak Out About Violence*; Ministry of Women's Equality, *Family Violence in Aboriginal Communities: A First Nations Report*; Canadian Arctic Resources Committee, "Violence Toward Women and Children" in *Gossip: A Spoken History of Women in the North*; Emma Laroque, *Violence in Aboriginal Communities*; Ontario Native Women's Association, *Breaking Free: A Proposal for Change to Aboriginal Family Violence* . . . to identify just a few.

6   See Government of Canada, Government of Saskatchewan, Federation of

Saskatchewan Indian Nations, Joint Study. "Reflecting Indian Concerns and Values in the Justice System", (1985) pp. 36– 8.

7 Royal Commission on Aboriginal Peoples, Volume 4: *Perspectives and Realities, Part 2. Women's Perspectives, Health and Social Services – a Priority on Healing.*

8 Royal Commission on Aboriginal Peoples, Volume 4, *Perspectives and Realities, Part 2: Women's Perspectives, Aboriginal Women and Indian Policy: Evolution and Impact.*

9 Royal Commission on Aboriginal Peoples, Volume 4, *Perspectives and Realities, Part 2. Women's Perspectives, Aboriginal Women and Indian Policy: Evolution and Impact.*

10 In effect, Bill C-31 merely moved the discrimination down one generation. For example, if a brother and sister both married non-Aboriginal people before Bill C-31 was passed in 1985 and had children, those children would now have unequal status. The brother would never have lost his status and so his children would always have been status Indians. The woman would have lost her status and have had to reapply for it after 1985 with her children. They would therefore have 6(2) status, which would not allow them to pass on their status to their children. This would put them on unequal footing with their first-cousins because of the Indian Act provisions.

References

Dickason, Olive. 1992: *Canada's First Nations: A History of Founding Peoples from Earliest Times.* Oklahoma: University of Oklahoma Press.

Dion Stout, Madeleine and Kipling, Gregory D. 1998: *Aboriginal Women in Canada Strategic Research Directions for Policy Development.* Ottawa: Status of Women of Canada Research Directorate.

Government of Canada, Government of Saskatchewan, Federation of Saskatchewan Indian Nations. 1985: *Reflecting Indian Concerns and Values in the Justice System.*

Lapachelle, Caroline. 1982: Beyond Barriers: Native Women and the Women's Movement. In Maureen Fitzgerald and Connie Guberman (eds), *Still Ain't Satisfied, Canadian Feminism Today.* Toronto: Women's Educational Press, 257–64.

LaRocque, Emma. 1990: Tides, Towns and Trains. In Joan Turner (ed.), *Living the Changes.* Winnipeg, University of Manitoba, 76–90.

Loomis, Mary E. 1991: *Dancing the Wheel of Psychological Types.* Wilmette, Illinois: Chiron Publications.

Maracle, Lee. 1996: *I Am a Woman: a Native Perspective on Sociology and Feminism.* Vancouver: Press Gang Publishers.

Mercredi, Ovide and Turpel, Mary Ellen. 1993: *In the Rapids: Navigating the Future of First Nations.* Toronto: Viking.

Monture-Angus, Patricia. 1995: *Thunder in My Soul: A Mohawk Woman Speaks Out.* Halifax: Fernwood Publishing.

Roach Pierson, Ruth, Cohen, Marjorie Griffin, Borne, Paula, and Masters,

Philinda. 1993: *Canadian Women's Issues, Volume 1: Strong Voices*. Toronto: James Lorimer & Co.

Spielman, Roger. 1998: *You're So Fat, Exploring Ojibwe Discourse*. Toronto: University of Toronto Press.

Vickers, Jill. 1993: (Spring–Fall/Printemps/Automne): The Canadian Women's Movement and a Changing Constitutional Order. *International Journal of Canadian Studies/Revue Internationale détudes canadiennes*, 261–84.

Chapter 10

Where Metaphor Meets Materiality: The Spatialized Subject and the Limits of Locational Feminism

REBECCA WALSH

O VER THE LAST few years, feminist theorists have increasingly turned to spatial models as a way to account for the multiple and shifting aspects of female identity neglected by previous feminisms. This emerging "locational feminism", as Susan Stanford Friedman has called it, gives spatial coordinates to the subject, whose complex, fluid and often contradictory relationships to gender, race, class, and sexuality are determined by the places she occupies (1998: 5). In large part, locational feminism owes its turn to geography to the work of women of color in the late 1970s and early 1980s, which criticized feminism's exclusionary academic practices, in particular its unexamined assumption that the experience of middle-class white women could serve as the barometer for *all* women's experience. Adrienne Rich's 1984 essay "Notes Toward a Politics of Location", for instance, is very much responsive to this critique as it puts into spatial terms an awareness of the vast differences among women and recognition of the multiple and interlocking nature of oppression. Rich asserts that what is important is "recognizing our location, having to name the ground we're coming from, the conditions we have taken for granted" (1986: 219) so that we may understand how racial and economic privilege affect female experiences. To embrace the variety of female perspectives, Rich urges us to "get back to earth – not as paradigm for 'women,' but as place of location" (1986: 214). This "grounded" analysis considers material contexts in which the female subject is located, thus avoiding "grandiose assertions" about the body or generalizations about universal female experience (Rich 1986: 215). Her foundational text lays out a valuable site-specific approach that considers multiple forms of alterity, or differences that are designated as "other" by dominant society, and situates them within a web of political alliances and disconnections. For literary critics and cultural theorists as well as geographers, then, place or location has provided a useful way to track the conjunctions and disjunctions among gender, race, class, and sexuality, without taking gender for granted as a privileged and insulated identity category.[1] Compared to prospects offered by temporally weighted, developmental models of identity such as Marxism or psychoanalysis, a locational approach opens up a much more complex understanding of the subject's protean relationship to difference and privilege.

However, this emergent paradigm also raises important questions about the kinds of female experience that often remain hidden by and in space. If attempts to locate a subject's multiple and shifting relationships to privilege necessarily involve reading and interpreting context, the temptation for locational feminism is to trust that difference is identifiable and mappable, and to assume that what is mappable is most determining, important, "real". As Patricia Yeager warns in *The Geography of Identity*, "One criterion of social space is its attempt to be thematic or real, to convince us of its solidity or authenticity even when we are skeptics or disbelievers: to treat something as real is to endorse it. How do we deal with the devilish impenetrability of social space, with our bodies' temptation to misremember the categorical struggles that have founded our world?" (1996: 25). What I want to consider here are the difficulties inherent in trying to make identity "thematic" through the use of a geographical epistemology and its accompanying metaphors and tools. For somewhere in the attempt to map geography onto identity, or identity onto geography, locational feminism risks privileging and making more legitimate or, as Yeager puts it, "endorsing" those aspects of identity that are most easily seen. Friedman notes the shift that locational feminism has inaugurated "from an earlier emphasis on silence and invisibility" to "the geopolitics of identity within differing communal spaces of being and becoming" (1998: 3). However, the geographical strategies exhibited in essays by June Jordan and Minnie Bruce Pratt[2] indicate that the issue of (in)visibility remains a concern within locational feminism, and is in fact exacerbated by the very geographical mode that seeks to theorize beyond it.

The prominence of geography and visibility in Jordan and Pratt's texts reveals locational feminism's reliance upon the logic of visibility.

This emphasis upon the seen at the expense of obscuring the unseen becomes particularly problematic when the female subject in question is bisexual or lesbian.[3] That some forms of race and homosexuality are not always performed on the body has been the subject of considerable discussion. While racial invisibility has been carefully addressed by others,[4] I focus on the complicated nature of the relationship between sexual alterity and metaphorical and material space as a way of indicating how locational feminism might consider more substantially the difference it makes that some kinds of difference are more visible than others. In charting gender, class, race, and desire, locational feminism needs to be more self-conscious about the nature of what it is trying to consider as well as how its project feeds into existing debates within the gay and lesbian community about issues of visibility, categorization, subversion, and the public sphere. What this involves, I want to suggest, is a resituating of the historical within locational analyses. For while few theorists would enforce a strict separation between time and space, the temporal in locational analysis has perhaps played a role too diminished to carefully consider identities that are dynamic, unstable, and/or in a state of constant becoming such as lesbian and bisexual subjectivities.

For many theorists, locational feminism's use of space as a flashpoint for understanding the complexities of difference has meant liberation from the difficulties of defining the subject and its role in identity politics. The noteworthy contributions of Rich and other theorists move us away from essentialist formulations of identity and embrace more flexible and contingent understandings of female experience. A number of scholars have taken up Rich's geographic rhetoric, commonly focusing on the subject's embeddedness in particular contexts and analyzing how these contexts call into play multiple and often paradoxical aspects of selfhood. While Donna Haraway thinks of this mathematically as a "geometrics of difference and contradiction" (1991: 170), Linda Alcoff, for instance, uses the apt metaphor of chess, conveying the complex and shifting power dynamics that grow out of each individual arrangement of the pieces; the pawn may be weak or strong depending upon its relation to other pieces. She observes that this positional approach circumvents essentialism since it makes the subject's identity "relative to a constantly shifting context, to a situation that includes a network of elements involving others, the objective economic conditions, cultural and political institutions and ideologies, and so on" (Alcoff 1988: 433).

On many fronts, essentialism has prevented feminism from being able to devote its energies to political mobilization, coalition building, and action. As Diana Fuss observes in *Essentially Speaking*, for lesbian feminists at least, the pressure to "claim" or "discover" one's true identity before going on to generate a political stance has created gridlock

(1989: 100). This has led Michael Warner to wonder if the non-identity politics of queer theory is attractive, in part, because it releases this pressure to define the subject (1992: 17). Similar to queer theory's celebration of the freeing and potentially subversive nature of performance,[5] locational theory moves beyond arguments about identity *per se* to consider the conditions of space as determining identity. As Alcoff suggests, in focusing on position, and not essence, locational models register the need to analyze women's lack of power in social and political networks without constructing the female subject as naturally lacking agency (1988: 432). The relational field of women's studies thus remains sensitive to the shifting power dynamics that race, gender, class, or sexual desire might introduce into female coalition building, even while allowing room for women to actively engage with their environments.

And yet the spatial focus of locational feminism is tied to a politics of visibility that makes it difficult to track differences constituted by forms of female-female desire. Indeed, locational feminism is caught between two kinds of visibility often fused or conflated: political visibility (metaphor) and practical visibility (materiality). On a political level, visual metaphors are hard to avoid in describing the process by which an oppressed group asserts itself in the public arena and measures how well it has transformed hegemonic ideology and practice. Making one's identity manifest and highlighting particular forms of alterity in public consciousness have become familiar strategies in oppositional politics. Such tactics participate in larger, firmly entrenched tendencies to link vision to power and knowledge.[6] Both Martin Jay (1992) and Jonathan Crary (1993) have discussed the "scopic" nature of western modernity, marked by competing ocular fields vying for truth. In the US, as in other western societies, this cultural trust in the palpable and perceptible is vested in the epistemological habits of natural history. What results from that discipline's scientific practices is an implicit faith that the truth will come from "objective" observation. This visual empiricism, accordingly, naturalizes what it sees and depends upon the fiction that visibility and reality come hand in hand.[7] The modern scopic regime pretends that the "truth" of differences can be noticed and that what is noticed represents the truth. The powerful role that has been afforded to vision has infiltrated even the most basic unit of being – the formation of the subject itself – in psychoanalytic theory.[8] And since establishing selfhood relies upon vision, taking control over the scopic regime becomes at its core a way to stake a claim for self-definition.

In this struggle to control what is seen and how it is seen in the cultural imagination, visibility politics has come to depend upon "real" visibility, making it extremely difficult to account for sexual alterity. As socially marginalized groups take charge of this scopic regime, they make difference visually noticeable on the body in order to reclaim the machinery by which cultural status is assigned. Real visible difference thus operates as the preferred route to political agency. As Lisa Walker observes, "privileging visibility has become a tactic of late twentieth-century identity politics, in which participants often symbolize their demands for social justice by celebrating visible signifiers of difference that have historically targeted them for discrimination" (1993: 868). Judith Butler provides a telling list of the ways in which queer-identi-fied groups have used public performance to draw attention to and reclaim difference: die-ins by ACT UP, designed to make AIDS a publicly visible concern rather than a stigmatized issue for gays alone; kiss-ins by Queer Nation that move homosexuality out of the private sphere and into the public; as well as drag balls, instances of cross-dressing, and butch-femme performances, just to name a few (1993: 233). These scenes of activist intervention rely upon the ability of performance to disrupt and alter heterosexist ideology. For the lesbian, organized efforts such as staged, public performances of excess sexuality can successfully challenge the dominant discourse which has desexualized her, as Butler points out (1993: 233). Yet as important as public performance has become to queer politics and activism, many bisexuals and lesbians, femme lesbians in particular, find it quite challenging to use gender performance to subvert heterosexist and patriarchal discourse and, therein, alter the standard of vision or the frame of reference for what is seen and what can be seen.

This privileging of visibility in locational feminism – both on a polit-ical level and on the level of the body – can also lead to prioritizing race over sexuality, since the hierarchy of what is most visible tends to leave bisexuality and certain forms of lesbianism, such as the femme, in the shadows. Skin color functions as the most visible feature of alterity in the role it has come to play in racial categorization.[9] In the United States in particular, the black/white binary is so thoroughgoing that it is hard to consider forms of alterity other than color. Even theorists who attempt to analyze sexuality and race simultaneously have trouble preventing sexuality from slipping out of focus. Lisa Walker, in her analysis of the relationship between race, sexuality, and visibility, has demonstrated that theorists' attempts to consider race and sexuality together can end up privileging racial difference while relegating lesbianism to a supplementary position. Haraway's "A Manifesto for Cyborgs", for instance, tracks skin color as a definitive marker of alterity and under theorizes the equally important role that lesbianism plays in Cherrie Moraga's *Loving in the War Years* (Walker 1993: 872–3). Haraway concludes that Moraga's writing marks her body as colored, thereby preventing her, as a fair-skinned woman not visibly Chicana, from passing as white. Yet what this argument does not consider, Walker points out, is that Moraga sees her lesbianism as marked on her body first, a realization that then fuels her understanding of racial difference (1993: 871). This slippage of lesbian identity that occurs at the intersection of race and sexuality, Walker concludes, contributes to the triple erasure of women of color who are femme lesbians: they are seen first as women of color, not lesbians; their skin color makes them unrecognized within the white lesbian community; and their particular sexual style renders them unrecognizable within the general lesbian community (1993: 886). The convergence of these layers of invisibility hinges upon the assumption that visible markers of difference – skin color along with gender performance – constitute the presence of difference itself.

In texts upheld as exemplars of locational feminism, such as June Jordan's "Report from the Bahamas", analysis becomes constrained when the axis of vision encounters female-female desire, though Jordan's essay does illustrate quite powerfully the dynamic and contradictory nature of identity, as well as the equally complicated task of forging alliances with others. In it, Jordan retraces her movements on a vacation in the Bahamas and details her life in New York as a professor at a public university; she narrates her experiences as a professor, feminist activist, single mother and as an African-American woman with West Indian roots, and charts her growing awareness of how social encounters in different locations pull various aspects of her identity into play. While in the Bahamas, she expects to find identification on the level of race and gender with the Afro-Caribbean women there. However, Jordan feels discomfort at the thought of haggling with "these other Black women" over the price of the hand-woven tokens they sell, as most American tourists – black and white – tend to do:

> This is my consciousness of race and class and gender identity as I notice the fixed relations between these other Black women and myself. They sell and I buy or I don't. They risk not eating. I risk going broke on my first vacation afternoon. We are not particularly women anymore; we are parties to a transaction designed to set us against each other. (1985: 41)

What Jordan finds is dis-identification with the Bahamian women she encounters, as gender is undone by difference: they are not "particularly women anymore". Her separation from them is echoed by the repeated reference to "these other Black women" throughout this section of the essay. Here, the products of colonization, racism, and economic oppression become the salient characteristics of identification and the dictators of affiliation, effectively complicating the connections that Jordan and the Bahamian women would make with each other based on gender alone. The consciousness-raising produced by these encounters becomes a haunting refrain throughout the essay. Using the formula "this is my consciousness of race and class and gender identity" (Jordan 1985: 41) to describe each situation, she continually modulates the phrase to capture the new combinations of race, class, and gender specific to each new context in which she finds herself. Jordan is aware that mapping (dis)identification along and across the lines of difference requires careful attention to how multiple alterities interact; she warns against using race, class, and gender as "automatic concepts of connection", acknowledging that however much they can indicate shared pain, as absolute foundations for connection "they seem about as reliable as precipitation probability for the day after the night before the day" (1985: 46).

While the essay paints an important picture of the complexity of affiliation building, its geographic epistemology benefits from visuality because Jordan's heightened consciousness about difference depends upon the markers on the bodies that she encounters: accents, hairstyle, skin color, clothing. It is the "frequently toothless Black women seated on the concrete in their only presentable dress", humbling themselves to the American's "careless" games at haggling, that fuel Jordan's considerations of her positionality (1985: 40). Visible markers clearly compel her to consider race and class in her interactions with her maid, Olive, as well. In the leisure space of her hotel room, Olive's working class status comes into stark contrast with Jordan's position as an American tourist. After all, Jordan notes, "Olive is older than I am and I may smoke a cigarette while she changes the sheets on my bed" (1985: 41). Economic difference colludes with national difference and imperialism; the relative lack of power in Olive's low paying job is only heightened by the fact that the hotel in which she cleans is the tellingly named Sheraton British Colonial, and Jordan seems to bump into statues of Christopher Columbus, the western hemisphere's ur-colonizer, at every turn.

Yet while Jordan carefully considers the intersections among gender, race, nationality, and class, issues of sexuality remain under interrogated by the text's locational analysis. Though Jordan ruminates "This is my consciousness of race and class and gender identity as I . . . " (1985: 41), sexuality is never part of the list of categories that form Jordan's consciousness of her identity. In the case of her maid Olive, such signs as skin, accent, name card, and uniform usefully signal to Jordan how she might connect or disconnect with her through race, class, nationality, or gender. But what if Olive is a lesbian? Nowhere in the essay does Jordan contemplate Olive's sexuality, or directly identify her own sexual orientation. Clearly, Olive's skin and dress do not encourage

Jordan to think about the role sexual identity plays in their interaction in the same way that they do race and class; this gap is not one that the essay recognizes as hindering full analysis of Jordan's shifting positionality. In fact, though Olive never actually speaks to her, the comment Jordan imagines she would make draws upon heterosexual discourse to fill the gap between visibility and knowledge. Jordan presumes that Olive would ask her where her husband is, saying that she would "probably allow herself one indignant query before righteously removing her vacuum cleaner from my room; 'and why in the first place you come down you without your husband?" (1985: 41). Not only is Olive constructed as straight, but her question works to inscribe Jordan into heterosexuality as well.[10] The "indignant" and "righteous" posture Olive strikes thereby allows her "heterotextuality" to take on a particularly aggressive form. In the absence of visual markers to indicate otherwise, Olive's sexual options are limited to heterosexuality, which allows Jordan to take on the oppositional power that Olive has represented up to this point.

The unmarked potential in the essay for Olive to participate in female-female desire illuminates the larger issues at stake for the bisexual or femme lesbian in locational feminism. The hot pursuit of political visibility via bodily difference reifies a new binary of visible/invisible in which the femme lesbian in particular cannot win. The femme has always struggled to carve out a legitimate space for her desire for other women. The butch lesbian's readily apparent challenge to traditional gender roles, in contrast, has been celebrated by feminists and lesbians alike (Grahn 1984), and this particular articulation of lesbian sexuality is becoming increasingly popular in the media, if we are to take the success of figures like K. D. Lang as any indicator (Stein 1994: 12–13). Much to the frustration of critics like Biddy Martin, less political potential is seen in the femme because her ability to visually subvert traditional scripts of gender and sexual desire is "compromised" by her ability to pass as a heterosexual woman.[11] While some theorists argue that the femme lesbian can in fact challenge heterosexist discourse through the parodic mimicry of heterosexual desire,[12] she is only visible when accompanied by her butch partner whose presence can make her desire signify as queer. As JoAnn Loulan points out, positing the femme lesbian's subversive potential in these terms defines her through her partner, just as heterosexual women have been defined through their husbands in patriarchal discourse (1990: 90). Instances of excess femininity do not always succeed in signaling a lesbian identity to all audiences. Carole-Anne Tyler identifies the limits of queer performances that do not always signify as subversive, pointing out that middle-class audiences might take Dolly Parton for a female impersonator, but for working-class audiences she might be the finest embodiment of natural femininity (1991: 57). It all depends upon the specificity of context, determined in large part by the dynamics between performer and audience.

Jordan's essay seemingly passes over the active role that lesbian sexuality might play in coalition and action as it focuses on connections between women based on "what we can do for each other" (1985: 47). While Jordan and Olive's fictional conversation indicates the beguiling ease with which locational feminism can assume straightness in the absence of visible difference – gender performativity or signs of butch behavior – Jordan's elusive response to Olive's imagined question, however, illustrates the way in which the relative lack of epistemological control over sexual identity can jam locational feminism's determination to map positionality. For even as Olive's question, "why in the first place you come down you without your husband?", participates in heterosexual discourse, Jordan's answer, set apart in its own paragraph, undermines it: "I cannot imagine how I would begin to answer her" (1985: 41). Not an admission of divorce, nor a declaration of privacy, Jordan's confession hints that her account of her own sexual identity cannot fit into a traditional fixed model, heterosexual or otherwise. Just two years before publishing "Report", Jordan points to her "continuing self-denial around the 'issue' of my bisexuality" in her essay "Civil Wars" (1980: 110), effectively putting her bisexual identification into public circulation. And yet here, Jordan's response admits a curious inability to express herself, which acknowledges and masks the alternative sexualities that would fall outside of the heterosexual default zone. The open-endedness of her answer confronts the overall nature of gay and lesbian identity and the challenges in self-definition and self-disclosure. As Eve Sedgwick argues, homosexual identity, unlike race in most cases, is a debatable issue, wherein others feel free to question whether it is "just a phase", or how one "really" knows one is gay. These challenges, she argues, "reveal how problematical at present is the very concept of gay identity, as well as how intensively it is resisted and how far authority over its definition has been distanced from the gay subject her- or himself" (1990: 79). So even while Jordan's text reveals locational feminism's reliance upon visibility for markers of difference, it also illustrates the epistemological problem that a lesbian or bisexual identity would pose to efforts to fix its existence and chart its location.

Perhaps in placing Olive within a fixed, heterosexual category, Jordan actually creates an opportunity to stage for us her active refusal of the narrow sexual options of the dominant discourse. Jordan's position here echoes Marilyn Frye, who celebrates lesbian desire as existing beyond definitions, in a "strange nonlocation beyond the pale", dancing around "a region of cognitive gaps and negative semantic spaces" (1983: 154). The passage becomes an occasion for Jordan to leave all sexual possibilities open for herself, a multiplicity that is preserved by the absence of visible markers that could be used to "fix" her as a lesbian or as a bisexual. As part of her passionate pursuit of political equality, she claims that any type of sexual oppression or limitation preempts freedom at its most basic level. Bisexuality, she has said, is a kind of sexual freedom that is inseparable from freedom in general (Erickson 1994: 145). Her essay "Bisexuality and Cultural Pluralism" proclaims her to be a "sexual pluralist" in her rejection of heterosexuality as the dominant, supposedly singular sexual option, celebrating instead the boundlessness of sexual freedom. Though Jordan appeals to the category of bisexuality in several other essays as well as her love poetry, she revels in the fluid continuum of sexual object choice that is performed stylistically by her text:

> Given men who desire women and women who desire men and men who desire men and women who desire women and men who want to become women and women who want to become men and men who desire men and women both, and women who desire women and men both, what else could I be, besides a sexual pluralist? (1998: 137)

Just as the long subordinated clause here articulates a multiplicity of desire, so her open-ended response to Olive refuses to fix her own sexuality within the positional framework she has set up in this encounter between North and South, rich and poor, educationally privileged and educationally poor. In this respect, Jordan's resistance to categorizing her own sexuality in "Report to the Bahamas" offers a silent protest against the fixing tendencies of locational feminism.

Like Jordan, Minnie Bruce Pratt also explores the complex and geographically contingent nature of identity, and yet her essay, "Identity: Skin Blood Heart", offers a model of locational analysis more overtly self-conscious about the limitations of vision. Although most critics celebrate Pratt's essay for checking Western feminism's blindness to its indifference to the experiences of women of color and Third World women, I find that it is instrumental in indicating how to extend locational feminism's ability to account for the nonvisible. Pratt's essay records her geographical and ideological movement away from her white, bourgeois, Southern upbringing, a nexus of privilege linked to her father. What enables this careful interrogation of her own privilege, according to Martin and Mohanty (1986: 193), is the rigorous attention she pays to the geography and architecture of the communities she finds herself in. For example, Pratt's father's habit of surveying the architecture of their town with an air of propriety from the courthouse tower symbolizes his patriarchal, white entitlement; he wants Pratt to climb the tower to take visual possession of the town as he had done as a boy. Pratt declines, however, saying:

> What I would have seen at the top: on the streets around the courthouse square, the Methodist Church, the limestone building with the county Health Department, Board of Education, Welfare Department (my mother worked there), the yellow brick Baptist church, the Gulf station, the pool hall (no women allowed) . . . Dr. Nicholson's office, one door for whites, one for Blacks . . . Yet I was shaped by my relation to those build-ings and to the people in those buildings, by ideas of who should be working in the Board of Education, who should be in the bank handling money, of who should have the guns and the keys to the jail, of who should be in the jail; and I was shaped by what I didn't see, or didn't notice, on those streets. (1984: 17)

Pratt's rejection of the white privilege that she might share with her father is one of many rejections of privilege she discusses. In beginning a lesbian relationship, her desire alienates her from her father, strains her relationship with her mother, and, through the process of divorce, reduces her relationship with her children to the occasional, supervised visitation. This precipitates her growing awareness of how her position as someone who is upper-middle class, educated, and white entitles her to privilege in some contexts, while her lesbian identity and her gender deny it in others. A white lesbian living in a predominantly Black neigh-borhood in Washington, D.C., she discusses her geographic and economic marginalization from the white community and her racial and sexual marginalization from her neighbors. These complex displace-ments, significantly, do not completely insulate her from the history of her relationship to her father's white privilege, which Pratt thinks of in spatialized terms: "Each of us carries around those growing-up places, the institutions, a sort of back-drop, a stage-set" (1984: 17).

Pratt's use of space as a way to address privilege, however, does not rely solely upon visible markers of difference. One of the lessons that she learns is the danger of viewing geography as static and fixed. In looking back on her memory of what she left behind in the rural south, Pratt notes that she was "shaped by what I didn't see, or didn't notice, on those streets" (1984: 17). After gathering details about the history of her hometown's cruelty and mistreatment of African Americans, she notes that she learned "a way of looking at the world that is more accu-rate, complex, multi-layered, multi-dimensional, more truthful" (Pratt 1984: 17). Pratt goes on to say, "I feel the *need* to look differently" because "I've learned that what is presented to me as an accurate view of the world is frequently a lie" (1984: 17). Though she repeatedly points to the importance of vision and geography in shaping identity, her solution is to develop a way of seeing beyond the simple appearances presented by her surroundings.

The significant qualifications her essay places on vision inform an awareness of the non-visibility of particular kinds of difference – Jewish identity as well as lesbian identity. Sexual desire, rather than race or class, becomes the impetus for her careful attempts to strip away privilege of all kinds; Pratt's lesbianism "broke through the bubble of skin and class privilege around me" (1984: 20), allowing her to understand her connections to other women's struggles, particularly to those who are different from herself. Yet she realizes how those sympathetic connections might be hampered by misrecognition. In describing her movements in her predominantly African-American neighborhood, arm in arm with her lover, she points out the relative invisibility of her lover's Jewish identity. To the black women in her building, Pratt and her lover "look like sisters, because we're close and they can see that we love each other" (1984: 13), despite the contrast between Pratt's blond hair and blue eyes and her lover's darker features. She wonders how the knowledge of her lover's Jewish identity might dampen the warmth of her black neighbor women and the friendliness of the white people they encounter. The slipperiness of identity categorization thus exceeds the type of knowledge that comes from visible appearance alone; for her neighbors would not only assume that they are both white, but they would also interpret their closeness as familial, and not as sexual. Pratt's self-consciousness about her sexual identity makes strikingly clear the tenuous relationship between knowledge and vision. As she considers the privileges that she has given up for her lesbianism, she bemuses that she could very easily hide her sexual desire for women and thereby pass to her neighbors, as well to as the readers of her essay. Pratt observes, "I fit neatly into the narrow limits of what is 'normal' in this country. Like most lesbians, I don't fit the stereotype of what a lesbian looks like; unless my hair is cut quite short and unless I am wearing the comfortable, sturdy clothes and shoes that are called 'masculine', I look quite stereotypically 'American', like the girl in the toothpaste ad" (1984: 20). Acknowledging the dominant but single-sided view of the butch, she steps back from examining her relationship to place and location to reflect on what sometimes does not present itself in space – articulations of lesbian identity. Self-reflection, in this case, seems to enable a locational feminism that stops short of conflating political visibility with measurable physical difference. Rather, the gaps that Pratt recognizes help to mark the places where locational feminism might not be able to map formulations of sexual desire, as well as other alterities, that are not easily seen.

Beyond merely marking what might be unseeable, or in the case of Jordan, that which resists categorization, I want to suggest that locational feminism needs to foreground more strongly the role that the temporal plays in analysis of space; by focusing more explicitly on history in its interpretation of place and positionality, locational feminism might avoid relying upon visual epistemologies and reifying visibility politics so problematic for certain kinds of subjects. While feminist theorists readily note the historical and dynamic dimensions to space, very rarely have they pointed to the critical need to actively pursue the kinds of histories that might not be readily apparent or visible in the spatial scene, particularly in the interactions between specific bodies.[13] As Liz Bondi warns in her survey of the field, geographical metaphors of contemporary politics, in order to be useful, "must be informed by conceptions of space that recognize place, position, location, and so on as *created*, as *produced*" (1993: 99). If we conceptualize a lesbian identity as a continual process of becoming, as Shane Phelan has argued, then locating historical as well as spatial coordinates seems crucial for understanding how sexual identity might be determined by space. The role of history in Pratt's narrative about coming into her sexual desire in this way enhances locational feminism's ability to register difference. As Martin and Mohanty mention, Pratt's "personal history acquires a materiality in the constant rewriting of herself in relation to shifting interpersonal and political contexts" (1986: 210), and this strategy, they argue, could translate into a larger political collectivity in which the range of female sexual desire might be recognized. For Rich, personal history is also important: "I need to understand how a place on the map is also a place in history" (1986: 212). Although "Notes Toward a Politics of Location" is not without its problems, one of its strengths, as Kathleen Kirby points out, is its ability to "incorporate into our theoretical framework personal history and the particular shaping forces of specific kinds of bodies" (1996: 29). However, this attention to the importance of the temporal needs to go beyond the mere historicizing of the subject, and requires searching for the histories of the people one is surrounded by; the full solution lies in uncovering the situated histories of the other pieces on the chessboard, to use Alcoff's metaphor, in order to track forms of difference that resist fixity, continually reconstitute themselves, or are otherwise not necessarily visible.

Recognizing the limitations that visibility puts on locational analysis and looking for the histories behind various subjectivities better prepares us to consider location without mistaking alternative sexualities for straight, or reducing the sexual options to straight or butch. However, if we consider how locational feminism might work best, we also need to remain sensitive to the complicated relationships that lesbians have to metaphorical and real spaces. Since space has always (over)determined lesbian and gay identity, forms of sexual alterity have a very different relationship to metaphorical space than other kinds of difference. On one level, metaphorical space for homosexual identities, as Diana Fuss points out, revolves around the cultural opposition between heterosexuality and homosexuality, philosophically and politically conceived as "inside" and "outside" (1991: 1). Yet, the "out" position is not only the marginalized position in the hetero/homo binary; it is also bound up with the metaphor of the closet, suggesting the processes of coming out, a "movement into a metaphysics of presence, speech, and cultural visibility" (Fuss 1991: 4). It is at this level that political space and the space of being and identity become so tangled as to make fixed space of any kind impossible: "To be out, in common gay parlance, is precisely to be no longer out; to be out is to be finally outside of exteriority and all the exclusions and deprivations such outsiderhood imposes. Or, put another way, to be out is really to be in – inside the realm of the visible, the speakable, the culturally intelligible" (Fuss 1991: 4); control even over this paradox is unstable. Rather than a simple inversion of inside/outside, there are actually multiple insides and outsides that are themselves mutable. For the queer subject, articulating one's sexual identity from a position of strategic outsiderhood is a difficult project indeed, as boundaries and spaces, insides and outsides, carry with them different valences. As a result, there's no luxury of centrality from which to idealize the outside (Fuss 1991: 5) and the fixed, visible position from which subversive performativity might take shape. And yet whatever strategic potential destabilized space offers is also a horizon from which lesbian and gay subjectivity can never fully be free. Fuss notes that the "figure inside/outside cannot be easily or ever finally dispensed with; it can only be worked on and worked over – itself turned inside out to expose its critical operations and interior machinery" (1991: 1).

While Jordan's essay, for instance, refuses fixity on one level, its play with Jordan's sexuality necessarily negotiates the various and shifting levels of metaphorical space bound up with the terms of the closet. In answering Olive's question about her husband, Jordan's indeterminate response, "I cannot imagine how I would begin to answer her", may signify her bisexuality to those in her readership who already know, constituting her as "out" in this sense, but constituting her as "in" to those new to her work. For as several queer theorists have observed, speaking one's sexual identity or coming out, as Jordan in a sense does here, actually has the effect of creating more closets. As Butler notes, for gays and lesbians the work of complete self-assertion and circulation of public knowledge is never over (1991: 15–16). The effect of Jordan's essay is the prying open of these shifting and multiplying spaces, which are as difficult to see as they are to pinpoint and map.

Considering locational feminism in relation to cultural practice also requires that we theorize lesbians' and bisexuals' relationship to material space. For many lesbians, to be in a public space in the first place dictates that desire must be routed into the private sphere. Gill Valentine notes that a recent US survey found that heterosexuals commonly have no objection to homosexuals provided their sexuality is not flaunted in public. Yet this routing of homosexuality to the private sphere is based on the premise that the public sphere is neutral, that heterosexuality is also limited to private space. In fact, the heterosexual nature of public space is naturalized through repeated performances of heterosexual desire and culture, causing most lesbians and gays to veil their sexuality in public (Valentine 1996: 146). In the event that lesbians and gays do not, public order laws are often brought to bear on them in discriminatory ways or citizens use violence to "stabilize the heterosexuality of the street" (Valentine 1996: 148).

Even when lesbians do carve out a safe space for themselves in the public sphere, they expose themselves to health risks that are unique to their experience. The public spaces that lesbians claim for themselves often bring with them the dangers of alcoholism and substance abuse. In the US in the 1950s, lesbians were marginally successful at creating social institutions, such as softball leagues, that would offer socializing opportunities. Lesbian bars became an important meeting place, since they were public, roomy and yet separated out from the mainstream public enough so as to ensure privacy, where lesbians could socialize in a reasonably safe atmosphere (Faderman 1991: 161; Kennedy and Davis 1993: 29).[14] These bars fostered a sense of community and common culture, since lesbians often had to work together to identify which bars were problematic and which would be safe (Kennedy and Davis 1993: 65). Working-class lesbians in the 1950s experienced pressure to drink while at these bars; Faderman notes that "alcoholism was high among women who frequented the bars, much more prevalent, in fact, than among their heterosexual working-class counterparts" (1991: 163). Drinking and substance abuse became a particularly seductive outlet for many lesbians who had to endure the pressure of working at low-paying jobs at a time when few women were entering the workforce. Alcoholism continued in the 1970s despite the advances women made in the business world and, even with the successes of the "clean and sober" efforts of the 1980s (Faderman 1991: 282–3), it remains an important issue.

Conclusion

It is no wonder that locational feminism has used geography to expand its capabilities. As Friedman has observed, this approach has reinvigorated feminism as a singular movement unified around gender even as it wields viable explanatory power for a wide range of female experience (1998:4). Spatial rhetoric has retained a sustained focus on gender, but at the same time it facilitates considering the relationship between gender and other constituents of identity (Friedman 1998: 17). In the process, it encourages greater cross-pollinations of theory and experience based on different identity categories within the space of a single movement.

Not only does space concretize a coherent, inclusive feminism, but it also makes the strange familiar. As Smith and Katz observe, metaphor works by using one familiar meaning system, the source domain, to clarify another unfamiliar system. It is precisely the familiarity of space that makes it attractive as a metaphoric tool (1993: 69). This recourse to spatial metaphor is symptomatic of the inadequacy of language, which becomes an opportunity, as Kirby argues, for us to "flesh out" the materiality of the signified. Despite the fact that post-structuralist theorists have tried to "loosen the link between 'language' and the real'", language is nevertheless "predicated on, and enabled by, an idea of correspondence of words to 'things' – to objects, which are necessarily dimensional and necessarily exist in space, even when this substantiality appears only in the dimensionality of signifieds" (1996: 5).[15]

Yet in our intense longing for a problem-free language that would bring us closer to the objects of our theoretical inquiry, we need to confront the blindnesses that accompany spatial rhetoric. As Edward Soja points out in *Postmodern Geographies*, "[w]e must be insistently aware of how space can be made to hide consequences from us, how relations of power and discipline are inscribed into the apparently innocent spatiality of social life, how human geographies become filled with politics and ideology" (1989: 6). For locational feminism, the heft and feel of the familiar often masks the social and ideological challenges posed by the surroundings that we perceive. What is masked for aspects of lesbian desire is the fact that it is often unseeable in a specular economy that has come to prize queer performativity, and in the wake of attempts to make gay and lesbian desire visible to the public through gender inversion, the presence of the lesbian femme seems particularly precarious. More attention needs to be focused on the ways that locational feminism can account for aspects of sexuality that do not present difference by sight.

The attempt to map and mark difference hits on the tension in queer theory and lesbian studies between viewing the homosexual as a fixed, oppositional category, and viewing it as unstable, shifting, and erotically elusive. Whereas a gay sexuality posits a relatively stable identity, mappable onto fixed locations, queer sexuality, as Nancy Duncan notes, conveys a "destabilizing oppositional politics of sexuality which is associated with a fluid spatiality and multiplying and moveable sites or resistance" (1996: 246). Locational feminism seems caught between dual impulses, to both recognize fluidity when it is salient, and map positionality so as to make power relations visible, familiar. The use of space needs to be accompanied by a similar sensitivity to the way in which space (over)determines lesbian identities on multiple and mutable levels. Addressing these issues seems integral to constructing a singular feminism, geographically inflected, that is as careful in examining the intersections of sexuality with other forms of alterity as it has been in examining the intersections of gender with other forms of alterity.

Acknowledgements

I would like to thank Susan Stanford Friedman and Susan Walsh for their helpful comments on an early draft of this essay.

Notes

1 For feminist theorists who draw upon ideas of location, see Anzaldúa (1987), Bondi (1993), Kaplan (1996), Duncan (1996), Friedman (1998), Higonnet (1994), McDowell (1996), and Rose (1993).

2 For discussion of the locational strategies in Jordan, see Friedman (1998: 48–51). For discussions of Pratt and location, see Martin and Mohanty (1986), Rose (1993: 156–9), Kirby (1996: 12), Friedman (1998: 50).

3 This paper targets the non-visible aspects of female-female desire and sexual behavior that the discourse and practice of location excludes. I do not assume that all lesbians fall into categories of either butch (which visually performs sexuality) or femme (which is visually indistinguishable from heterosexuality). However, the butch/femme binary is reified by the categories of visible/invisible maintained by the politics of visibility. Therefore, I use the terms "unseen" or "nonvisible" to recognize the range of sexual identities, but where I touch upon binarized butch/femme positions, I use the terms "visible" and "invisible".

4 For discussion of racial instability and passing, see Ahmed (1999).

5 See Butler (1993; 1991), de Lauretis (1993), and Case (1989).

6 See Foucault's *Discipline and Punish* for the role of surveillance (1979). This emphasis on vision resonates with a number of years of feminist theory, particularly the critique of the specular economy of western thought in Irigaray's *Speculum of the Other Woman* (1985), and the Lacanian feminist critique of the male gaze in film studies that we see advanced by Mulvey (1989) among others. For the role of the gaze in the visual arts in general,

see Berger (1972), and for the connection between vision and colonialism, see M. L. Pratt (1992).

7   See Weigman (1995: 9), Fraser (1999: 110), and Phelan, P. (1993: 2).

8   Kathleen Kirby provides an overview in *Indifferent Boundaries* of the role vision plays in subject formation in psychoanalytic and film theory (1996: 122–45).

9   For discussion of the relationship between skin color and racial identification, see Ahmed (1998).

10 And yet, Olive's question about her husband might, on another level, operate as an indirect way to feel out Jordan's sexual preference. After all, if Olive were a man asking this question, alone in a hotel room with a female tourist, sexual attraction would be as likely a subtext as any. Olive's supposed impatience suggests this could be an erotic challenge to Jordan's presumed heterosexual status. However, Jordan's aligning of Olive with the loyal wife of the Talmudic scholar–father in Anzia Yezierska's *The Bread Givers* (1985: 42) links her to heterosexuality. Perhaps Olive's presumed heterosexuality reflects upon locational reading strategies, given the heterosexual imperative's strong foothold in some Afro-Caribbean cultures.

11 The femme lesbian has fared unfavorably when compared to the butch's more aggressive stance; since, as Pat Califia notes, femmes are sometimes seen by butch lesbians as passively finding a refuge from patriarchy in lesbianism (1992: 10–11). Biddy Martin defends the femme lesbian from assertions that, when not camped up, she is capitulating to patriarchy (1996: 73).

12 See Butler (1990: 123), Case (1989: 294), and Tyler (1991: 55).

13 Though Kaplan's work does not focus on the unique problems that sexuality poses, her recent study *Questions of Travel* astutely articulates the need for locational theory to consider history and process in order to address national, racial, economic, and gender differences in the global arena (1996). Mariam Fraser also focuses on the relationship between the spatial and temporal in her analysis of queer performativity and class (1999).

14 Karla Jay (1999) points out that though these bars did, in fact, provide a space in which lesbians could socialize, mafia ownership or control resulted in lesbians being overcharged or treated like perverts.

15 In Lacanian psychoanalysis, the "real" lies beyond signification and language, and yet can only be accessed through the signifiers that language gives us. Spatial theory, in Kirby's view, gives us the illusion of coming closer to the real by giving more body to the materiality of the signifiers themselves.

References

Ahmed, S. 1998: Animated Borders: Skin, Colour and Tanning. In M. Shildrick and J. Price (eds), *Vital Signs: Feminist Reconfigurations of the Bio/logical Body*, Edinburgh: Edinburgh University Press, 45–65.

——. 1999: She'll Wake Up One of These Days and Find She's Turned into a

Nigger: Passing through Hybridity. *Theory, Culture, and Society* 16 (2), 87–106.

Alcoff, L. 1988: Cultural Feminism Versus Poststructuralism: The Identity Crisis in Feminist Theory. *Signs* 13 (3), 405–36.

Anzaldúa, G. 1987: *Borderlands/La Frontera: The New Mestiza*. San Francisco: Spinsters/Aunt Lute.

Berger, J. 1972: *Ways of Seeing*. London: Penguin.

Butler, J. 1990: *Gender Trouble: Feminism and the Subversion of Identity*. New York: Routledge.

——. 1991: Imitation and Gender Insubordination. In D. Fuss (ed.), *Inside/Out: Lesbian Theories, Gay Theories*, New York/London: Routledge, 13–32.

——. 1993: *Bodies that Matter: On the Discursive Limits of "Sex"*. New York/London: Routledge.

Bondi, L. 1993: Locating Identity Politics. In M. Keith and S. Pile (eds), *Place and the Politics of Identity*, London/New York: Routledge, 84–101.

Califia, P. 1992: Clit Culture: Cherchez La Femme . . . *On Our Backs* 8 (4), 10–11.

Case, S. E. 1989: Toward a Butch-Femme Aesthetic. In L. Hart (ed.), *Making A Spectacle*, Ann Arbor, Michigan: University of Michigan Press, 282–99.

Crary, J. 1993: *Techniques of the Observer: On Vision and Modernity in the Nineteenth Century*. Cambridge, MA: MIT Press.

de Lauretis, T. 1993: Sexual Indifference/Lesbian Representation. In H. Abelove, M. A. Barale, and D. M. Halperin (eds), *The Gay and Lesbian Studies Reader*, New York/London: Routledge, 141–58.

Duncan, N. (ed.) 1996: *Bodyspace: Destabilizing Geographies of Gender and Sexuality*. London/New York: Routledge, 245–7.

Erickson, P. 1994: After Identity: A Conversation with June Jordan and Peter Erickson. *Transition* 63, 133–49.

Faderman, L. 1991: *Odd Girls and Twilight Lovers: A History of Lesbian life in Twentieth-Century America*. New York: Penguin.

Foucault, M. 1979: *Discipline and Punish: The Birth of the Prison*. A. Sheridan (trans.). New York: Vintage.

Fraser, M. 1999: Classing Queer: Politics in Competition. *Theory, Culture & Society* 16 (2), 108–31.

Friedman, S. S. 1998: *Mappings: Feminism and the Cultural Geographies of Encounter*. Princeton, New Jersey: Princeton University Press.

Frye, M. 1983: *The Politics of Reality: Essays in Feminist Theory*. Trumansberg, New York: The Crossing Press.

Fuss, D. 1989: *Essentially Speaking: Feminism, Nature, and Difference*. New York: Routledge.

——. (ed.) 1991: *Inside/Out: Lesbian Theories, Gay Theories*. New York/London: Routledge, 1–12.

Grahn, J. 1984: *Another Mother Tongue: Gay Words, Gay Worlds*. Boston: Beacon.

Haraway, D. 1991: *Simians, Cyborgs, and Women: The Reinvention of Nature*. London: Free Association Books.

Higonet, M. and Templeton, J. (eds). 1994: *Reconfigured Spheres: Feminist Explorations of Literary Space*. Amherst: University of Massachusetts Press.

Irigaray, L. 1985: *Speculum of the Other Woman*. G. C. Gill (trans.). Ithaca, NY: Cornell University Press.

Jay, K. 1999: *Tales of the Lavender Menace: A Memoir of Liberation*. New York: Basic Books.

Jay, M. 1992: Scopic Regimes of Modernity. In S. Lash and J. Friedman (eds), *Modernity and Identity*, Oxford/Cambridge, MA: Blackwell, 178–95.

Jordan, J. 1985: Report from the Bahamas. In *On Call: Political Essays*. Boston: South End Press, 39–49.

——. 1989: Civil Wars. In *Moving Towards Home: Political Essays*. New York: Virago, 107–15.

——. 1998: On Bisexuality and Cultural Pluralism. In *Affirmative Acts: Political Essays*. New York: Anchor Books, 132–8.

Kaplan, C. 1996: *Questions of Travel: Postmodern Discourses of Displacement*. Durham, North Carolina: Duke University Press.

Kennedy, E. L. and Davis, M. D. (eds) 1993: *Boots of Leather, Slippers of Gold*. New York: Penguin.

Kirby, K. 1996: *Indifferent Boundaries: Spatial Concepts of Human Subjectivity*. New York: Guilford.

Loulan, J. 1990: *The Lesbian Erotic Dance: Butch, Femme, Androgyny and Other Rhythms*. San Francisco: Spinsters Press.

Martin, B. 1996: *Femininity Played Straight: The Significance of Being Lesbian*. New York/London: Routledge.

—— and Mohanty, C. T. 1986: What's Home Got to Do With It? In T. de Lauretis (ed.), *Feminist Studies/Critical Studies*. Bloomington, Indiana: Indiana University Press, 191–212.

McDowell, L. 1996: Spatializing Feminism: Geographic Perspectives. In N. Duncan (ed.), *Bodyspace: Destabilizing Geographies of Gender and Sexuality*, London/New York: Routledge, 28–44.

Mulvey, L. 1989: *Visual and Other Pleasures*. Bloomington, IN: Indiana University Press.

Phelan, P. 1993: *Unmarked: The Politics of Performance*. London/New York: Routledge.

Phelan, S. 1993: (Be)Coming Out: Lesbian Identity and Politics. *Signs* 18 (4), 765–90.

Pratt, M. L. 1992: *Imperial Eyes: Travel Writing and Transculturation*. London/New York: Routledge.

Pratt, M. B. 1984: Identity: Skin Blood Heart. In E. Bulkin, M. B. Pratt, and B. Smith (eds), *Yours in Struggle: Three Feminist Perspectives on Anti-Semitism and Racism*. Brooklyn, NY: Long Haul Press, 9–64.

Rich, A. 1986: Notes Toward a Politics of Location. In *Blood, Bread, and Poetry: Selected Prose, 1979–1985*. New York: Norton, 210–31.

Rose, G. 1993: *Feminism and Geography: The Limits of Geographical Knowledge*. Minneapolis, Minnesota: University of Minnesota Press.

Sedgwick, E. K. 1990: *The Epistemology of the Closet*. Berkeley, CA: University of California Press.

Smith and Katz, C. 1993: Grounding Metaphor: Towards a Spatialized Politics. In M. Keith and S. Pile (eds), *Place and the Politics of Identity*. London/New York: Routledge, 67–83.

Soja, E. 1989: *Postmodern Geographies: The Reassertion of Space in Critical Social Theory*. London: Verso.

Stein, A. 1994: Crossover Dreams: Lesbianism and Popular Music Since the 1970s. In D. Hamer and B. Budge (eds), *The Good, the Bad, and the Gorgeous: Popular Culture's Romance with Lesbianism*, London: Pandora, 15–27.

Tyler, C. A. 1991: Boys Will Be Girls: The Politics of Gay Drag. In D. Fuss (ed.), *Inside/Out: Lesbian Theories, Gay Theories*, New York/London: Routledge, 32–70.

Valentine, G. 1996: (Re)Negotiating the "Heterosexual Street": Lesbian Productions of Space. In N. Duncan (ed.), *Bodyspace: Destabilizing Geographies of Gender and Sexuality*, London/New York: Routledge, 146–55.

Walker, L. 1993: How to Recognize a Lesbian: The Cultural Politics of Looking Like What You Are. *Signs* 18 (4), 866–90.

Warner, M. 1992: From Queer to Eternity: An Army of Theorists Cannot Fail. *The Voice Literary Supplement* 37 (23), 17.

Weigman, R. 1995: *American Anatomies: Theorizing Race and Gender*. Durham, North Carolina: Duke University Press.

Yeager, P. (ed.) 1996: *The Geography of Identity*. Ann Arbor, Michigan: University of Michigan Press, 1–38.

Part IV

Finding a Different Voice

———

BELLA ADAMS' ESSAY, *Feminism and the Aesthetic*, treats the theoretical and political problems that the concept of the aesthetic raises for feminism, particularly Anglo-American feminisms. Adams explores why feminists are divided into pro- and anti-aesthetic camps and the implications for feminist theory and practice of arguing the possibility of a specific feminine aesthetic versus either its unfeasibility or undesirability. Over and against a critique of the work of the prominent feminist linguist Rita Felski, who argues the impossibility of developing a feminist aesthetic, Adams asserts that a progressive feminism cannot do without a theory of the text and a rhetoric that seeks to understand the complex relationship between women's writing and the world of actions and events. The essay offers insights into how feminists may negotiate between their epistemologies and their politics so that they reliably correspond to the full range of female identities and experiences.

Bodily Transactions: Jean Genet in the Feminist Debate explores the diverse ways in which the work of Genet has been appropriated by Continental and Anglo-American feminisms. The thrust of Liz Barry's argument focuses on French feminist Hélène Cixous' use of Genet, especially how it informs her theory of écriture féminine, and what she describes as the more pragmatic treatment Genet receives from Kate Millet. The essay draws attention to the highly problematic absence of the material female body from both Cixous' and Millet's reading of Genet. Neither the poststructuralist textual body identified by Cixous nor the equally abstract social body highlighted by Millet as marking the feminine in Genet, Barry argues, ultimately has much to do with the lives of women. She contends that a reliance on Genet, a male writer with scant interest in female experience, ultimately radically shortchanges the feminist cause. For a reliance on this kind of exclusionary model renders it more difficult for feminist thought to progressively address differences among real women's experiences.

———

Michele Hunter's *"Doing" Judith: Race, Mixed Race and Performativity* problematizes Judith Butler's seminal theory of gender as performance. This essay seeks to rework Butler's theory by revising it in color. Hunter persuasively argues that it is only from a reconfigured racially-centered perspective, one that allows for the complexities of race/gender epistemologies, that the profound liberatory possibilities of Butler's theory can begin to be realized for feminist theory and practice.

In *Mary Wollstonecraft: Feminist, Lesbian or Transgendered?* Ashley Tauchert outlines the degree to which understandings of Wollstonecraft's "maternal" status for feminism stands as radically challenged by feminist theory that has attempted to come to terms with the proliferation of queer identities in the 1990s. The essay explains how Wollstonecraft has been firmly situated as the "mother" of Anglophone feminism since the suffrage movement and that she has been routinely depicted by second-wave feminists as an icon and historical mentor for feminist representations of women's social and sexual roles. Therefore, Tauchert argues, when the challenge to Wollstonecraft's maternal status is followed through to a conclusion, it offers feminism a new vision of the feminist subject, one that allies partial female-embodied identities with "feminist claims on behalf of 'woman'".

Chapter 11

Feminism and the Aesthetic

BELLA ADAMS

T
HE 1990s SAW a number of English-speaking radical intellectuals "endors[ing] the return of the aesthetic, not in some enfeebled academic condition but in the enlarged form of a politics of culture" (Regan 1992: 15). Endorsement was justified because this philosophical category apparently empowered ideology critique. More specifically, an enlarged aesthetic unmasks the ideological underpinnings of dominant discourses and "offers a generous utopian image of reconciliation" (Eagleton 1990: 9). Whether it occurs between men and women or between linguistic and natural reality, reconciliation is assumed fundamental to radical theoretico-political critique. Although this understanding of the aesthetic is dominant among a number of radical intellectuals, it overlooks the complex debate among feminist scholars regarding philosophical aesthetics. The latter, particularly those associated with Anglo-American feminism, either ratify or resist the aesthetic. For instance, Hilde Hein and Carolyn Korsmeyer (1990: 4) affirm a feminine aesthetic, albeit provisionally. In marked contrast to this, Rita Felski argues that "we need to go 'beyond feminist aesthetics'" (1995: 431). Contradictory responses such as these draw attention to the fact that the aesthetic is a problematic category for feminism.

The first part of this discussion involves an analysis of why it is that some feminists say "yes" and other feminists say "no" to the aesthetic. This analysis also necessitates examining the aesthetic as understood in ancient, medieval and modern philosophies. Felski's contribution to the debate about philosophical aesthetics constitutes the second part of this discussion. *Beyond Feminist Aesthetics*, along with two of her later essays, is targeted because it articulates a dominant assumption among feminist scholars. In asking whether "'feminism' and 'aesthetics' [can] be brought together, should they be, and what is the value or cost of such a reconciliation" (Felski 1994: 203), the assumption is that the aesthetic is simply a matter of choice for feminists. Whichever answer they choose is beside the point because both "yes" and "no" presuppose the possibility of exteriority regarding the aesthetic. As it turns out, this philosophical category is interior to feminist theoretico-political critique. The third part of this discussion problematizes moving beyond and, for that matter, returning to the aesthetic because it really already informs "some of our deepest, most 'natural' and perhaps . . . ineradicable ideas about language and experience" (Norris 1988: 15). Its ineradicability seems to imply that the aesthetic is not susceptible to critique in the sense that feminists can be either for or against it.

However, the final part of this discussion proposes that critique is possible if feminism responds to the linguistic workings of the aesthetic, with Paul de Man's "'critical-linguistic analysis' of 'aesthetic ideology'" (Warminski 1996: 1) providing the theoretical model. This movement towards de Man raises a problem because his preoccupation with linguistic questions seems incompatible with a feminism that focuses on women's experiences, particularly if binary logic is assumed. However, de Man's understanding of the complex, if not contradictory, relationship between linguistic and natural reality, and the part played by rhetoric in negotiating this relationship, promotes theoretico-political insights that feminism cannot (afford to) exclude. Indeed, if feminism is going to "unmask . . . ideological aberrations, as well as . . . account for their occurrence" (De Man 1986: 11) in both patriarchal and feminist discourses, it has no alternative but to address linguistic questions. This is because these ideologies have their bases in language. More specifically, the rhetorical dimension of language is aestheticized so that these ideologies can reliably mean and reference. Rhetoric also resists the aesthetic reconciliations that it makes possible, ensuring that ideological aberrations, whether patriarchal or feminist, are vulnerable to a radical theoretico-political critique. The fact that resistance is as ineradicable as the aesthetic itself does not prevent feminists from making proclamations about "the woman" and so on. Rather, "the woman" is strategically negotiated with an insight into its linguistic and ideological underpinnings. Feminism thus realized is vigilant about the implications of its own project, especially with respect to the cost or value of aesthetically reconciling linguistic and natural reality. All in all, then, the ideological category of the aesthetic cannot be excluded from feminism, although it is liable to a strategic negotiation.[1] Strategy acknowledges that the aesthetic is both ineradicable and impossible, which in turn makes certain a future for feminist debate.

Why do feminists either endorse or exclude the philosophical category of the aesthetic? This question necessitates a discussion of the way in which the aesthetic is formulated by the western philosophical tradition. Although this tradition is not a homogenous entity, a general trend is discernible regarding the relationship between the cognitive and the aesthetic. More specifically, this relationship is hierarchical, organized according to the dictates of binary logic. The inequality between cognition and aesthetics is suggested by the fact that the latter receives less attention than "'hard core' . . . philosophy that includes metaphysics, epistemology, and philosophy of science" (Hein and Korsmeyer 1990: 1). Its inferior status is reinforced because the aesthetic is given the task of negotiating a realm that is typically underprivileged by western philosophy, namely the realm of materiality: "things, sensations . . . the business of affections and aversions . . . and all that arises from our most banal, biological insertion into the world" (Eagleton 1990: 13). As it turns out, this realm is also cast as feminine, which helps to generate the notion that "the aesthetic is a woman" (Armstrong 1993: 222). Following this binarized logic, a small, soft, material and feminine aesthetic is set against a large, hard, immaterial and masculine cognition. The notion that "reason and form are aligned with maleness and formlessness and matter are aligned with femaleness" (Rooney 1991: 79) constitutes a norm for the western philosophical tradition from Pythagoras to the present day. Phyllis Rooney succinctly documents the concept of the feminine as it is represented by ancient, medieval and modern philosophies, reinforcing the point that aesthetic theory is up against a project that is largely opposed to a feminized materiality.[2] In order to achieve the privilege of objectivity, these philosophies ultimately adopt a policy of exclusion in relation to that which disrupts cognition's capacity to mean reliably. Not only do they exclude worldly materiality, these philosophies also attempt to exclude the materiality of the word from their respective analyses. That the word is material owes much to de Man, with the rhetorical dimension of language in particular rigidly resisting western philosophy's endeavour to formulate meaning once and for all.

Back as far as Plato, matters related to both perception and poetry problematize the formation of an Ideal State based on *theoria*. From a theoretical viewpoint, they are associated with the visible realm of appearances. The fact that the senses deceive and the allegorical deludes compels Plato to exclude both from ancient philosophy. As he remarks in relation to poetic representation, "[it] had better be buried in silence" (Plato 1888: 60). The "burial" of sensible objects, shadows and reflections is assumed to make possible cognition of "the things themselves, which can only be seen with the eye of the mind" (Plato 1888: 212). At the same time, however, "burial" ensures that neither perception nor poetry is limited by Plato's Ideal State, potentially affording them the privilege of objectivity. For this reason, Plato manages their "exhumation", which in turn influences the development of two distinct areas of philosophy – *aisthesis* and the philosophy of art. Management helps to ensure that materiality, whether experiential or linguistic, does not trouble ancient philosophy's cognition of the intelligible realm of forms. Censorship is Plato's preferred means of dealing with the allegorical: "let the censors receive any tale of fiction which is good, and reject the bad" (1888: 59). It is of no small consequence that bad fiction in part represents woman, and a sensuous woman at that.[3] Her deficiency in most matters also helps to ensure that woman and all she represents is designated as "the *other* of reason, and the *other* of philosophical discourse" (Rooney 1991: 95). According to this perspective, pre-modern philosophies, including those that apparently acknowledge perception, poetry and femininity, ultimately exclude matters related to the visible realm by rendering them compatible with the intelligible realm.

Modern philosophies apparently offer a different understanding of the relationship between cognition and aesthetics. As Terry Eagleton remarks, "the aesthetic . . . show[s] signs of overreaching its humble status of handmaid of reason" (1990: 110). Rational investigation is limited because it empties materiality of its content, a limitation that German idealism attempts to avoid by investing heavily in the modern category of the aesthetic. Investment is justified because the aesthetic makes possible the link between philosophical discourse and sensuous experience. This investment is also significant from a feminist viewpoint: "the aesthetics of Enlightenment Europe . . . first made the feminine visible, as a topos in philosophical discussion" (Armstrong 1993: 221). That a feminized materiality is theoretically valuable seems to upset the long-standing authority of philosophical discourses committed to masculine immateriality. Modern philosophers tend to respond to this upsetting situation by affirming the aesthetic and, for that matter, "the woman", albeit in terms of an appropriation. For example, Immanuel Kant provides an effective way of minimizing the upset generated by a feminized materiality when he concedes that woman "has as much understanding as the male", although it is considered "beautiful" and not "deep" (1995: 581). This difference between the sexes is important because it functions to protect man's high insights from woman's infantile, trivial, useless and pleasure-seeking philosophizing.[4] Were she to reflect in a manner more properly befitting a man, woman would "always do very poorly". This is because it would be "contrary to nature's will" (Kant 1995: 586). In other words, woman is permitted to participate in the modern philosophical enterprise as long as she agrees to her feminization. She is not really doing philosophy proper since her meditation is neither deep nor long sustained, but at least beautiful philosophizing keeps woman entertained and, most importantly, quiet. Like the picture of a naked woman in a gentleman's club, the presence of the fair sex in modern philosophy is "a fine thing as long as it is kept in its proper place" (De Man 1996: 36).

Following the logic of the last point, it seems that the aesthetic does not come to terms with "real" woman and all that she represents. In order to avoid the scandal of engaging its other on equal terms, modern philosophy offers an abstract picture of a feminized materiality, ensuring also that woman's participation occurs in straitened circumstances. Far from moving beyond its own abstractions via the aesthetic, modern philosophy renders particularity ascetic. With otherness asceticized from the outset, radical theoretico-political critique looks unlikely. The reliability of modern philosophy's method, along with its ability to determine the facts of materiality, does not seem compromised by matters related to the aesthetic. According to this perspective, reason has found a "way of penetrating the world of perception, but [without] . . . put[ting] at risk its own absolute power" (Eagleton 1990: 15). Furthermore, the discontinuity between picture and referent is carefully effaced, with the aesthetic functioning to reconcile these two different entities. Aesthetic reconciliation is important because it renders modern philosophy all-inclusive, representing both the cognitive and the aesthetic on its own terms. Critique is in this way pre-empted; it is as improbable as the appearance of a woman in a gentleman's club, and as inconceivable as the picture of a naked woman speaking out about her objectified status.

That the aesthetic ultimately serves the interests of a male-dominated philosophy, one that is responsible for the hierarchical arrangement that imagines form as masculine and matter as feminine, gives Felski good reason to exclude this modern philosophical category from feminism. The idea that "the aesthetic is a woman" (Armstrong 1993: 222) is ultimately compatible with the logic of patriarchal ideology, a logic that feminism is supposed to problematize. However, it is also the case that a reasoned aesthetic relates feebly, if at all, to materiality, regardless of reason's attempt to create the opposite illusion by rendering itself immaterial. The difference that a feeble or a non-existent relationship implies is exploited by those feminists who endorse "the aesthetic as that one final realm which has not (cannot be) subsumed into reason" (Ingrid Richardson in Felski 1995: 437). It also empowers feminists to highlight the limitations of an enfeebled aesthetic, limitations that make plain its ideological underpinnings. Even when western philosophies claim not to be limited by ideology, whether autonomy is achieved via the cognitive or the aesthetic, they are ideological. This is not simply because autonomy is identified as a patriarchal concept; it is also because "we are never so much 'in' ideology as when we think ourselves to be 'outside' it" (Warminski 1996: 10). Indeed, inside/outside is a metaphor, functioning reliably only if an ideological understanding of the rhetorical dimension of language is assumed. As significant as the argument is for a feminist analysis of philosophical aesthetics, a significance that Felski acknowledges only later, she does not abandon her original policy of exclusion regarding the aesthetic. It is Felski's contention that the abstract philosophical category of the aesthetic is incompatible with a feminist discourse that is concerned with the particularities of women's experiences. Not only is it limited both theoretically and politically, the aesthetic is also problematic with respect to literature, particularly feminist literature. Indeed, this aesthetic form is encumbered by the category of the aesthetic because the latter ensures the separation of literature from political matters, a separation that generates problems for a feminist literary critic like Felski.

According to Felski, "'feminist aesthetics' [is] any theoretical position which argues a necessary or privileged relationship between female gender and a particular kind of literary structure, style, or form" (1989: 19). By any theoretical position she means "feminist formalism", which "implausibl[y] . . . claim[s] that aesthetic radicalism equals political radicalism" (Felski 1994: 205; 1989: 161). In other words, the form women's writing assumes is not sufficient to identify it as feminist. Contesting the notion that formal complexity, as it occurs in modernist, postmodernist and deconstructive texts, is necessarily radical *vis-à-vis* patriarchal ideology, Felski asserts that accessible, comprehensible and presumably (non-classic[5]) realist forms are more enabling for feminism. This is because realism "relate[s] . . . to the lives of large numbers of women, [and] stresses the issue of political content" (Felski 1989: 6). It is worth noting that Felski's dialecticism apparently prevents a total rejection of feminist formalism. In relation to feminist literature, for example, she defines it as "all those texts that reveal a critical awareness of women's subordinate position and of gender as a problematic category, *however* this is expressed" (1989: 14; my emphasis). This remark aside, the fact that the dialectic is a hierarchical concept compels Felski to privilege "'instrumental' [over] 'aesthetic' theories of the text" (1989: 3). The "aesthetic" or formalist theories that emerge from *l'écriture féminine* in particular are no match for a theory like Felski's, which is based on something more substantial than "metaphors, analog[ies] . . . and homologies" (1989: 5, 8). In short, then, Felski's "view is that there exists no necessary relationship between feminism and experimental form, and that a text can thus be defined as feminist only insofar as its content or the context of its reception promote such a reading" (1989: 31–2).

Rather than reversing the logic of Felski's argument by citing examples that contradict her view of specific literary genres, this discussion stays with Felski's texts. More specifically, it promotes a critique that radically problematizes her theorization of the aesthetic, a theorization that also underpins her claims about both avant-gardism and realism. As it turns out, this critique acknowledges that Felski is right when she remarks that the rhetorical dimension of language renders avant-garde forms feminist. Rhetoric's involvement makes certain that "[t]here is no . . . necessary connection between symbolic transgression and political transgression, between stylistic rupture and processes of social change" (Felski 1995: 439). Felski supports this remark by arguing that *l'écriture féminine*'s "canon" of "esoteric" texts is off-limits to large numbers of women, compromising the radical possibilities of experimental form. Further, French feminism offers a reductive understanding of femininity, along with "generat[ing] intense anxiety by claiming that women's writing must be radically *other* than anything which has gone before" (Felski 1989: 6, 43–4). French feminism is also questionable insofar as its emphasis on the indeterminacy of language, a rhetorically generated indeterminacy, compromises the articulation of a determinate politics. Felski's charge of conservatism, if not apoliticism, also makes sense in relation to *l'écriture féminine*'s "aesthetic" theory, which apparently excludes women's experiences by analyzing formal linguistic structures instead, notably tropes and figures.

According to Felski, then, two main problems emerge from the "aesthetic" theory favoured by the feminist formalists working in France. First, form is not in itself sufficient to render women's writing feminist. This is less because the rhetorical dimension of language moves unreliably and more because both content and context properly function to ensure that women's writing is feminist. Second, rhetoric is unlikely to function substantially with respect to women's emancipation: "It is still not clear *why* it is so important to show that certain literary practices break up the structures of language, when they seem to break up little else" (Toril Moi in Felski 1989: 6). All in all, then, Felski argues that "aesthetic" theory is problematic because it overestimates the rhetorical dimension of language. Rhetoric is overestimated when it is assumed to secure a necessary link between formal complexity, a feminist meaning and women's experience. The transgressive possibilities of rhetoric are also overestimated. However, Felski's point about overestimation only makes sense if a naive binary opposition is assumed between linguistic and natural reality. This is not to say that language and experience are identical; in point of fact, the two are radically different. However, "[t]his does not mean that . . . narratives are not part of the world and of reality; their impact upon the world may well be all too strong for comfort" (De Man 1986: 11). In other words, there is a discontinuous relationship between language and experience. For example, "the woman" comes into being via language, sharing no substantial relationship with women apart from structuring their lives. In relation to "the woman" as imagined by western philosophy, say, it affects women theoretically, politically, economically and so on. Feminism needs to understand this relationship of discontinuity if it is to "progress from purely linguistic analysis to questions which are really already of a political and ideological nature" (De Man 1986: 121).

More specifically, it is impossible for language to function reliably as regards meaning and reference because of the difference between linguistic and natural reality and because of the unreliable movement of rhetoric. Commenting on this predicament, de Man discusses "the impossibility for . . . language . . . to appropriate anything, be it as consciousness, as object, or as a synthesis of both" (1979: 47). In relation to feminism, this predicament renders problematic "feminist literature". The bringing together of these two different entities is impossible once and for all, as is suggested by the debate among feminists regarding what constitutes "feminist literature". It is also worth noting the impossibility of eradicating the idea of "linguistic structures [as] somehow truly consubstantial with the world of natural processes and forms" (Norris 1988: 14). At once impossible and ineradicable, appropriation is nevertheless "a mere *effect* which language can perfectly well achieve, but which bears no substantial relationship . . . to anything beyond that particular effect" (De Man 1986: 10). For example, catachresis enables feminism to designate "feminist literature". That this literature refers to female experience depends on deixis, a rhetorical effect that makes possible referentiality. The assumption that these effects function reliably constitutes an ideological understanding of the rhetorical dimension of language. It is ideological insofar as it leaves unacknowledged rhetoric's ability to "take you in a completely different direction" (De Man 1986: 87). In short, tropes and figures enable reconciliations that they also have the potential to disable. The disabling dimension of rhetoric raises problems for certain feminists, risking the critique of patriarchal ideology, along with jeopardizing the utopian possibility of harmony, whether between language and experience or between women. Feminism thus realized needs to assume that rhetoric functions reliably, anything else would seem to make it "epistemologically highly suspect and . . . ethically and politically shameful" (De Man 1986: 10). Given this criticism, it is hardly surprising that certain feminists privilege an understanding of rhetoric that takes for granted its capacity to direct them towards a particular meaning and a particular referent. This understanding of rhetoric has its basis in the aesthetic. The fact that the aesthetic masks the way in which tropes and figures move unreliably renders it an ideological category. From this perspective, the aesthetic reconciliation of linguistic and natural reality proves problematic: "whenever the aesthetic is invoked as an appeal to clarity and to control, . . . a great deal of caution is in order" (De Man 1986: 64).

The reasons for de Man's cautionary advice become apparent in relation to Felski's discussion of "aesthetic" or formalist theory. In some respects, both advocate a critical attitude regarding the aesthetic. However, there are also crucial points of difference. Felski demands that feminism move beyond the aesthetic, a situation that de Man finds impossible because this ideological category is built into ideas about language and experience. That it is a built-in constituent of all theories, de Man's and Felski's included, would seem to make the aesthetic invulnerable to critique were it not for the fact that vigilance regarding its linguistic workings unsettles aesthetic reconciliations. Rather than responding to the way in which tropes and figures "avoid and resist the reading they advocate" (De Man 1986: 19), Felski marginalizes the matter of form. Admittedly, she is insightful about the affects of French feminism, notably the discomfort generated by formal complexity. However, Felski does not apply this insight to her own argument. In claiming that both content and context render literature properly feminist, she unwittingly assumes an aesthetic ideology. That this literature is realist, utilizing the apparently more stable trope of metonymy, perhaps explains her oversight as regards the aesthetic and, indeed, the rhetorical dimension of language. However, it is also the case that Felski's attempt to exclude the aesthetic from an "instrumental" theory is destined to fail because her concern[6] with "'hermeneutic' presuppositions depend[s] on the category of the 'aesthetic', indeed, on a certain 'aestheticization', to negotiate the passage between formal linguistic structures and the meaning of the literary texts [she] interpret[s]" (Warminski 1996: 2). The idea that it is possible to say anything at all about either the content or the context of literary language, irrespective of what is actually said, mistakenly assumes the smooth running of rhetorical effects, including metonymy. In this respect, then, Felski's details about what makes literature feminist are beside the point because underpinning them is an unacknowledged assumption, one that takes for granted the possibility of both meaningfulness and referentiality in relation to a formal linguistic structure. De Man remarks on this problematic: "Language can only be about something such as [wo]man, but in being about [wo]man, it can never know whether it is about anything at all including itself, since it is precisely the *aboutness*, the referentiality, that is in question" (1979: 161). In short, aboutness is a rhetorical effect, only becoming reliable in terms of an aesthetic ideology. From this perspective, the aesthetic is ineradicable, even informing a theory that claims to move beyond it.

Felski's theory also depends on rhetoric to reconcile linguistic and natural reality, in spite of an aversion to metaphors, homologies and analogies. That she successfully completes this task raises a theoretico-political problem, suggesting also that Felski underestimates the discomfort brought about by her own texts on the lives of women, whether they constitute the majority or a minority. In Felski's opinion, this minority group of women comprises of elite feminists who experiment with form apart from political matters. However, it is also the case that "minority" women from non-white races engage a postmodern style in their literature. Perhaps small numbers of women, however this group is formulated, are worth excluding if (the) majority (of) women are enabled. Perhaps the feminist critique of patriarchal ideology is the main issue for Felski, even if it occurs at the expense of the radically other. If the radically other is understood as both linguistic and experiential, an understanding that relies on a catachresis, then it is possible to argue that much is at stake in Felski's analysis. Not only does the exclusion of the rhetorical dimension of language, along with a minority of women, raise serious epistemological and ethico-political questions, it also leaves unacknowledged the way in which the other of Felski's discourse resists marginalization. As regards the matter of rhetoric, it resists her attempt to render it immaterial. How can Felski exclude that which enables her aesthetic reconciliation of linguistic and natural reality? Moreover, how can she exclude tropes and figures when they are the only material available, despite their capacity "to confuse the materiality of the signifier with the materiality of what it signifies[?]" (De Man 1986: 11). In short, the radically other, whether linguistic or experiential, resists Felski's effort to exclude it from feminism.

Rather than arguing for an all-inclusive feminism, "which can . . . in the long run lead to totalitarianism" (Spivak 1990: 118), this discussion moves in the direction of a critical-linguistic analysis. This analysis acknowledges that aesthetic reconciliation is at once ineradicable and impossible. In other words, the aesthetic is susceptible to a strategic negotiation. A strategic aesthetic compels feminists to acknowledge that they "*are* committed to th[is] concept, whether [they] acknowledge it or not". Since it "is irreducible, . . . let us become vigilant about our own practice and use [the aesthetic] as much as we can rather than make the totally counter-productive gesture of repudiating it" (Spivak 1990: 11). On the one hand, a strategic aesthetic achieves some control with respect to the rhetorical dimension of language. Feminism needs to and, indeed, has to assume that tropes and figures function reliably for the sake of theoretico-political critique. Without this ideological assumption, feminism cannot assert that a formal linguistic structure "is" feminist, let alone offer a critique of patriarchal ideology. Moreover, a strategic aesthetic demands that feminism acknowledge its basis in language, which allows it to use various tropes and figures for the purposes of self-empowerment. For instance, "paleonomy – that is to say, the charge which words carry on their shoulders" (Spivak 1990: 25) is liable to a feminist appropriation. "Suffering" is one such word, and its charge is exploited by feminism in order to criticize women's experiences of patri-archal ideology. On the other hand, a strategic aesthetic compels feminism to acknowledge the limitations of its respective projects, whether in relation to theory, politics or literature. These limitations not only involve the exclusion of radically other women, but also the exclusion of the unreliable movement of rhetoric. Insofar as it is unreliable, resisting feminism's endeavour to essentialize, homogenize and univer-salize via the aesthetic, rhetoric ensures a future for feminist debate. Feminism thus understood promotes vigilance as regards the linguistic workings of its own, as well as patriarchy's aesthetico-ideological activ-ities, which is also significant for radically other women. The latter are neither excluded nor appropriated by a feminism that takes seriously its own limitations.

In conclusion, this discussion proposes that feminism develop an insight into the complex relationship between language and experience. The assumption that formal linguistic structures move towards a femi-nist meaning and a female referent depends on an aestheticized understanding of the rhetorical dimension of language. This movement is ineradicable, ensuring that the category of the aesthetic is not simply a matter of choice for feminists, whether it is ratified or resisted. Nowhere is this more obvious than with Felski's "non-aesthetic" theory, which reconciles linguistic and natural reality "*only* thanks to a phenom-enalizing (and hence aesthetico-ideologizing) trope!" (Warminski 1996: 12). Although feminism cannot move beyond the aesthetic, this does not mean that the aesthetic is beyond feminist analysis, particularly if it takes the form of a critical-linguistic analysis. The latter negotiates the aesthetic strategically, affording an insight into the discontinuous relationship between linguistic and natural reality. An emphasis on discontinuity problematizes patriarchal ideology, along with putting feminist ideology into question. However, vigilance regarding discon-tinuity makes for a properly radical feminism, one that is unable to designate once and for all the meaning of "feminist literature", "the woman" and, indeed, "feminism". Rhetorically generated categories such as these cannot help but be formulated, although they are only reli-able in terms of an aesthetic ideology. That "feminist literature", "the woman" and "feminism" have their bases in language, as opposed to natural reality, opens them up to other possibilities, which also makes certain a future for feminist debate. In turning towards the matter of language, feminism is thus able to do something for women in all their heterogeneity by unmasking and accounting for the aesthetico-ideological aberrations that impact on their experiences.

Notes

1   "Strategic" is informed by deconstruction, negotiating critically with the liberal humanist concept of strategy. "Strategic because no transcendent truth present outside the field . . . can govern theologically the totality of the field. . . . [T]his strategy is not a simple strategy in the sense that the strategy orients tactics according to a final goal, a *telos* or theme of domination, a mastery" (Derrida 1982: 7).

2   Aristotle: "The rational part of the soul 'naturally' rules the irrational part – the 'natural' authority of master over slave and of a free man over a free woman". Augustine: "'Just as in man and woman there is one flesh of two, so the one nature of the mind embraces our intellect and action'." "Descartes, Hume, Rousseau, Kant, and Hegel all relied to some extent on the sense of a deepening division between a private feminine realm of domestic retreat and a realm of public action that was central to development toward fully rational, autonomous self-consciousness" (Rooney 1991: 82–3).

3   "Woman, whether young or old, quarrelling with her husband, or striving and vaunting against the gods in conceit of her happiness, or when she is in infliction, or sorrow, or weeping, and certainly not one who is in sickness, love, or labour" (Plato 1888: 80).

4   Like a child, woman "can be entertained by trivialities". "[P]refer[ring] the beautiful to the useful, . . . [w]oman is intolerant of all commands and all morose constraint. They do something only because it pleases them" (Kant 1995: 581, 583).

5   Felski demands a revaluation of realism by feminism. She challenges Catherine Belsey's and Colin MacCabe's argument that realism *per se* is complicit with dominant ideologies. Non-classic realism, then, criticizes classic realism without giving up radical possibilities for other realisms.

6   "[M]y main concern lies in . . . hermeneutic[s]" (Felski 1989: 84).

References

Armstrong, Isobel. 1993: So What's All this About the Mother's Body?: The Aesthetic, Gender and the Polis. In Judith Still and Michael Worton (eds), *Textuality and Sexuality: Reading Theories and Practices*, Manchester: Manchester University Press, 218–36.

De Man, Paul. 1979: *Allegories of Reading: Figural Language in Rousseau, Nietzsche, Rilke and Proust*. New Haven/London: Yale University Press.

——. 1986: *The Resistance to Theory*. Minneapolis: University of Minnesota Press.

——. 1996: *Aesthetic Ideology*. Minneapolis/London: University of Minnesota Press.

Derrida, Jacques. 1982: *Margins of Philosophy*. New York: Harvester Wheatsheaf.

Eagleton, Terry. 1990: *The Ideology of the Aesthetic*. Oxford: Blackwell Publishers.

Felski, Rita. 1989: *Beyond Feminist Aesthetics: Feminist Literature and Social Change*. Cambridge, MA: Harvard University Press.

——. 1994: Does the Concept of Feminist Aesthetics Facilitate or Inhibit Cultural Activism? In Philip Goldstein (ed.), *Styles of Cultural Activism: From Theory and Pedagogy to Women, Indians, and Communism*, Newark: University of Delaware Press, 203–12.

——. 1995: Why Feminism Doesn't Need an Aesthetic (And Why It Can't Ignore Aesthetics). In Peggy Zeglin Brand and Carolyn Korsmeyer (eds), *Feminism and Tradition in Aesthetics*, University Park, Pennsylvania: Pennsylvania University Press, 431–45.

Hein, Hilde and Carolyn Korsmeyer. 1990: Introduction. *Hypatia* 5, 2 (Summer), 1–6.

Kant, Immanuel. 1995: The Fair Sex. In Isaac Kramnick (ed.), *The Enlightenment Reader*, New York/London: Penguin Books, 580–6.

Norris, Christopher. 1988: Paul de Man and the Critique of Aesthetic Ideology. *AUMLA* 69, 3–47.

Plato. 1888: *The Republic of Plato*. Trans. B. Jowett, 3rd edn. Oxford: Clarendon Press.

Regan, Stephen. 1992: Introduction. In Stephen Regan (ed.), *The Politics of Pleasure: Aesthetics and Cultural Theory*, Buckingham, Philadelphia: Open University Press, 1–16.

Rooney, Phyllis. 1991: Gendered Reason: Sex Metaphor and Conceptions of Reason. *Hypatia* 6, 2 (Summer), 77–103.

Spivak, Gayatri Chakravorty. 1990: *The Postcolonial Critic: Interviews, Strategies, Dialogues*. New York/London: Routledge.

Warminski, Andrzej. 1996: Introduction: Allegories of Reference. In Paul de Man, *Aesthetic Ideology*, Minneapolis/London: University of Minnesota Press, 1–33.

Chapter 12

Bodily Transactions: Jean Genet in the Feminist Debate

Liz Barry

THE FEMININE IN FRANCE has become a "metaphor without brakes", in the words of Roland Barthes, and a metaphor that finally seems to have very little to do with women (Jardine 1985: 34). In this respect, it could be compared to the idea of the body in critical discourse, which has become a catch-all, a fetishized index of meaning that once possessed can yield the key to any literary text. French theories of the feminine have given relatively little importance to cultural determinants of gender. As Mary Jacobus in a survey of theories of *l'écriture féminine* commented, "Utopian attempts to define the specificity of women's writing [. . .] either founder on the rock of essentialism (the text as body), gesture toward an avant-garde practice which turns out not to be specific to women, or, like Hélène Cixous, do both" (1982: 37). Cixous does indeed seem to want to have it both ways, predicating a notion of feminine writing on the plural and diffuse quality of female sexuality, yet opening up this category to male writers such as Joyce, Proust and, most consistently, Jean Genet. I want in this piece to balance Cixous's reading of Genet's work with the more pragmatic treatment he has received from Anglo-American feminists such as Kate Millett and to assess the impact of Genet's "female" body for gender studies.

Cixous's labelling of male writers' work as *feminine* is complicated by her emphasis on homosexual writers, whose sexual orientation might seem to be directly implicated in the features of their style. This would seem to return us to some sort of essentialist relation between writing and sexual practice. Hélène Cixous's translators have not helped to untangle the issue. Betsy Wing's translation of Cixous's writing on Genet in *La Jeune Née* (*The Newly-Born Woman*) gives the following translation of the key sentence about Genet: "Thus, what is inscribed under

Jean Genet's name, in the movement of a text that divides itself, pulls itself to pieces, dismembers itself, regroups, re-members itself, is a proliferating, maternal femininity" (Cixous and Clement 1986: 83). When Ann Liddle translated Cixous for the earlier Marks and Courtivron *New French Feminisms* reader of 1981, however, she added to Cixous's original the word *pederastic*, giving "an abundant, maternal, pederastic femininity", without there being any authority for this decision in the French text. This discrepancy raises the question of what Cixous means by *femininity* here. What sense can *pederastic* femininity have? How far is this identical with the femininity ascribed to a woman? And if this quality cannot be mapped onto tangible sexual practice, is it simply rhetorical flourish?

Cixous is adamant in her writing that it is not the empirical sex of the author that matters, but the kind of writing they produce. She warns against getting "trapped by names" (1981: 52). Yet her subsequent reliance on the vocabulary of psychoanalysis to characterize the kinds of textuality under discussion leads her to describe certain features as *male* and to link the masculine libidinal economy with fear of castration. Toril Moi, in *Sexual/Textual Politics*, also charts the slippage from "feminine" to "female" and "woman" in "The Laugh of the Medusa" (1985: 113). Cixous's meaning seems finally to rely on traditional assumptions about the realms of the male and the female, despite its gesture towards a Lacanian Real (a sphere existing prior to and beyond analysis and language) where all difference has been abolished.

Cixous holds that woman has an inherently *bisexual* nature, whereas man has been "trained to aim for glorious phallic monosexuality". The suggestion is that textual practice such as Genet's is also "bisexual", open to the idea of the "other", and as such can instantiate some (albeit phantasmic) unity. The non-linearity, abundant wordplay and proliferating imagery of Genet's text create a mobile and open text that escapes a monologic Symbolic order.[1] If we consider this unity from the position of the reader, however, it is not unproblematic. In discussing the passage on Genet, and its English versions, Gregory Woods suggests that it is a "condescending" idea on Cixous's part to intimate that a gay man's cultural production is less "flawed" by his being male than a straight man's. Woods's objection underlines the fact that it is difficult not to read Cixous's argument as suggesting that gay men themselves are somehow *less male* than straight men (1993: 169).

A feminism attentive to the pragmatics of female reading practice might also cavil at Cixous's optimism as to how far a woman can appropriate Genet's text. If feminine pleasure is located in Genet's open and playful rhetoric, creating a *jouissance* (a pleasure akin to sexual bliss) which disrupts the univocal patriarchal voice, it has no place in what is

represented in the novels, where sexual activity is relentlessly masculine and reverent of the phallus. How far does the referential content
disrupt the effect of the signifier? To cite Genet's overt affiliation to the
Symbolic order in its most rigid and hierarchical forms, or his investment in the status quo, as problematic thorns in the side of Cixous's
argument may be naïve essentialism. To read Genet, however, so
against the grain of all his avowed intentions and in the face of his manifest disinterest in the 'empirical' female and female sexual experience
might give a more literalist female reader cause for unease.

Yet Genet's novels and plays do provide answers, of a kind, to what
"pederastic femininity" might entail in practice. There are several
explicit discussions of the qualities of femininity and maternal feeling
in relation to his male characters. Divine in *Notre-Dame-des-Fleurs* (*Our
Lady of the Flowers*) provides the most sustained picture of how Genet
might conceive of femininity as a category open to appropriation. Genet
makes it clear, however, that there is no sense in which Divine is a
woman: "she was womanly only through her submission to the impe-
rious male" (1957a: 176). Her "organs hindered her" from further
identification with the empirical female; if Cixous eschews essentialism,
Genet does not. Divine talks of "real" women in terms of abhorrence;
their physical difference is a source of disgust rather than fascination.
They are "those horrible titty females [*ces horribles femelles à tétons*] [. . .]
those vile sailors' tarts, those tramps, those dirty nasties" (Genet 1957a:
180).

If one avoids the simplistic equation of a passive sexual role and the
female, Divine's femininity is strangely incorporeal. The only descriptions of her body are androgynous, characterizing it as white, thin and
hairless like the "ivory body of Jesus on an eighteenth-century crucifix"
(Genet 1957a: 109). When her body comes into focus it is to register its
ageing and the withdrawing of any sexual identity: "She ate her grief
and drank it; this sour food had dried her body and corroded her mind.
Nothing – neither her own personal care nor the beauty parlours – kept
her from being thin and having the skin of a corpse" (Genet 1957a: 124).
What remains of her beauty is "artfully" contrived, yet "powder and
cream" do not disguise the fact that she wears a wig. Just as society's
construction of a "homoseckshual" is as a "monster", a "chimera or
griffin" (Genet 1957a: 63) painted on a wall, Divine's identity is a
monstrously artificial contrivance. Darling "steeped himself in all the
monstrosities of which she was composed" (Genet 1957a: 125).

Femininity here is a matter of effect and gesture, of pastiche. Fredric
Jameson writes of pastiche that it is, "like parody, the imitation of a style,
the wearing of a stylistic mask, speech in a dead language: but it is a
neutral practice of mimicry, without parody's ulterior motive [. . .],

without that still latent feeling that there is something normal compared to which what is being imitated is rather comic" (1989: 114). Despite the sometimes humorous effects of Genet's extravagant prose, the female impersonation that Divine enacts has this deadened quality. We are not presented with any "real" women who act the way that "she" does. Her repertoire consists of over-delicate, highly-strung bird-like gestures and rituals that are unlikely to be mirrored in the behaviour of the "sailors' tarts" who appear fleetingly in a one-dimensional representation. This femininity aims for the bodilessness of the saint, the dead icon.

In *Sexual Politics*, Kate Millett contends that Genet ironizes and parodies conventional roles, and makes masculinity a pastiche as well as femininity. In the context of her polemical work, Genet is seen to give an insight into the stark imbalance of power in the patriarchal structure. She claims that in his position as a gay writer he nevertheless "penetrates to the heart of what heterosexual society imagines to be the character of 'masculine' and 'feminine'" (1977: 17). The implication is that we are shown in exaggerated but graphic terms – the terms of pastiche – the monstrous society we have created.

All Genet's characters are destined to become images. The difference is that his men can choose the form of their metamorphosis; his few woman characters have theirs dictated for them. Yet the implication of pastiche is, as we have said, that it is difficult to perceive the "normal" situation that it feeds on. There is a flip side to Genet's commitment to the idea that women are confined in society to stylized and emblematic roles that leave them powerless. Pretence and illusion are seen as *inherent* features of femininity, leaving no room for genuine feeling or experience. Femininity indeed becomes accessible for either sex, as Cixous suggests, but this empowers the male still further as only he possesses the true token of worth, the phallus at the center of the social power structure. I would argue that Genet might expose this situation, as Millett proposes, but that he also has a deep investment in preserving it and in denying the existence of the different strengths and genuine energies of a true femaleness.

Genet's play *The Balcony* can lay greater claim than his novels to the kind of incisive social comment that Millett reads into his work. Even here his perspective is ultimately quietist, however. We are given the alternative of two kinds of hollow masquerade: the tacit rituals of society and the candid role-playing of the brothel. Women are characterized more fully in this play than elsewhere, but are still seen to invest wholeheartedly in the illusions society requires of them. Femininity is equated with pretence, just one step away from deceit. The language of the play makes this perfectly explicit. Even when talking among themselves, the women characterize speaking openly and candidly as talking "man to man" (Genet 1957b: 37). The real "men" are those who do not get involved in the game of the brothel, as is conveyed by the following exchange:

> Irma: Roger. The plumber. An idiotic affair. It's not easy for men to get into this place: it's a convent. By "men" you know whom I mean . . . ?
> The Chief of Police: The ones who keep their heads.
> Irma: Very neatly put. (Genet 1957b: 50)

Even the women who do not get involved in the games of the brothel (or those who leave them), such as Georgette and Chantal, are condemned to role-playing as iconic beauties or simply nurses, a "woman's job" as a casualty of the revolution puts it. When Irma asks Carmen in the brothel whether she wants to get married, Carmen gives a Pavlovian response: "Orange blossom, tulle. . ." Irma responds: "Wonderful! To you, getting married means masquerading. Darling, you certainly are one of us" (Genet 1957b: 42).

Irma here means that Carmen is a true member of the brothel, but she might be talking of women in general, as Roger's comment later on underlines. He suggests that women *want* to distance themselves from genuine desire in favour of playing a role or becoming an 'icon': [to Chantal]: "You'll be what you've always dreamt of being: an emblem forever escaping from her womanliness" (Genet 1957b: 64). The most significant and redemptive moment of the play in this respect is when Irma is given access to what has been an exclusively masculine perspective in Genet's other work. Wondering whether to take on the entirely symbolic role of Queen, she says: "I haven't yet decided to go along with you in this adventure. I love love and I love power and I want to experience them with my body" (Genet 1957b: 101). Nonetheless the alternative is a narrow one: symbolic social power that is exposed as empty, or power predicated upon the ephemerality of the body and sexual pleasure.

In most of Genet's dramatic situations, however, it is the complete powerlessness of the feminine role that is emphasized. A passage in *Our Lady of the Flowers* illustrates Kate Millet's idea that the sexual balance of power also characterizes the social structure, and suggests why. Darling has picked a bunch of flowers, which disturbs some ingrained principle of Divine's that is linked to her rural beginnings. "A cherry branch, supported by the full flight of pink flowers, surges stiff and black from a vase" (Genet 1957a: 75). This provokes a flight of hysteria from Divine, an over-pronounced instance of "feminine" behavior. Divine "tears the flowers to shreds. Slaps. Shrieks". There is a richly symbolic sexual reading to be made of this passage. The unmistakably phallic stiff black branch could be seen to represent Divine's "lost" or stolen masculine self that Darling has "plucked". He has taken possession of this self by submitting his passive partner to his dominance. The narrator comments: "The broken branch shocked her as you would be shocked by the murder of a nubile young maiden." The pronouns are significant here. In the world of Genet's bourgeois reader, the canonical sexual "theft" is that of a maiden's virginity; in Genet's world, it is the theft of the potency of one partner in the sexual unit. Both acts of appropriation disempower the victim in a much more generalized sense than the local sexual one.

In Genet's account, the unity that the sexual act provides can – momentarily, at least – compensate for this loss of potency, this symbolic castration. Divine says to Gabriel: "you're myself. My heart or my sex. A *branch* of me" (Genet 1957a: 118), a comment that picks up on the sexual sense of this image suggested earlier in the text. Divine also uses a female image of herself in addressing Gabriel, however: "I love you as if you were in my belly" (Genet 1957a: 118). The only form of possession available to the female (or this pseudo-female) is a maternal one. Genet wants it both ways and openly admits to mixing masculine and feminine attributes in the imaginative transformation of his characters. He writes in *The Thief's Journal* of old male criminals who have a "maternal element" that is not feminine:

> The tenderness that makes them unbend is not femininity, but the discovery of ambiguity. I think they are prepared to impregnate themselves, to lay and hatch their eggs, but without any blunting of their cruel male sting. (1967: 226)

Once more Genet endorses Cixous's idea that sexual characteristics can be linguistically appropriated, but Genet uses this possibility not to celebrate femininity but to empower the male position.

The feature of Genet's writing that connects most closely with Cixous's ideas is the sense in which sexuality is linked to linguistic choices. Unlike Cixous, however, Genet cuts these away from psychoanalytic or physical relations, at least in constructing his version of "femininity". The narrator of *Our Lady of the Flowers* says blithely: "I shall speak to you about Divine, mixing masculine and feminine as my mood dictates" (Genet 1957a: 61). This virtual femininity has its limitations, however. Divine's self-perception fluctuates between the power of her gestures and the evidence of her "organs". The narrator comes clean later in the text:

> For if, to define a state of mind that she felt, Divine dared to use the feminine, she was unable to do so in defining an action which she performed. And all the "woman" judgements she made were, in reality, poetic conclusions. (Genet 1957a: 176)

This distinction has implications for the narrator's investment in his "persona". The bodily Divine is inaccessible to him, and – we have seen – cannot fully embody the feminine in any case. In this sense, she is the "object" of the discourse. Her thoughts and feelings, on the other hand, are accessible to the narrator, and are interleaved with the narrator's own experiences of desire and revelation. The narrator establishes a communion with Divine and his other characters by speaking of "our" world and (to us, the reader) "your[s]". Through such economical linguistic means, the writer can inhabit positions that allow him to explore the "other" of bisexuality.

This is developed most significantly toward the end of *Our Lady of the Flowers* at the moment of Divine's death. At this point, Divine remembers and reincarnates her former self, Culafroy, the "he" subject position. In turn, she relives the death of her (his) old cousin Adeline, whose shoes Culafroy used to have to wear to school, already taking on the identity of this old woman to some degree. In the guise of her former self, Divine is invaded by Adeline's soul – that is to say, returns to being a "she.

Finally, the *narrator* takes on the persona of Divine, he too lying motionless and rigid, figuring an imaginative death for himself:

> So here she is dead. The Quite-Dead. Her body's caught in the sheets. It is, from head to foot, forever a ship in the breaking-up of ice-floes, motionless and rigid, drifting toward infinity: you, Jean, dear heart, motionless and rigid, as I have already said, drifting on my bed to a happy Eternity. (Genet 1957a: 236)

The narrator suddenly, without signalling the transition, addresses himself in the third person, and then slips back into the first person almost immediately. What is going on here? This is a "limit situation", the end of the book, and an exploration of several boundaries as the subject (the narrator) and the object (Divine) approach their vanishing point. The imaginative embodiment of the narrator in his subject has its apotheosis as this subject disappears, or rather changes into a permanent "image" in death. But this image is far from stable. This is a Kristevan "borderline", and the text challenges what Kristeva describes as "the prohibitions that found the inner and outer borders in and through which the speaking subject is constituted – borders also determined by the phonological and semantic differences that articulate the syntax of language" (1982: 69). This passage provides a fictional enactment of the collapse of these prohibitions between subject and object, male and female, which is ultimately of course the collapse of discourse itself. The events of the narrator's text come to a definitive end with the death of his fictional "representative"; this projected female part of himself, his "other", could be seen to "rejoin" him at this moment, occasioning the vertiginous instability of the gender and position of the subject that we see in the passage above.

Both Cixous and Millett concur that Genet gives us an insight into what "feminine" and "masculine" might mean in textual and social terms. The most radical difference between their views on Genet is their stance on the writer's agency. Kate Millett is interested in the political position that Genet adopts – in the broadest sense of the word "political": the shifts that he effects in the power relations between his characters, the social networks of their world, the connection of the "feminine" position with that of the colonized, the black, the proletariat, the social outcast. He is, beneath the bombast of his rhetoric, a shrewd social observer, whom Millett contrasts starkly with the big-hearted whore that Divine represents (Millet 1977: 344, 19). Hélène Cixous, on the other hand, true to the deconstructive turn, erases the subject position to allow language itself to speak, a position resulting from the openness, mobility, and flexibility of Genet's writing, and Genet's recognition of, and submission to, his own femininity and passiveness in the face of the other. This division, characteristic of the two strands of feminism, Anglo-American and Continental, creates two distinct feminine bodies in Genet's work. Millett's is the social body, an abstraction of the disempowered body in the sexual act; Cixous's is the body of the text, on the surface of the text, in which words become physical objects, and Genet creates, in Sartre's words, "a work of the mind that smells of bowels and sperm and milk" (1977: 11). What is missing in both cases is the actual referent, the woman's body. The object of pastiche is by its nature absent.

The fact remains then that the female body is essentially excluded from Genet's text while the male body is all-pervasive. The feminist appropriations of Genet's work which we have discussed are ingenious and convincing, but we are radically short-changing the feminist cause to rely for a model on a male writer with so little interest in female experience. Genet may write at the borders of gender and circumvent the hegemonic discourse of a patriarchal society, but, ultimately, his ludic disruption of society involves a reiteration of its very forms.

Note

1   Lacan's Symbolic order is the domain of language, where desire is represented, and the subject consequently constituted, through social and cultural processes.

References

Cixous, Hélène. 1981: Castration or Decapitation? Annette Kuhn (trans.), *Signs* 7, 1, 41–55.

—— and Cathérine Clément. 1986: *The Newly-Born Woman*, Betsy Wing (trans.). Minneapolis: University of Minnesota Press.

Genet, Jean. 1957a: *Our Lady of the Flowers*, Bernard Frechtman (trans.). London: Penguin.

——. 1957b: *The Balcony*, Bernard Frechtman (trans.). London: Faber and Faber.

——. 1967: *The Thief's Journal*. London: Penguin.

Jacobus, Mary. 1982: The Question of Lanugage: Men of Maxims and *The Mill on the Floss*. In Elizabeth Abel (ed.), *Writing and Sexual Difference*. Brighton: Harvester.

Jameson, Fredric. 1989: Postmodernism and Consumer Society. In Hal Foster (ed.), *The Anti-Aesthetic: Essays on Postmodern Culture*, 3rd edn. Washington ,D.C.: Maisonneuve Press, 111–25.

Jardine, Alice. 1985: *Gynesis: Configurations of Woman and Modernity*. Ithaca: Cornell University Press.

Kristeva, Julia. 1982: *The Powers of Horror: An Essay on Abjection*, Léon S. Roudiez (trans.). New York: Columbia University Press.

Millett, Kate. 1977: *Sexual Politics*. London: Virago.

Moi, Toril. 1985: *Sexual/ Textual Politics: Feminist Literary Theory*. London/New York: Routledge.

Sartre, Jean-Paul. 1957: Introduction. In Jean Genet, *Our Lady of the Flowers*, 9–44.

Woods, Gregory. 1993: The Injured Sex: Hemingway's Voice of Masculine Anxiety. In Judith Still and Michael Worton (ed.) *Textuality and Sexuality: Reading Theories and Practices*. Manchester: Manchester University Press, 160–72.

Chapter 13

"Doing" Judith: Race, Mixed Race and Performativity

MICHELE HUNTER

Introduction

C OMING TO FEMINISM, like mathematics, is a cumulative process. Consciousness-raising groups, introductory Women's Studies courses and politicization through unjust treatment are the basics, like addition, subtraction and multiplication. A feminist consciousness would equal zero, it would bear little or no value, without the collective agreement that women daily endure oppression, just as mathematics would lose its grounding without (real) numbers. But what happens to women's experience when we enter the realm of imaginary numbers, or the high math of feminist theory? Do the real (female) numbers disintegrate into meaningless linguistic aberrations? Are they devalued, zero-summed? This essay will answer that question yes and no.

Judith's Butler

Until the appearance of *Bodies That Matter* (1993), Judith Butler's early writing on gender and sexuality had considerably failed to engage a rigorous race/gender analysis. Theorizing the body, desire and sex, Judith argued that "There is no subject prior to its constructions, and neither is the subject determined by those constructions; it is always the nexus, the non-space of cultural collision . . . It is the space of this ambivalence which opens up the possibility of a reworking of the very terms by which subjectivation proceeds – and fails to proceed" (1993: 124). Thus, queer enactments of gender, or "performances", which seem to mock the masculine and the feminine are perpetually subordinate to the effect of power which legislates gender norms even as these acts resist this legislation.

As she argues in her discussion of the historic discursive construction of the female body, "Without the temporal prioritization of primary characterizations, it would be unclear which characterizations were to serve as substance and which as attributes" (1990a: 331). Reasoning that desire is not necessarily rooted in biological sex, Judith invalidates the notion of a natural (female) self and consequently legitimates lesbianism and bisexuality by dismissing the essentialist concept of a fixed female core. Alluding to the internal fragmentation of the category woman due to class, race, ethnic and other identifications, Judith extends her gender analysis to ask: "But how do we know what exists prior to its discursive articulation?" (1990a: 327). Just as the body (as in gender and sex) has been historically constructed, and we see it and talk about it with phallomorphic vision, propaganda and language, Judith suggests that similar explanations can be made for race. However, she does not proceed with this statement, nor is she explicitly addressing race in this essay. As a white feminist who is racially privileged, it is in her best interest not to. As a black feminist, I assume this responsibility.

Allotted even less space in the margins of intellectualism and history, black lesbians and feminists have fewer resources with which we may control representation, debunk myths and redefine dominant conceptions of blackness. Black feminist theory, and the activism that led to the theories, practices and spaces that facilitate Judith's notoriety encompass, in my mind, Judith's "Butler": she who buttresses Judith's intellectual work and remains in the background, invisible. Only from a racially-centered perspective, one that responsibly acknowledges a race/gender epistemology, can Judith's theory even begin to explore its profound possibilities.

In the interest of pursuing a racially-sophisticated truth, a reading of Judith that is informed by black feminism, I aim to change the invisible condition of black women to a visible one. Notably, Judith's linguistic tools render the black woman the same status as the lesbian: "Lesbianism . . . has not even made its way into the thinkable, the imaginable . . . How then, to 'be' a lesbian in a political context in which the lesbian does not exist?" (1990c: 20). Certainly, Judith does not envision *a* lesbian identity. Her efforts are to reinscribe a lesbian-centered discourse into the dominant ideology that would transform ideology and the notion of lesbianism to meaninglessness without undervalued invisibility. This would entail the thorough restructuring of sexuality and gender to an ideal community in which lesbians will not be called lesbians because heterosexuality will no longer be compulsory behavior. To this extent, Judith ultimately does not want gender to exist.

As I revisited Judith's theory from a racially-inclusive viewpoint, it quickly became apparent to me that the foundation of black feminist theory *is* agency. The black feminist model for subverting the limits of gender, and the point at which Judith and her Butler meet, resides in black creativity, black feminist theories and the *revaluation* of black lesbianism, women and womanhood. These black feminist acts do not connote embracing sexist stereotypes and reinforcing female subordination (a.k.a. essentialism). Instead, they assume that which is most devalued and set apart in the margins and reinvent it. They give zero a value. As a brief, but informative, example, Barbara Christian, in her essay "The Race for Theory", embraces racial difference and explores its worthiness: "For people of color have always theorized – but in forms quite different from the Western form of abstract logic . . . often in narrative forms, in the stories we create, in riddles and proverbs, in the play with language, because *dynamic rather than fixed ideas seem more to our liking*" (1987: 68). Judith might sense that this last clause sounds a bit familiar.

Doing Gender

During my first encounter with Judith's theories as an undergraduate, I bought lipstick. At the time, I hadn't worn makeup for about a year for many reasons, most of them feminist. I wanted to be able to like myself without it. I didn't need it. It was a difficult habit to break at first. But, I adjusted. My lips were always getting chapped, so I bought Chapstick. I then grew accustomed to having an extra five or ten minutes that I usually spent in the mirror on other things. However, I didn't get used to still being catcalled and invaded. You see, makeup to me was a chief signifier in and of women's oppression. If women stopped wearing it, I naïvely believed we would stop being oppressed, have the extra five to ten minutes and be able to live unnoticed. Without lipstick, women could be invisible and, thus, unavailable to discriminate against.

So how did I come to buy lipstick? I thought about woman-loving; I thought about marking my "sex" so that I, too, could "be" a woman. Because if a feminist ignores the feminine, if she too devalues all that is "woman", then whose cause does she support? I worry about sounding essentialist, but what I wanted was to value our difference(s). I could not do that as a "man" (in the sense that manhood is merely performative). Did I want to uphold the notion that there are two sexes? I wanted women to feel comfortable with our expressions of gender.

One day, at a street fair on the Eastern edge of Washington Square

Park, I searched for lipstick on a table covered with makeup. I examined a few colors, but felt extremely out of place and hesitant. I noticed the other women checking out the eyeliners and blushes and felt a connection to them that mattered more to my self-love than theirs. I felt that buying lipstick might force me to relive that feminine experience I had so long denied, and this could clue me into a deeper understanding of what woman-loving really was.

I returned to the library and went to the women's bathroom. I pulled out the small lipstick, looked into the mirror and put on the orange. I didn't like the color very much, but I kept staring at my mouth. I puckered my lips and tried all sorts of gestures with my newly marked mouth, my mouth in the feminine. I got used to the near-gawdy color and slathered more on, watching the orange brighten into a neon shade. I considered that lipstick was a phallus, but chose to reinvent a woman-centered vision that metaphorically depicted the case as a vagina, and the pouring out of color, the beauty which pours out of a woman. I walked out of the bathroom into the reading room hoping someone would notice me. I looked at everyone, daring them to stare at my mouth and take note that I was doing woman well. Of course, I passed as a woman quite successfully – without a hitch!

But I couldn't stop thinking, in the midst of my ideas, about another lipstick I had tried at the vendor's booth. I also wanted to look at myself in the mirror to see what I looked like, because the one minute of indulgence did not impress my memory well enough. I had to have another look.

On the way out, again, I went to the bathroom and looked in the mirror. I collected some toilet paper and wiped it all off only to start over. I applied more and more. Then I stopped and went out to seek another color.

The vendor was still there, but most of his wares had been packed away. I asked him about a certain color for which I had no name, my lips blaring orange to him. "I'd know it if I saw it", I said to him, very desperate for his assistance. He remembered me and even recalled which color I wanted. After much searching, he found it, in the way Santa Claus finds just the perfect toy, and I bought it.

Heading back to the library, I observed the many women walking around me and others sitting at tables selling their wares. There was a table full of Afrocentric merchandise. I looked at the black woman sitting there and wondered if I was betraying her by doing this "white" theory: by performing not only a gender that was defined by whiteness, but feeling a crush on Judith coming on.[1]

Passing, Queering: Judith Butler's Mixed Desires

Subsequent to my performance of gender, I viewed Douglas Sirk's 1959 film *Imitation of Life* and recognized myself in Sara Jane, the mixed-race daughter of Annie Johnson. Like Sara Jane, I found myself negotiating between two polarized versions of femininity, exhibited in the film by Lora and Annie. In that the homoerotic elements of Annie's relationship with Lora ("just let me come and do for you") collude with her Mammy stereotyping and its accompanying invisibility ("Why Annie", Lora exclaims, "I didn't know you *had* any friends!"), the film projects a skewed vision of single black motherhood and the intimacy of domestic work.[2] It is no surprise, then, that Annie's daughter Sara Jane shows off how well she has learned what it means to be "colored" by bringing in a tray of hors d'oeuvres to Lora and her guests. Just as Sara Jane's performance pronounces the racial status of gender, her ability to pass as white *and* black forces our notions of engendered blackness and whiteness outside of the terms of performativity. In so far as Sara Jane is capable of adopting either pole of representation, she distorts their respective coherence and exhibits the core which can maneuver itself in and outside of the protocols of race. In this sense, Sara Jane's act does not counter the legislation of gender. Instead, in that it belies the whiteness of whiteness, it totalizes the function of miscegenation.

Moreover, Sara Jane's unrelenting resistance to blackness introduces a racial self that defines itself in opposition to its "self". Played by a white actress, Sara Jane's desire to pass for white requires the audience's temporary suspension of belief. Yet her racial difference is repeatedly upheld by her assertions that she *is* white. To this extent, she inhabits her own forbidden racial double. At school, Sara Jane is humiliated when her mother pays her a visit and the classroom discovers the truth. "I hope I die!" Sara Jane screams. "They didn't ask me, why should I tell them? Why do you have to be my mother? Why?! Why?!" At Christmas, she asks her mother if Jesus was white or black. Before anyone gives an adequate answer, she daringly declares: "He was like me – white."

In that its assertion is truly a denial, Sara Jane's whiteness is not "really" white, it is colored. And more than simply expressing the limits of conventional racial categories, Sara Jane's obsession paints a frustrated portrait of mixed-race subjectivity to the degree that her flawed characterization reveals a limited vision of *this* "category".

To the extent that the film defines black womanhood as domestic servitude, Sara Jane desires a social and economic alternative. The facility with which Sara Jane may improve her condition supports Laura Harris's claim that "to be of mixed parentage could define one's class standing" (1996: 11). Thus, Sara Jane's performance of "whiteness" incorporates race, gender and economic status such that her act of passing testifies to the multiple means of social maneuverability available to, and presumed to be definitive of, the mixed-race woman.

In her analysis of Sara Jane's performances, Judith misses the interconnection between mixed-race and sex, except when she describes Sara Jane's beating: "[that whiteness enacts the] compulsory normative requirement for desirability, . . . becomes clear when Sara Jane, mulatto and anxious to pass, becomes involved with a white boy who, after learning that she's 'colored', beats her and throws her in the mud" (1990b: 5). Recognizing the "cruelty of whiteness", Judith fails to address the mixed-race specificity of Sara Jane's act. When Annie and Lora discuss what it means to raise Sara Jane in a racist country, Annie asks, "How do you teach your child that she was born to be hurt?" Because Sara Jane can pass for white, and chooses to do so as a direct consequence of both her mother's inadequate model and Lora's "glamorous" one, she is vulnerable to bitter disappointment. Passing for a white woman is thus Sara Jane's gendered and mixed-race confrontation with racism.

Sara Jane's mixed desires come to a head at the end of the film when Annie Johnson visits her daughter in Los Angeles, where Sara Jane is passing for white. "Are you happy here? Are you finding what you really want?" her mother pleads. In response, Sara Jane defends: "I'm somebody else. I'm white! White! White! White! Does that answer your question?" (Sara Jane's determination to pass acutely echoes Lora's desire "to go up and up and up".) However pained by her chosen alienation from her mother, Sara Jane is successful in her mixed-race performance. And yet the bitterness in her words reveals the disturbing price of her adopted lifestyle and the failure of performativity. What Sara Jane's figurative and literal escape from her mother's condition further confirms is that class mobility is always at odds with black authenticity.

In her reading of Nella Larsen's *Passing*, Judith argues that passing for straight is "inextricably linked" to passing for white. Yet passing for straight is only "inextricably linked" to passing for white if marginalized sexuality and blackness occur in separate bodies. By positing passing for straight, or being in the closet, as equivalent to passing for white, Judith invents a falsely interdependent relationship between these acts. Race thus becomes essential to Judith not as an integrated signification *vis-à-vis* sexuality, but as a borrowed concept which, like the Mammy character, only exists in support of practices performed by white people. In her ambition to confront heterosexism and essentialism, Judith's reasoning guarantees the perpetuation of essentialist race segregation and thus renders invisible queer people of color – contrary to her political desires. Although she offers a compelling explanation for the construction of gender, in her reassertion of white privilege, she reestablishes inequalities and fails to get what she wants.

Conclusion: Toward a Black Woman-Loving Theory

I want to return to this question of zero with a geometrical if-then statement. If women are negative, or of zero-value, meaning of *no* value, then feminism must revalue zero and *all* that is in the margins, including race.

Yet as I lie here in bed with Judith, she does not see the world as I do – in color. Judith, in her subtle language, also does not provide me with a concrete form of woman-loving, a tangible sex act, just as lesbian feminism doesn't. Does Judith love women? And "am I the dark exotic?" (Omosupe, 1991: 104). Would this interracial relationship truly "confront and challenge . . . our stereotypes, assumptions, and prejudices toward those who are different?" (Garcia *et al.* 1987: 143).

I would like to think that Judith and I could enjoy each other's differences, even celebrate them. It would be inappropriate for Judith to remain closed to black consciousness or for her to perform an uncritical vision of whiteness. Our differences would perhaps be the locus of our mutual love, quite unlike the dominant notions of difference in which "the other is almost unavoidably either opposed to the self or submitted to the self's dominance . . . always condemned to remain in its shadow while attempting at being it's equal" (Mihn-ha 1990: 371).

Instead, "Our energy would be . . . spent on naming, confronting, owning, and resolving [racist] feelings rather than trying to evade, deny, or suppress them" (Piper, 1996: 265). Judith's whiteness would have to constantly endure its undoing while my racial difference would find meaning beyond alterity. Her privilege would be countered with woman-loving: loving the woman she is, and from this all women, and from this another woman who is different. As women-loving women, our differences would be enriching to both of us, to our theoretical concerns and to feminism as a movement. As it is envisioned here, my fantasy is responsible because I nurture my feelings and insist that I be nurtured.

Like a natural woman.[3]

Notes

This essay began as an undergraduate paper in the Spring of 1992. I presented part of it, in a different form, at the CUNY Center for Lesbian and Gay Studies'

Michele Hunter

"Relatively Speaking Conference", held at New York University May 3–5, 1997. I am indebted to Dr. Barrie Karp, who encouraged my thinking as an undergraduate with rare enthusiasm and engagement, Judith Butler, for her immediate responsiveness to earlier versions of this paper, and Mary Brewer, for her useful editorial suggestions.

1 This crush is a metaphor for my intense passion for theory, this theory I am calling Judith. See also Barbara Christian's discussion of people of color who are "wooed by [the academy]" (77) and the hooks and West conversation concerning black intellectuals' feelings of ambivalence about academia (1991). I am also deliberately objectifying Judith Butler, who, until now, was the (white) Subject.

2 As Adrian Piper writes, "I've also been thinking about the legions of African American women whose survival has depended on their submission to the intimate interpersonal roles, traditional for black women in this culture, of nursemaid, housekeeper, concubine, cleaning lady, cook; and what they have been required to witness of the whites they have served in these capacities" (261, my emphasis).

3 To avoid the risk of being misunderstood, I should explain my irony. Judith, in her article "Gendering the Body: Beauvoir's Philosophical Contribution", interprets the song "You Make Me Feel Like a Natural Woman", sung by Aretha Franklin, as an outright example of the impossibility of attaining a "true" or "natural" womanhood. I, on the other hand, am exploiting this biologically rooted and racially deterministic concept of natural womanhood (and Judith's misappropriation of the song) to demonstrate my ability to subvert it.

References

Butler, Judith. 1989: Gendering the Body: Beauvoir's Philosophical Contribution. In Ann Garry and Marilyn Pearsall (eds), *Women, Knowledge and Reality: Explorations in Feminist Philosophy*, Boston: Unwin Hyman, 253–62.
——. 1989 (Winter): The Body Politics of Julia Kristeva. *Hypatia* 3 (3), 104–17.
——. 1990a: Gender Trouble, Feminist Theory and Psychoanalytic Discourse. In Linda Nicholson (ed.), *Feminism/Postmodernism*. New York: Routledge, 324–40.
——. 1990b (Fall): Lana's "Imitation": Melodramatic Representation and the Gender Performative. *Genders* 9, 1–18.
——. 1990c: *Gender Trouble: Feminism and the Subversion of Identity*. New York: Routledge.
——. 1991: Imitation and Gender Insubordination. In Diana Fuss (ed.), *Inside/Out: Lesbian Theories, Gay Theories*, New York: Routledge, 13–31.
——. 1993: *Bodies That Matter: On the Discursive Limits of "Sex"*. New York/London: Routledge.
Christian, Barbara. 1987 (Spring): The Race for Theory. *Cultural Critique* 6, 67–9.
Collins, Patricia Hill. 1989 (Summer): The Social Construction of Black Feminist Thought. *Signs* 14 (4), 745–73.

Combahee River Collective. 1982: A Black Feminist Statement. In Gloria T. Hull, Patricia Bell Scott, and Barbara Smith (eds), *All the Women Are White, All the Blacks are Men, But Some of Us are Brave: Black Women's Studies*. New York: Feminist Press, 13–22.

Garcia, Norma, Cheryl Garcia, Sarah F. Pearlman and Julia Perez. 1987: The Impact of Race and Culture Differences: Challenges to Intimacy in Lesbian Relationships. In The Boston Lesbian Psychologies Collective (eds), *Lesbian Psychologies: Explorations and Challenges,* Urbana/Chicago: University of Illinois Press, 142–60.

Harris, Laura Alexandra. 1996 (Autumn): Queer Black Feminism: The Pleasure Principle. *Feminist Review* 54, 3–30.

hooks, bell and Cornel West. 1991: *Breaking Bread: Insurgent Black Intellectual Life*. Boston: South End Press.

Lorde, Audre. 1984: "Uses of the Erotic: The Erotic as Power". *Sister/Outsider: Essays and Speeches*. Freedom, California: The Crossing Press.

Mihn-ha, Trihn T. 1990: Not You/Like You: Post-Colonial Women and the Interlocking Questions of Identity and Difference. In Gloria Anzaldúa (ed.), *Making Face, Making Soul: Haciendo Caras: Creative and Critical Perspectives by Women of Color*, San Francisco: Aunt Lute, 371–5.

Omosupe, Ekua. 1991: Black/Lesbian/Bulldagger. *differences* 3 (2), 101–11.

Piper, Adrienne. 1996: Passing for White, Passing for Black. In Elaine K. Ginsberg (ed.), *Passing and the Fictions of Identity*, Durham/London: Duke University Press, 234–69.

Chapter 14

Mary Wollstonecraft: Feminist, Lesbian or Transgendered?

Ashley Tauchert

Introduction

MARY WOLLSTONECRAFT has been firmly situated as the "mother" of Anglophone feminism since the suffragists claimed her *Vindication of the Rights of Woman* (1792) as a historical precedent for their otherwise unprecedented claims for women's suffrage.[1] In this paper, I will outline the degree to which Wollstonecraft's "maternal" status in feminism is challenged by "third-wave" feminisms, characterized by a coming to terms with lesbian, bisexual and transgendered claims to female-embodiment through the 1990s.[2] This challenge, moreover, offers a new vision of the female-embodied subject by integrating claims to at least partial female-embodied identities with feminist claims on behalf of "woman". This paper will focus these concerns through a consideration of the compelling and ambiguous iconic figure of Mary Wollstonecraft.

The apparent fragmentation of feminist methodologies and categories has, somewhat inevitably, located itself in and on the female body, since female-embodiment remains that which grounds claims to a feminist position in the first place (Kemp and Squires 1997: 4). The feminist claim to "woman" that had already been criticized as a hetero-sexist and racist construct by lesbian and black criticism and theory by the end of the 1970s, seemed to some to have collapsed (whether successfully or in defeat remains open to debate) under the intensification of deconstructive pressures in the 1980s (Riley 1988; Felski 1989; Brooks 1997).[3]

Wollstonecraft appears to shift between *either* feminist, *or* lesbian, *or* transgendered categorization, with differing aspects of her biography and written work coming into focus to support each identification. These categories make discrete – if overlapping – claims to female-embodiment, and ultimately coalesce to imply the diasporic condition of female-embodied subjectivity. This is not to claim that the category "woman" as such is atomized and made redundant by these competing identities, but rather that the category itself needs reactivating under new critical conditions to provide the hub of a diasporic female-embodied Imaginary.

Contested Boundaries of "Woman"

Lesbian theory and criticism is grounded on the primary lesbian iden-tification of the theorist, and is perhaps best exemplified as a theoretical stance in Wittig's classic paper "One is Not Born a Woman" (1981):

> Lesbian is the only concept I know of which is beyond the categories of sex (woman and man), because the designated subject (lesbian) is not a woman, either economically, or politically, or ideologically. For what makes a woman is a specific social relation to a man, a relation that we have previously called servitude, a relation which implies personal and physical obligation as well as economic obligation [. . .], a relation which lesbians escape by refusing to become or to stay heterosexual. (226)

What is broadly at stake *between* the lesbian and feminist position is the category "woman". For Wittig "woman" denotes a mythological cate-gory which screens a complex history of enslavement; she calls for the destruction (rather than de-construction) of "woman" as a class.[4]

Feminist theory stages itself upon the assumption/belief that "woman" is a political and material category that holds purchase and which cannot be simply subsumed into a more diffuse post-post-struc-tural model of universalized difference. Feminist theory also contends that a focus on "patriarchy" can only be sustained by careful and conscious identification of the female-embodied subject as positioned differently from the male-embodied subject in the material structures and processes that constitute history: in access to the body-politic, in the Symbolic, in culture, in discourse. Sexual difference provides the primary marker of status across cultural, racial, ethnic, class and ability borders. The boundaries between feminist and lesbian theory are ambiguous, and, if tidied up, tend to suggest a demarcation of "femi-nism" as "straight" women's theorizing.

Female-embodiment is no longer considered the reserved domain of "birth women", but is claimed as an identificatory strategy also by male-to-female (mtf) transsexuals and transgenderists, as well as constituting a necessarily central aspect of intersexed identities.[5] Judith Butler's work on the gender performative and phantasmatic identifications is a key catalyst to third-wave feminist theory.[6] The same work is cited by lesbian, queer and transgendered theorists. This is partly explicable in the context of transgender as post-queer theory, evidenced, for example, in the shift between Judith Halberstam's work under the sign of lesbian to Jude Halberstam's work under the sign of transgenderist (Halberstam 1995, 1998).[7] What is at stake in feminist, lesbian and trans-gendered claims to "woman", then, are the contested boundaries of female-embodiment itself.

Transgender calls upon a multitude of identities *between* the norma-tive ideals of masculine-male and feminine-female – identificatory lines that cross and recross the sex/gender binary until there remains no stable sexually-embodied reference to be cited beyond an infinity of embodied singularities.[8] Feminism *per se* (if such a thing exists) has had little to say to transgender. What *has* been said has been said most powerfully by Germaine Greer, who in a recent interview rejected mtfs' claim to identity as women outright on the grounds of "how would [they] *know*"?[9] I'll return to Greer's both familiar and controversial posi-tion in my concluding remarks.

Mary Wollstonecraft and Female-embodiment

We are comfortable with the figure of Wollstonecraft as a proto-femi-nist.[10] Wollstonecraft's writings also demonstrate evidence of a fragmented, often displaced, narrative of same-sex desire – figured in her fiction in encodings of "Romantic Friendship" or same-sex nursing, or maternal desire, but perhaps most often and most influentially located in a transgendering of female-embodied subjectivity, and iden-tification with the masculine, in her two monumental *Vindications*.[11] This unquiet and insistent desire maps easily onto the largely accepted biographical evidence of Wollstonecraft's intimate adult relationship with Fanny Blood, which she novelizes in *Mary, A Fiction*; her passionate adolescent relationship with Jane Arden; a later intense encounter with Margaret King (one of Wollstonecraft's wards as a governess); a variety of remarks about "pretty women" in *Letters from Sweden* and private letters; and her off-the cuff, but intriguing, remark in the *Vindication of the Rights of Woman* that "[m]any women have not mind enough to have an affection for a woman" (Wollstonecraft 1995: 200).[12] Moore argues that while "it would be unwise to categorize Wollstonecraft's and Fanny's friendship as lesbian", it would be "equally mistaken to ignore the depth of Wollstonecraft's feeling for Fanny" (Moore 1999: 13).

When Wollstonecraft's biographic evidence of same-sex desire and relations is acknowledged by critics and feminist theorists, it tends to be contained within a narrative of adolescent role-play, an "experiment in female sexuality", to which Blood's death swiftly put an end (Kelly 1997: 148).[13] Wollstonecraft is given her moment of same-sex desire and potentially erotic intimacy, but usually swiftly returned to the familiar and easier to digest narrative of her more central and significant relationships with men (particularly Fuseli, Imlay, and Godwin).[14] However, even this familiar, if promiscuous, narrative (which Emma Goldman famously represented in terms of Wollstonecraft as a "sexually starved" woman) is transformed by a sustained understanding of the evidence for female-embodied same-sex desire in Wollstonecraft's life and writings (Elam and Weigman 1995: 140; Johnson 1995: 54). Wollstonecraft's infamous offer to co-habit with the painter Fuseli and his wife (a reiteration of her plans to live with Blood and Hugh Skeys after their marriage, and reiterated in her later offer to co-habit with Gilbert Imlay and his new mistress after her rejection by Imlay) appear less irrational in the context of the actively liminal sexual position readable in her writings.[15]

However, the arguments between feminist and lesbian theory are central rather than peripheral to our understanding of Wollstonecraft's life and work as a woman. The question of her lived experience of same-sex desire, and to what extent she was acting out this desire in her own relations with women, as well as its (often displaced) circulation in her fictional and non-fictional writings, raises the stakes in the study of women's literary history and the history of feminism. When considered in this light, Wollstonecraft's writings reveal struggles between feminist, lesbian and transgendered claims to female-embodiment manifested as unanswered questions about the kind of desire in circulation, and what this implies for the "mother" of feminisms, as well as for the feminism that claims her as its mother.

Wollstonecraft's Desire

It is a commonplace to observe that in the *Vindication of the Rights of Men* Wollstonecraft stages her argument in the style of a "manly" rationality in contrast with the artificial and effeminate sentimentality she claims to find in Burke's *Reflections on the Revolution in France* with which she is arguing.[16] This *Vindication* famously feminizes Burke, and, in turn, makes a claim for its writer (in the first edition anonymous) as a more "manly opponent", deploying imagery of dueling to convey this macho stance. While this move has usually been read as a feminist agenda, it can also be read as a symptom of displaced lesbian subjectivity. According to Teresa de Lauretis' reworking of Freud's theory of castration and femininity: "[l]esbian desire [. . .] is constituted against a fantasy of castration, a narcissistic wound to the subject's body-image that redoubles the loss of the mother's body by the threatened loss of the female body itself" . . . That "loss" is replayed through multiple prohibitions of access to female bodies in culture (in the form of incest, perversion and masturbation taboos) and "compounded" both by the social and economic devaluing of women in general, and the aphasia that demands its non-perception as a significant absence. For de Lauretis, lesbian desire can be understood in the context of a more general displacement of this desire for the "missing female body" – which circulates for women as the lack of a lack – onto pre-fetishized objects representing that otherwise unnamable and unknowable desire in cultural terms. A drive appropriating pre-coded signifiers when there is no social space in which it can otherwise symbolize? Lesbian fetish objects often denote masculinity, since masculinity functions as our only culturally available semiotics of "sexual (genital) activity and yearning toward women" (de Lauretis 1994: 261–3).

In Wollstonecraft's first novel, *Mary, A Fiction* (1789), the eponymous heroine's "disposition" is expressed as a taste for the Sublime, and accompanying "accoutrements" of masculinity. Since this novel narrates a passionate and sexually intimate same-sex relationship, we can deduce that the masculinization of its same heroine functions as a displaced trace of a female-embodied same-sex desire that is, as Johnson notes, otherwise "indiscursible" (Johnson 54). The valorization of the "manly", which underpins Wollstonecraft's *Vindications*, can be argued by extension to mediate in writing a similar displacement of female-embodied same-sex desire: the transgendering of female-embodied same-sex desire.

Extraordinary "Women"

In her *Rights of Woman,* Wollstonecraft claims association with Sappho and Chevalier d'Eon (Wollstonecraft 1995: 87). It is uncertain to what degree Sappho was circulated as a sign of lesbian desire or writing womanhood in Wollstonecraft's period; d'Eon offers a clear reference to sexual ambiguity.[17] Susan Gubar has noted Wollstonecraft's tendency to identify those "few extraordinary women" who have escaped oppressive and demeaning femininity as "virtually transsexuals" (Gubar 1997: 137). Wollstonecraft's desire for female-embodied masculinity (as the Sublime, as "history", as philosophy, as lover to the feminized love object, as self-identification in opposition to despised femininity) tends towards a transgendering of the writing subject, and, in some instances, the positing of an imaginary body in discord with the writer's female-embodiment. In *Mary, A Fiction*, the openly self-projecting heroine is marked out as "different from those generally portrayed" by her "thinking powers". The "Author" notes the cultural paradox implicit in situating this attribute in a female-embodied character (Wollstonecraft 1989: 1, 5). Butler conceives of such a split between embodiment and self-identification as definitive of the transsexual condition, since: "Transsexuals often claim a radical discontinuity between sexual pleasures and bodily parts [. . .] This imaginary condition of desire always exceeds the physical body through or on which it works" (Butler 1990: 71).

Wollstonecraft makes a point of setting herself apart from the general run of women, and identifying herself with what she called the "few extraordinary women who have rushed in eccentrical directions out of the orbit prescribed to their sex". She describes these extraordinary women as "*male* spirits, confined by mistake in female frames" (Wollstonecraft 1995: 39). This phrase returns us to Greer's provocative question: *how would [she] know*, and, at the same time, returns us to the contested boundaries between feminism and transgender.

Feminist – Lesbian – Transgendered Woman?

We might argue – following Biddy Martin – that as Queer Theory "grew out of" feminist theory (in both senses of the phrase) – then transgender as post-Queer theory can also be said to have grown out of and emerged from the critical and identificatory spaces opened by ground-breaking feminist work. Transgender may then also claim Wollstonecraft as its "maternal" genealogy. There is of course another way to stage this argument: that feminism has been founded on a fundamentally *transgendered* text. From this perspective, what we read as Wollstonecraft's proto-feminism may be read differently, for a trace of the evaporation of female-embodied same-sex desire in writing. Since love between women has no formal mode of self-expression in the late eighteenth century, we could argue that it would be expected to manifest as a claim to encoded masculinity in writing, as well as in figurings of an Imaginary transgendered body. Feminism might in this context be considered a mode emerging from the transgendering of female-embodied same-sex desire.[18]

The question that remains is that of chicken-and-egg: is Wollstonecraft transgendering an otherwise "indiscursible" proto-lesbianism, or is her partial lesbian biography the surface trace of a transgendered subjectivity? As an iconic figure for feminism, in either case, she represents female-embodied desire for equality, which somewhat inevitably collapses into a desire for masculinity and a repudiation of traditionally feminine skills and techniques.[19] What is at stake in this analysis and its conclusions are the very borders marking the territory of the female-embodied subject claimed by feminism, lesbianism and – at least partially – by transgender/transsexualism.

Conclusion

I would not wish to stand judge on whether feminism had any greater or more *authentic* claim to female-embodied subjectivity than lesbian or transgendered identities. Following Irigaray, I would contend that a chronic frustration of the "drive" to find symbolic support for affective and significant social exchanges between women establishes lesbian, feminist, *and* transgendered female-embodied subjectivities under different historical and contextual conditions. Because female-embodied same-sex exchanges have no symbolic apparatus by which to represent themselves other than the "relation to origins" of the phallic economy (castration and penetration), women's longing for affective contact with women manifests through radical parodies of masculine subjectivity, since this is the only subject position from which post-oedipal intimate contact between women can be re-established. What this contesting of Wollstonecraft – and of female-embodiment – might imply, then, is a derelicted diasporic female-embodied Imaginary without the social conditions to represent itself, except in partial, often parodic or contradictory forms.

However, Greer's concern with the mistaking of self-castration for womanhood is worth considering further:

> Governments that consist of very few women have hurried to recognize as women men who believe that they are women and have had themselves castrated to prove it, because they see women not as another sex but as a non-sex. No so-called sex-change has ever begged for a uterus-and-ovaries transplant; if uterus-and-ovaries transplants were made mandatory for wannabe women they would disappear overnight. The insistence that man-made women be accepted as women is the institutional expression of the mistaken conviction that women are defective males. (1999: 81)

The question of what constitutes "woman" for mtfs has very little to do with questions of sexual difference and more to do with the disembodying of gender and the pervasiveness of castration fantasy. We may trace in Wollstonecraft a radical displacement of a disinherited femininity into cultural forms denoting female-female desire and exchange through masculine identification: through transgendering of the subject. As "daughters" of Wollstonecraft's desire, we have some work to do on coming to terms with her. This work will impact on our own critical acts of displacement.

Greer acknowledges: "There has always been a confederacy between women and rebels against masculinist conditioning, be they homosexual, transvestite or transsexual, and these are relationships that feminists should continue to foster but not at the cost of denying their own perception of female reality" (1999: 422). I would contend that our "perception of female reality" cannot be delimited to the traditional borders of "woman', but exceeds these in a diasporic dispersal of modes of female-embodied subjectivity. Acknowledging diasporic female-embodied subjectivity demands a greater degree of cross-border negotiation, and – as Greer notes – confederacy between the borderlands of the female-embodied subjective claims, as well as the "woman" to whom they make reference, and through whom these claims are staked.

Notes

1   For references to Wollstonecraft's "maternal" status in feminism, see Gilbert and Gubar 258; Showalter 216; Todd 1988 103; Hill 391; George 3; Lundberg and Farnham 33; Mulvey, Roberts and Mizuta xi; Jacobus 54. For suffragist appropriation of Wollstonecraft's *Vindication* see: Pennell; Fawcett 1970.
2   Third-wave feminism is feminism that has encountered and been transformed by poststructuralist and postmodernist arguments concerning essentialism and universalism, but which does not collapse into the position of post-feminism. I would cite in particular Whitford 1991; Bock and James 1992; Barrett and Phillips 1992; Irigaray 1985a, 1985b; Schor 1994; de Lauretis 1994; Braidotti 1994; Grosz 1994, 1995; Gatens 1996; Battersby 1998; Weiss 1999; Walker 1999.
3   For full discussions of the dangers and opportunities exposed by the collapse of "woman" as an identificatory term, see Soper 1997; Alcoff 1988; Braidotti 1989; Walby 1992; de Lauretis 1993; Morris 1993; Fraser and Nicholson 1993. For the argument in favour of the collapse of "woman" as an essentialist category, see Adams; Braidotti 1994; Butler 1990.
4   Race, class and ability "difference" have also been brought to bear on the feminist "woman", but for the purposes of the argument I am proposing in this paper I have limited my focus artificially to the gender/sex/sexuality triad. However, it is a fundamental recognition of this argument that subjectivity is never embodied as *only* sexed, but is always also raced, classed and subject to ability indices. In general terms, I am arguing that the

object of critical and theoretical work on embodied subjectivity must shift to the normative embodied ideal against which *all* singular embodied subjectivities are marked as different, but to markedly different degrees. See Audre Lorde on the "mythic norm" of Eurowestern cultures (1997). See also for a fuller discussion of the specificities of racial difference bearing on the category of "woman": hooks 1984; Riley 1988; Kanneh 1992; Amina 1995. Margrit Shildrick gives an interesting account of the discursive construction of disability (1997).

5 "Transsexual" refers to subjects undergoing full sexual realignment procedures. "Transgendered" refers to subjects situating themselves *between* sex and/or gender binaries, signaling sexual and/or gendered ambivalence, and popularly defined as an identity defined through flux or fluidity. "Intersexed" denotes subjects with embodied characteristics associated with male *and* female identities, to a lesser or greater degree (i.e. where sexual categorization is open to question with reference to embodiment).

6 Butler 1990, 1993; Battersby 1998; Grosz 1995; Halberstam 1995; Hale 1996; Benhabib *et al.* 1995; Butler *et al.* 1999; Cohen 1997.

7 For a fuller version of this argument see Tauchert 2000b.

8 See Butler's delineation of the task of transgendered linguistic and identificatory performances (Butler 1993: 223–42); Garber 1992.

9 A transcript of the interview on ABC Lateline 30 March 1999 runs as follows:

> "I'm born a women, I've got all the bits and pieces and the operations and the contraceptive history and the rest of it to prove it. But I don't know if I actually am a woman. What is 'being a woman'? Am I being a woman now? How would you know? I might as well say that I'm convinced I'm a cocker spaniel, I just was accidentally born a human. This is just such an extraordinary argument, that 'I'm in the wrong body' that you have to look at the sources of that certainty, and one of the people who is not consulted in the transsexual script that justifies the sex change is the child's, the person's, mother. Very often the change is made after the person has lived and married and become a father, and all the time the person was convinced that he was a woman, whatever that is. I don't know what womanhood is or the metaphysical womanhood that infests people who are actually gonally male. And I think to decide that they are right is a curious decision. And it's a decision that is difficult to expiate in terms of the rest of your life history". Full interview can be accessed at: <http://www.abc.net.au/lateline/stories/21783.ram>.

Greer is being interviewed following her argument in her most recent book that mtf transsexuals are exorcising their mothers. She makes no reference to ftm transsexuals, or to the transgendered identities emerging in recent theory and practice (Greer 1999).

10 See Woodward's account of proto-feminism in the eighteenth century, and Caine's excellent *English Feminism: 1780–1980*.

11 I am summarizing here the argument made in "Escaping Discussion: Liminality and the Female-embodied Couple" in *Romanticism on the Net*, 18 (May 2000).

12 See Johnson 1995; Faderman 1996 and Todd 2000 for fuller discussions of Wollstonecraft's experiences of same-sex desire and how this gets redirected in her writing and in literary history.

13 Todd's recent excellent biography of Wollstonecraft goes some way to reclaim the Wollstonecraft/Blood relationship as the most significant in her life, with strong impact on her writing: "In *Mary, A Fiction* she had bade farewell to one meaning of Fanny Blood in her life – as an erotic object displacing romance and men – but the dead woman was a potent force . . ." (Todd 2000: 150).

14 Claudia Johnson's study of Wollstonecraft in *Equivocal Beings* remedies this neglect, but has been neglected as an important revisionary source in turn.

15 For a fuller discussion of the figure of same-sex desire and intimacy in Wollstonecraft's writings, see my forthcoming book, *Mary Wollstonecraft and the Accent of the Feminine* (Palgrave).

16 See Poovey, Zaw, and Kaplan's work in particular.

17 Chevalier d'Eon (Charles de Beaumont) was a French diplomat to the court of Empress Elizabeth of Russia and later to that of George III in Great Britain. He was a renowned and decorated military hero. Few knew that he had also worked for a French spying operation. In 1776, Louis XVI declared that d'Eon was actually a woman who had been masquerading as a man. His autopsy in 1810 disclosed that he was a man who had been masquerading as a woman. Burke wrote of d'Eon that "she was the most extraordinary woman of the age". Indeed. For an account of the debate concerning Chevalier d'Eon's ambiguous gender and sex in the 1770s, see Kates, 1991. Trumbach notes that in the eighteenth century Sappho was both "domesticated into a tragic heterosexuality" but also present in a libertine tradition that "makes clear her taste for girls" (Trumbach 1994, 520–1, n. 4).

18 See Rupp and Faderman for evidence of figures of transgendering and disavowal for female-embodied same-sex desire in literary history.

19 See Gubar for an account of Wollstonecraft's "feminist misogyny" and Jacobus for an account of Wollstonecraft claiming equality over women's dead bodies.

References

Adams, Parveen. A Note on Sexual Divisions and Sexual Differences. *m/f* 3 (1979): 51–9.

Alcoff, Linda. 1988: Cultural Feminism Versus Post-Structuralism: The Identity Crisis in Feminist Theory. *Signs* 13, 405–36

Amina, Mama. 1995: *Beyond the Masks: Race, Gender, and Subjectivity*. London/ New York: Routledge.

Armstrong, Isobel (ed.) 1992: *New Feminist Discourses: Critical Essays in Theories and Texts*. London: Routledge.

Barrett, Michèle and Phillips, Anne (eds) 1992: *Destabilizing Theory: Contemporary Feminist Debates*. Cambridge: Polity Press.

Battersby, Christine. 1998: *The Phenomenal Woman: Feminist Metaphysics and the Patterns of Identity*. Cambridge: Polity Press.

Benhabib, Seyle *et al.* (eds) 1995: *Contentions: A Philosophical Exchange*. New York: Routledge.

Bock, Gisek and Susan James. 1992: *Beyond Equality and Difference: Citizenship, Feminist Politics and Female Subjectivity*. London: Routledge.

Braidotti, Rosi. 1994: *Nomadic Subjects: Embodiment and Sexual Difference in Contemporary Feminist Theory*. New York: Columbia University Press.

———. 1989: The Politics of Ontological Difference. In Brennan (ed.) 89–105.

Brennan, Teresa (ed.) 1989: *Between Feminism and Psychoanalysis*. London/New York: Routledge.

Brooks, Ann. 1997: *Postfeminisms: Feminism, Cultural Theory and Cultural Forms*. London/ New York: Routledge.

Butler, Judith. 1990: *Gender Trouble: Feminism and the Subversion of Identity*. London/New York: Routledge.

———. 1993: *Bodies That Matter: On the Discursive Limits of Sex*. London/New York: Routledge.

———, John Guillory and Kendell Thomas (eds) 1999: *What's Left of Theory: New Work on the State and Politics of Literary Theory*. New York: Routledge.

Caine, Barbara. 1997: *English Feminism 1780–1980*. Oxford: Oxford University Press.

Cohen, Cathy. 1997: Punks, Bulldaggers, and Welfare Queens: The Radical Potential of Queer Politics? *GLQ: A Journal of Lesbian and Gay Studies* 3 (4), 438–64.

de Lauretis, Teresa. 1994: *The Practice of Love: Lesbian Sexuality and Perverse Desire*. Bloomington and Indianapolis: Indiana University Press.

Elam, Diane and Robyn Wiegman (eds). 1995: *Feminism Beside Itself*. London/New York: Routledge.

Faderman, Lillian. 1996: Who Hid Lesbian History? In Zimmerman, Bonnie and Toni A. H. Mcnaron (eds), 41–7.

Fawcett, Millicent Garrett. 1970: *Women's Suffrage: A Short History of a Great Movement*. New York: Source Book Press.

Felski, Rita. 1989: *Beyond Feminist Aesthetics: Feminist Literature and Social Change*. London: Radius.

Fraser, Nancy and Nicholson, Linda. 1993: Social Criticism Without Philosophy: An Encounter Between Feminism and Postmodernism. In Docherty, Thomas (ed.), *Postmodernism: A Reader*. New York/London: Harvester Wheatsheaf, 415–32.

Garber, Marjorie. 1992: *Vested Interests: Cross-Dressing and Cultural Anxiety*. New York: Routledge.

Gatens, Moira. 1996: *Imaginary Bodies: Ethics, Power, and Corporeality*. London: Routledge.

George, Margaret. 1970: *One Woman's "Situation": A Study of Mary Wollstonecraft*. Urbana, Chicago/London: University of Illinois Press.

Gilbert, Sandra and Susan Gubar. 1979: *The Madwoman in the Attic: the woman writer and the nineteenth-century literary imagination*. New Haven: Yale University Press.

Greer, Germaine. 1999: *The Whole Woman*. London, Doubleday.

Grosz, Elizabeth. 1994: *Volatile Bodies: Toward a Corporeal Feminism*. Indiana University Press: Bloomington/Indianapolis.

——. 1995: *Space, Time, and Perversion: Essays on the Politics of Bodies*. Routledge: New York/London.

Gubar, Susan. 1995: Feminist Misogyny: Mary Wollstonecraft and the Paradox of "It Takes One to Know One. In Elam and Weigman (eds), 133–54.

Halberstam, Jude. 1999: F2M: The Making of Female Masculinity. In Rivkin, Julie and Michael Ryan (eds), *Literary Theory: An Anthology*. Oxford: Blackwell, 759–68.

Halberstam, Judith and Ira Livingston (eds.). *Posthuman Bodies*. Bloomington, Indiana: Indiana University Press, 1995.

Hale, Jacob. 1996: Blurring Boundaries, Marking Boundaries: Who is Lesbian? *Journal of Homosexuality* 32 (1), 29–40.

Herdt, Gilbert (ed.). 1993: *Third Sex, Third Gender: Beyond Sexual Dimorphism in Culture and History*. New York: Zone Books.

Hill, Christopher. 1958: *Puritanism and Revolution: Studies in Interpretation of the English Revolution of the Seventeenth Century*. London: Secker and Warburg.

hooks, bell. 1984: *Feminist Theory: from Margin to Center*. Boston: South End Press.

Irigaray, Luce. 1985a: *Speculum of the Other Woman*. Gillian C.Gill (trans.). Ithaca: Cornell University Press.

——. 1985b: *This Sex Which Is Not One*. Catherine Porter (trans.). Ithaca: Cornell University Press.

Jacobus, Mary. 1989: The Difference of View. In Belsey, Catherine and Jane Moore (eds), *The Feminist Reader: Essays in Gender and the Politics of Literary Criticism*. Basingstoke: Macmillan, 49–62.

Johnson, Claudia. 1995: *Equivocal Beings: Politics, Gender, and Sentimentality in the 1790s: Wollstonecraft, Radcliffe, Burney, Austen*. Chicago/London: University of Chicago Press.

Kanneh, Kadiatu. 1992: Love, Mourning and Metaphor: Terms of Identity. In Armstrong (ed.), 139–52.

Kaplan, Cora. 1985: Pandora's Box: Subjectivity, Class and Sexuality in Socialist Feminist Criticism. In Greene, Gayle and Coppélia Kahn (eds), *Making a Difference: Feminist Literary Criticism*, London/New York: Methuen, 146–76.

——. 1986. Wild Nights: Pleasure/Sexuality/Feminism. In *Sea Changes: Essays on Culture and Feminism*. Cora Kaplan, London: Verso, 31–56.

Kates, Gary. 1991: d'Eon Returns to France: Gender and Power in 1777, in Epstein, Julia and Kristina Straub (eds), *Body Guards: The Cultural Politics of Gender Ambiguity*. New York/London: Routledge, 167–94.

Kelly, Gary. 1997: (Female) Philosophy in the Bedroom: Mary Wollstonecraft and Female Sexuality. *Women's Writing* 4 (2), 143–54.

Kemp, Sandra and Judith Squires (eds). 1997: *Feminisms*. Oxford: Oxford University Press.

Lorde, Audre. 1997: Age, Race, Class, and Sex: Women Redefining Difference.

Ashley Tauchert

In McClintock, Anne, Aamir Mufti, Ella Shohat (eds), *Dangerous Liaisons: Gender, Nature and Postcolonial Perspectives*, Minneapolis: University of Minnesota Press, 374–80.

Lundberg, Ferdinand and Marynia F. Farnham. 1947. *Modern Woman: The Lost Sex*. New York: Harper & Brothers.

Moore, Jane. 1999: *Mary Wollstonecraft*. Plymouth: Northcote House.

Morris, Meaghan. 1993: Feminism, Reading, Postmodernism. In Docherty, Thomas (ed.), *Postmodernism: A Reader*, New York/London: Harvester Wheatsheaf, 368–89.

Mulvey Roberts, Marie and Professor Tamae Mizuta (eds) 1994: *Perspectives on the History of British Feminism* (vol. 1). *The Radicals: Revolutionary Women*. London/Tokyo: Routledge/Themes Press.

Pennell, Elizabeth Robbins. 1885: The Life of Mary Wollstonecraft. *Athenaeum Journal of Literature, Science, the Fine Arts, Music, and the Drama* (July–December 80–1,143–4.

Poovey, Mary. *The Proper Lady and the Woman Writer: Ideology as Style in the Works of Mary Wollstonecraft, Mary Shelley and Jane Austen*. Chicago and London: University of Chicago Press, 1984.

Radstone, Susannah. 1997: Postcard From the Edge: Thoughts on "Feminist Theory: An International Debate. In Kemp and Squires (eds), 104–8.

Riley, Denise. 1988: *Am I That Name?: Feminism and the Category of "Women" in History*. Basingstoke: Macmillan.

Rupp, Leila. 1996: Finding the Lesbians in Lesbian History: Reflections on Female Same-Sex Sexuality in the Western World. In Zimmerman, Bonnie and Toni A. H. Mcnaron (eds), 153–9.

Schildrick, Margrit. 1997: *Leaky Bodies and Boundaries: Feminism, Postmodernism and Bioethics*. London/New York: Routledge.

Schor, Naomi. 1994: *The Essential Difference*. Bloomington: Indiana University Press.

Showalter, Elaine. 1971: *Women's Liberation and Literature*. New York: Harcourt Brace Jovanovich.

Soper, Kate. 1997: Feminism, Humanism, Postmodernism', in Kemp and Squire (eds), 286–92.

Tauchert, Ashley. 2000a: Escaping Discussion: Liminality and the Female-embodied Couple. *Romanticism on the Net*. 18 May.

——. 2000b: Beyond the Binary: Fuzzy Gender and the Radical Centre. In Haynes, Felicity and Tarquam McKenna (eds), *Unseen Genders: Beyond the Binaries*. New York: Peter Lang.

——. (forthcoming): *Mary Wollstonecraft: The Accent of the Feminine*. Basingstoke: Palgrave.

Todd, Janet. 1988: *Feminist Literary History: A Defense*. Cambridge: Polity Press.

——. 2000: *Mary Wollstonecraft: A Revolutionary Life*. London: Weidenfeld & Nicholson.

Trumbach, Randolph. 1994: London's Sapphists: From Three Sexes to Four Genders in the Making of Modern Culture. In Herdt, Gilbert (ed.), *Third Sex, Third gender: Beyond Sexual Dimorphism in Culture and History*, New York: Zone Books, 111–36.

248

Walby, Sylvia. 1992: Post-Post-Modernism? Theorizing Social Complexity. In Barrett & Phillips, 31–52.

Walker, Michelle Boulous. 1998: *Philosophy and the Maternal Body: Reading Silence*. London: Routledge.

Weiss. Gail. 1999: *Body Images: Embodiment as Intercorporeality*. New York: Routledge.

Whitford, Margaret and Kathleen Lennon (eds). 1994: *Knowing the difference, feminist perspectives in epistemology*. London: Routledge.

Wittig, Monique. [1981] 1997: One Is Not Born a Woman. In Kemp and Squires (eds), 220–6.

Wollstonecraft, Mary. 1989: *The Works of Mary Wollstonecraft*, 7 vols. Todd, Janet and Marilyn Butler (eds), London: Pickering.

——. 1995: *Vindication of the Rights of Woman*. Tauchert, Ashley (ed.), London: Dent/Vermont: Charles E Tuttle.

Woodward, Carolyn. 1994: Naming Names in Mid-eighteenth-century Feminist Theory. *Women's Writing* 1 (3), 291–316.

Zaw, Susan Khin. 1994: Appealing to the Head *and* Heart: Wollstonecraft and Burke on Taste, Morals and Human Nature. In Perry, Gill and Michael Rossington (eds), *Femininity and Masculinity in Eighteenth-Century Art and Culture*, Manchester/New York: Manchester University Press, 123–41.

Zimmerman, Bonnie and Toni A. H. Mcnaron (eds). 1996: *The New Lesbian Studies: Into the Twenty-First Century*. New York: The Feminist Press at City University of New York.

The Contributors

Bella Adams lectures in American Studies at Keele University. Her research interests include the concept of the aesthetic, critical theory, and contemporary American fiction. Her forthcoming publications include a book on Amy Tan for the Contemporary World Writers Series, Manchester University Press.

Julia Balén, Associate Director of Women's Studies at The University of Arizona, has a Ph.D. in Comparative Cultural and Literary Studies with a focus on issues of embodiment and power relations. She has published articles in the *The Intimate Critique: Autobiographical Literary Criticism; Doing Feminism: Teaching and Research in the Academy; In Language and in Love; Marguerite Duras: The Unspeakable*; and *Tickled Pink: Women and Humor*. She presents regularly on issues of diversity and brought the national -ISM (N.) Project to the University of Arizona. She also serves on the executive committee for Lesbian, Gay, Bisexual Studies. Her newest project is a study of identity and community in the Gay and Lesbian Association of Choruses.

Liz Barry completed her D.Phil. on Beckett, Modernism and Cliché at Oxford University. Her other research interests include modern theater, especially Jean Genet, Virginia Woolf, and English and French Modernism. She has published articles in *Beckett Aujourd'hui*, the *Journal of Beckett Studies*, and *Crossing Boundaries: Interdisciplinarity in the Humanities* (Sheffield University Press). She lectures in English at the University of Warwick.

Mary Brewer lectures in the School of English and Performance Studies at De Montfort University. She received her D.Phil. in English and American Studies from the University of Sussex, where her research focused on contemporary women's theater. Her other publications include *Race, Sex and Gender in Contemporary Women's Theatre: The Construction of "Woman"* (Sussex Academic Press, 1999). Her current research project, *Performing Whiteness* (Wesleyan University Press in association with Continuum Press, forthcoming 2004), addresses the political technology through which the category of Whiteness has been produced and endowed with cultural authority within the specific context of twentieth-century US and British theater estates.

Melissa Chinchillo is a doctoral candidate at the State University of New York, Stony Brook. Her research interests include nineteenth- and twentieth-century American fiction and poetry; chaos, feminist and poststructuralist theory, science fiction and film. She has published a critical biography of E. Ann Kaplan in Routledge's *Postmodernism: An Encyclopedia,* and her poetry has been published in *Venture, Meanie,* and *Sidelines* literary magazines. At Stony Brook, she has taught courses in Women's Studies, American literature, and science fiction film.

Michele Hunter is a Ph.D. candidate at the Institute for Women's Studies at Emory University. In 1995, she completed a Master's degree in French Literature at Harvard University. In 1992, she graduated from New York University, where she completed a Bachelor's degree in Women's Studies. Her "coming out" stories are included in the anthology *"does your mama know?" An Anthology of Black Lesbian Coming Out Stories"* (RedBone Press, 1997), and she has published an article on Danzy Senna's novel *Caucasia* in Brooks' and Hubel's *Literature and Racial Ambiguity* (Ropoi Press, 2001).

Kathleen Iudicello is a Ph.D. candidate at The George Washington University and is currently completing her dissertation (*Women Take Stage: Performance Art, Hip-Hop, and Punk Rock*). She teaches writing and literature at Estrella Mountain Community College in Avondale, Arizona. Kathleen is part of a writing collective that publishes *QueerJane,* a political on-line and print zine for queer women. Her interview with scholar-activist Kitty Krupat appears in *Workplace: The Journal for Academic Labor* and her interview with writer–sex educator Tristan Taormino can be seen in *Popmatters.* Kathleen is an activist for gay, lesbian, bisexual, and transgender rights in Phoenix, Arizona, and she plays bass in a punk rock band with three other women.

Sue Jackson is a lecturer in Lifelong Learning and Citizenship in the Faculty of Continuing Education at Birkbeck College, University of London. Her doctoral thesis, *Spinsters and Mistresses: Re-turning the 'Academic' to Women,* combined her interests in women's studies and education by examining learning experiences of women students in higher education, and she has published widely in this field. Sue is currently working on two books, a co-edited collection which explores challenges and negotiations for women in higher education, and a single authored book *Differently Academic? Widening Participation for Women in Higher Education*. Sue is currently co-chair of the Women's Studies Network (UK) Association, and an active member of the Women in Higher Education Network.

Alyssa O'Brien was awarded a doctorate in English Literature from the University of Rochester, where her research focused on gendered and textual mobility in the fiction of Joyce, Woolf, and Larsen. Her publications include articles in the *Quarterly Review of Film and Video* and the *Journal of Modern Literature*. She teaches on the Program in Writing and Rhetoric at Stanford University.

Doreen Piano, a Ph.D. candidate in Rhetoric and Composition at Bowling Green State University, has had short stories, reviews, and essays published in *Gulf Coast: A Magazine of Literary and Fine Arts, Iron Women: New Stories by Women, The Face,* and *Bust Magazine*. Her dissertation, *Congregating Women: Reading Ethos and Style in Feminist Subcultural Production*, analyzes how rhetorical and cultural features of third-wave feminist print and electronic media can inform writing practices in the classroom. A web-based publication, "Analyzing a Zine: Studying Subcultural Production on the WWW," will be published in Kairos, Summer 2002.

Angela Slaughter is an Aboriginal woman of Mi'kmaq heritage, raised in the Listuguj First Nation, Quebec, and educated at Carleton University in Ottawa, Ontario. She has worked as a Policy Analyst with the Department of Indian Affairs. She is active in the Aboriginal community in Ottawa as a long-standing Board Member of Gignul Housing, with the Odawa Native Friendship Center, and the Aboriginal Peoples Network. She would not label herself a "feminist" and is proud to be the stay-at-home mother of two beautiful children, Bradley and Josephine, and wife of David.

Ashley Tauchert lectures in English at the University of Exeter. She has edited the Everyman edition of Mary Wollstonecraft's *Vindication of the Rights of Woman* (1995). Her monograph, *Mary Wollstonecraft: The Accent of the Feminine,* is forthcoming from Palgrave Press, and she is co-editor with Gillian Howie of *Gender, Teaching and Research in Higher Education,* to be published by Ashgate Press. She is co-director of the Institute for Feminist Theory and Research — an independent body made up of researchers in English at Exeter University and members of the philosophy department at the University of Liverpool: http://www.ex.ac.uk/english/IFTR/IFTR.home.htm.

Margaret A. Villanueva holds a doctorate in Sociology from the University of California–Santa Cruz, and she is currently an Assistant Professor of Community Studies at St. Cloud State University, Minnesota. Her publications have appeared in *Anthropology and Education Quarterly, Women and Language, Studies in Latin American Popular Culture* and *Discourse-Theoretical Studies in Culture and Media,* and *The Illusion of Borders: The National Presence of Mexicanos in the United States,* Kendall-Hunt, 2001. She is currently investigating immigration and settlement of Mexicans in Midwestern towns of Illinois and Minnesota, and transnational family networks of Veracruz and the Midwest. Her website http://AdelanteSterling.tripod.com highlights the history of community-building among Latinos in Sterling, Illinois, as depicted on a Latino Mural painted in 1999.

Rebecca Walsh lectures in Women's Studies at the University of Wisconsin–Madison. She is completing a doctoral thesis entitled *The Geopolitics of Cultural Difference: Locating the Spatial Poetics of H.D., Langston Hughes, Ezra Pound, and William Carlos Williams.* Through her involvement with the Border and Transcultural Studies Research Circle at Wisconsin-Madison, she is putting together an interdisciplinary collection of essays on global diasporas.

Index

abject bodies, 154; *see also* prostitutes, prostitution
abjection, 134–5, 141–3; voice of, 135, 137
Aboriginal Women, 6, 147, 167–80; *see also* feminism, Canadian
Academy, the, 29–30, 37–8, 46; *see also* *First Amongst Equals*; language
ACT UP, 149, 154, 186
Acuña, Rodolfo, 60
Adam (Biblical), 98
Africa, 80–1, 97, 112–13; *see also* colonialism; *Nervous Conditions*; post-coloniality
agency, 88, 94, 118
Ahmed, S., 184n4, 186n9
AIDS, 149, 154, 161, 186
Alarcón, Norma, 54n9, 55
Albertine, Viv, 124; *see also* punk rock, women's
Alcoff, Linda, 184, 185, 194
America, 48, 52, 60; 92, 113; media in, 121
American Cancer Society, 160
Amina, Mama, 237n4
Andersen, Margaret, 57
Anderson, Laura, 139n5
anorexia nervosa, 102; *see also* *Nervous Conditions*
Anzaldúa, Gloria, 3, 48, 54n9, 56
Aparacio, Frances, 47–8, 50, 53, 54n9
Appiah, Anthony, 53n4
Appiah, Kwame, 93n2, 112
Arden, Jane, 238; *see also* Wollstonecraft, Mary
Aristotle, 207n2; *see also* feminist, aesthetics
Armstrong, Isobel, 207, 208, 209
Assembly of First Nations, 178; *see also* Aboriginal women
Astra, 43; *see also* language, women's
Augustine, 207n2
Austen, Jane, 59; *Mansfield Park*, 60

Baca Zinn, Maxine, 47n1, 49, 57
Bakhtin, M. M., 82, 83
Balcony, The, 221–2; *see also* Genet, Jean
Bangles, the, 125n4
Barnett, Claudia, 78n4
Barrett, Michèle, 236n2
Barthes, Roland, 218
Bataille, George, *Story of the Eye*, 122–3
Battersby, Christine, 236n2, 238n6
BBC2, 38; *see also* *First Amongst Equals*
Bedard, Yvonne, 168
Belén, Edna Costa, 55
Bell, Shannon, 133, 135
Belsey, Catherine, 210n5
Benhabib, Seyle, 238n6
Benmayor, Rita, 54n6
Bennett, Tony, 119
Berger, J., 185n6
Bhabha, Homi, 79, 85
Bhavnani, Kum-Kum, 47n1, 49, 50, 59
Bikini Kill, 125, 126, 128, 129; *see also* punk rock, women's
Bill C-31, 168, 174; *see also* Aboriginal women
biological fallacy, 152
Blondie, 125; *see also* punk rock, women's
Blood, Fanny, 238–9; *see also* *Mary: A Fiction*
Bock, Gisela, 236n2
Boleyn, Anne, 79; *see also* *The Owl Answers*
Bondi, L., 183n1, 194
Boob, Betty, 128
Borden, Lizzie, *Working Girls*, 144n6
Bordo, Susan, 152n3
Borne, Paula, 176–7
Brady, J., 154
Braidotti, Rosi, 140, 142, 236n2
Brando, Marlon, 86; *see also* *A Movie Star Has to Star in Black and White*
Brant, Clare, 177
Breast Cancer Action, 154
breast cancer narratives, 147–64

Index

Index

Dickens, Charles, 82; *see also The Owl Answers*
Dion Stout, Madeleine, 175–6
discourse, 29, 40, 95; localized, 151; master, 32; patriarchal, 78–9; prostitute, 134, 143; *see also* breast cancer narratives; language
Doezema, Jo, 136, 137
Dolan, Jill, 119–20
Dollimore, Jonathan, 76
Downing College, Cambridge, 39; *see also First Amongst Equals*
Duncan, Michael, 122
Duncan, Nancy, 183n1, 198
Dyer, Richard, 86

Eagleton, Terry, 205, 207, 208, 209
Ebert, Teresa, 152
Écriture féminine, 31–4, 211, 218; *see also* Cixous, Hélène
Eden, 98
Elam, Diane, 239
Elgin, Suzette Haden, 42; *Native Tonque*, 41; *The Judas Rose*, 41, 43
Eliot, T. S., 82; *see also The Owl Answers*
Embry, Marcus, 10, 59
Epstein, Dr. Samuel, 155n4
erasure, 47, 50, 94
Erickson, P., 191
essentialism, 37
Ethnic Studies, 2, 47–8
Eve, 93, 98
EyeBody, 119n1, 121–2; *see also* Schneeman, Carolee

Facio, Elisa, 54n8
Faderman, Lillian, 196, 238n12, 241n18
Fanon, Frantz, 73, 76, 93n1, 101–2
Farnhan, Marynia, 236n1
Fawcett, Millicent Garrett, 236n1
Federation of Saskatchewan Indian Nations, 170n6; *see also* Aboriginal Women
feedback mechanism, 109; *see also* chaos theory
Felini, Frederico, *Nights of Cabiria*, 144n6
Felski, Rita, 203, 205–6, 209–11, 213–15, 236; *see also* feminist, aesthetics
female body, 118–29, 132, 136–43, 186–7; *see also* breast cancer narratives, performance art, puck rock, women's, prostitution
feminism, Aboriginal, 168–80; Anglo-American, 74, 205–16, 225; African American/Black, 9 ,74 30, 34, 43, 227–34; borders, 61, 229; Canadian, 6, 167–80; Continental, 225; French, 9,

30–4; latina, 46–63; liberal, 2–3, 51; locational, 147, 152, 182–99; ludic, 152; mainstream, 2, 167–80; materialist, 152; postcolonial, 94, 111; postmodern, 74, 123; progressive, 4, 11–12, 73, 83; pro-sex, 133; radical, 50; second-wave, 2; third-wave, 236n2; Third World, 49–50, 133; white, 51, 167–80
feminist, aesthetics, 205–16; ideals, 23–4; pedagogy, 14–24, 47; praxis, 23, 58–62, 151–3
Fernández, Roberta, 54n9
Finch, Jennifer, 127
First Amongst Equals, 38n4, 38–41; *see also* Cambridge University; Academy, the
First City, 129
First Nations, 167, 169; *see also* Aboriginal women
Flood, Ann Barry, 162
Fluxus, 120; *see also* performance art
Foucault, Michel, 41, 185n6
Forte, Jeanie, 123
Frankenberg, Ruth, 3, 58, 86; *see also* whiteness
Fraser, M., 185n7, 194n13
Fraser, Nancy, 152n1
Fregosa, Rosa Linda, 54n9
Freud, Sigmund, 33; *see also* psycho-analysis
Friedman, Susan Stanford, 182, 183n1 and n2, 197
Frye, Martin, 190
Fuentes, Sylvia, 54n8
Funnyhouse of a Negro, 78, 80–1, 83, 84, 87; *see also* Kennedy, Adrienne
Fusco, Coco, 54n9
Fuss, Diana, 75–6, 85, 87, 184, 195

Gabriel, Susana, 56
Garber, Marjorie, 238n8
Garcia, Alma, 47n1, 56
Garcia, Jerry, 54n5
Garcia, Karen, 54n7
Garcia, Norma, 233
Gatens, Moira, 236n2
gaze, the, 80, 87, 102, 126, 135, 143; camera's, 141
Genet, Jean, 203, 218–20, 225; *The Balcony*, 221–2; *Notre-Dame-des-Fleurs*, 220, 222–4; *The Thief's Journal*, 223
George, Margaret, 236n1
Gilbert, Sandra, 2236n1
Gilligan, Carol, 40, 41
Gilman, Sander, 137
Glass on Body Imprints, 122; *see also*

Index

Mendieta, Ana
Glass on Face Imprints, 122; *see also*
 Mendieta, Ana
Gleick, James, 92, 93, 109
Go-Gos, the, 125
Goldman, Emma, 239
González, Juan, 48, 60
González, Sylvia, 47n1
Gordon, Betty, *Variety*, 134
Grahn, J., 189
Greer, Germaine, 238, 241, 242; *see also*
 transgender
Griffin, Gabriele, 78
Griffin, Marjorie, 176
Grosz, Elizabeth, 119, 236n2, 238n6
Gubar, Susan, 236n1, 240
Guy-Sheftall, Beverley, 55, 57

Halberstam, Judith/Jude, 238, 238n6
Hale, Jacob, 238n6
Hall, Stuart, 73, 76
Hanna, Kathleen, 128, 129
Haraway, Donna, 7, 11, 12n1, 13,14, 184,
 186; *see also* cyborg practices
Harding, Sandra, 152
Hardy-Fanta, Carole, 54n5
Harris, Laura Alexandra, 119
Harry, Debbie, 125
Harvard University, 40
Hawkins, Harriet, 93, 98, 99n7
Hay, Louise, 157
Hayles, N. Katherine, 93, 94, 95, 99, 101,
 110, 111
Hegel, Georg, 207n2
Hein, Hilda, 205, 207
Hellerstein, Erna, 48n2
Henderson, Joe, 162n5
Henreid, Paul, 86; *see also A Movie Star Has
 to Star in Black and White*
Herdt, Gilbert, 247, 248
Higgonet, M., 183n1
Hill, Christopher, 236n1
Hole, 125, 126; *see also* punk rock,
 women's
Holtzman, Linda, 19, 19n7
Hondagneu-Sotelo, Peirrete, 54n7
hooks, bell, 3, 35, 47n1, 48, 74 , 137, 237n4
Hooper, Judith, 160–1
Hopkins-Hausman, Joy, 157
Horno-Delgado, Eliana, 54n9
Hull, Gloria, 3, 56
Hull, Suzanne, 56
Hume, David, 207n2
Humm, Maggie, 132, 134, 141
Hurtado, Aída, 3, 47n1, 50, 52, 58, 59, 60,
 61

Hustling, 134; *see also* prostitutes;
 prostitution
hybridity, 85, 108–9
Hynde, Chrissie, 125

identification, 76, 79, 82, 85, 87
identity, black, 87; geopolitics of, 147, 183;
 inter-sexed, 238; mixed-race, 80,
 231–2; multiple, 36; politics, 74–5;
 race-gendered, 54, 79; sexualized,
 133; Third-World, 133, 136; white, 77,
 85–9
ideology, patriarchal, 214–15; *see also*
 patriarchy
Ignace, Vivian, 176–7
Imaginary, the, 30, 242; *see also* Lacan,
 Jacques
Imitation of Life, 231–2; *see also* passing
Imlay, Gilbert, 239
India, 92, 100, 113; *see also Jasmine*
Indian Act, 168, 173–4, 178; *see also*,
 Aboriginal women
In Mourning and In Rage, 121; *see also*
 performance art
Institute for Public Media Arts (IPMA),
 14, 15, 18
institutionalized racism, 47
invisibility, women's, 47, 50, 119; *see also*
 subject, viewing
Irigaray, Luce, 30–3, 131, 185n6, 236n2,
 242; *see also* feminism, French
-ISM (N.) Project, 14–15, 19; *see also* femi-
 nist, pedagogy

Jacobson, Matthew Frye, 86
Jacobus, Mary, 218, 236n1
Jagger, Alison, 51n3
Jakobsen, Janet, 12n1
James, Susan, 236n2
Jameson, Fredric, 220–1
Jane Eyre, 105–6
Jardine, Alice, 218
Jasmine, 93, 95–101, 105, 110, 112, 113; *see
 also* Mukherjee, Bharati
Jay, Karla, 196n14
Jay, M., 185
Jesus, 78, 80, 83; *see also A Lesson in Dead
 Language*
Jett, Joan, 125
Johnson, Claudia, 238n12, 239, 239n14,
 240
Johnson, Linda, 140
Jordan, June, 3, 183, 187–9, 190–1, 195
Joseph (Biblical), 83; *see also A Lesson in
 Dead Language*
Joseph, Barbara, 162–3
Joseph, Gloria, 47n1

Index

Index

Index

Index